The Science of

BOREDOM

The Science of

BOREDOM

THE UPSIDE

(AND DOWNSIDE)

OF DOWNTIME

SANDI MANN

ROBINSON

ROBINSON

First published as *The Upside of Downtime* in Great Britain in 2016 by Robinson

This paperback edition published in 2017 by Robinson

A CIP catalogue record for this book
is available from the British Library.

ISBN 978-1-47213-598-8

Typeset in Gentium by Initial Typesetting Services, Edinburgh
Printed and bound in Great Britain by Clays Ltd, St Ives plc

Papers used by Robinson are from well-managed forests
and other responsible sources

Robinson
An imprint of
Little, Brown Book Group
Carmelite House
50 Victoria Embankment
London EC4Y 0DZ

An Hachette UK Company
www.hachette.co.uk

www.theimprovementzone.co.uk

Dedicated to Dania, Elisha and Akiva,
who ensure that my life is never boring!

Acknowledgements

Thanks to everyone who has taken part in my boredom research over the years – I hope it was not too boring. Thanks too to my lovely agent, Chelsey Fox, who has put up with my obsession with boredom for many years now – without ever indicating that she was bored of it!

Contents

Introduction

My first ever graduate job was as a shop assistant in a very quiet high-street clothes shop, where I was so bored that I resorted to unfolding sweaters and refolding them, just to have something to do (unsurprisingly, the store has since closed down). So began a lifelong interest in boredom that was not quashed by my next job, which was only marginally less tedious; as a cytology screener, my job was to sit gazing down a microscope at cells all day in order to spot the occasional unhealthy one. I remember finding this vigilance task so dull that I begged to be permitted to listen to music via my headphones in order to provide some much-needed stimulation. This request was refused on the grounds that the music might be distracting; and so my mission to explore boredom and to research ways of coping with it was born. My subsequent years of research into boredom have taught me (amongst other things) what I instinctively knew then – that far from being a dis- traction, extra stimulation like music can help people cope with tedious, repetitive tasks. I would love to be able to go back to my ex-employer and show them my findings, but that job too has now gone, to be replaced by computers (who never get bored!).

This book then is the result of years of research that, unlike my first two jobs, has never been dull. It is for everyone who is ever bored and for those who go to great lengths to ensure they never are. In a world in which many of us seek ever more stimulation in an attempt to counter our lowering threshold for boredom, *The*

Upside of Downtime is about not just helping us cope with boredom, but also about harnessing its power. For the reality is that, despite the ever-increasing ways in which to entertain ourselves today, we appear to be more bored at school, at work and at play than ever before. Internet, DVDs, iPhones, Xboxes, PlayStations, 24-hour supermarkets, multiple TV channels, cinemas, bowling, retail parks, online chatrooms, Facebook, Twitter, MSN, texting ... today we have so many varied ways to spend our leisure time that we should all surely never know what boredom feels like. Yet boredom appears to be the curse of the twenty-first century; it seems that the more we have to stimulate us, the more stimulation we crave. The fast pace of the world means that in an environment characterised by change, speed and novelty, we are losing the ability to tolerate the routine and repetition of everyday life. We experience this lack of tolerance as the uncomfortable feeling of boredom, and it is the motivation to reduce this ennui that leads us in a never-ending quest for stimulation.

This quest brings a whole plethora of consequences: kids hang out on street corners causing trouble because they are 'bored'; people of all ages become addicted to drugs or gambling or pornography because they are constantly seeking more stimulation; others take risks or seek ever-more dangerous thrills (hence the growth in 'extreme' sports) in order to relieve the tedium of their lives; still more over-indulge in shopping or eating in order to bring much-needed stimulation into their lives.

How has this happened? And, how can we stop it? *The Upside of Downtime* examines the evidence and looks at the causes and consequences of boredom in the twenty-first century. This book will start with an exploration of the concept of boredom, debunking a few myths along the way (for example, that boredom is the result of having nothing to do). The central premise of the book, that boredom is actually beneficial for us, is suggested from the outset, with this idea being developed as the book progresses. Using my own groundbreaking research into boredom, as well as that of other international researchers, the text tells the story of what we do when we are bored; how we act, react and how we cope.

The causes of boredom are explored in detail, with the relative roles of environment, personality and other people being debated; are we bored because life now is too routine and repetitive? Or is it just that we are more boredom-prone? Or are we bored because other people are boring us (and, heaven help us, could we be that boring person?)?

Boredom within the education system is discussed with an exposé of how schools are creating a boredom-prone society with their increasing emphasis on 'whizzy' teaching involving ever-more interactive whiteboard technology. It will be argued that we are growing a nation of children who expect to be entertained to such an extent that they are unable to cope with lower levels of stimulation. Combined with all the instant and engaging (but soundbite-short) technology around them, our kids are growing up with ever-decreasing attention spans and thresholds for boredom. They are getting bored more easily and lack the skills to cure their ennui themselves. And yet, just when people's boredom thresholds are being lowered, and they need higher levels of stimulation to satisfy their quest for engagement, they find themselves entering a world of work that is increasingly boring (due to increased bureaucracy, paperwork, legislation and routinisation).

The consequences for society of all this boredom are worrying. Much of society's ills can be laid at the door of boredom, either because of our reactions to being bored (e.g. risk-taking, thrill-seeking, vandalism, drug-taking, etc.) or because of the effects that being bored have on our minds and bodies. Indeed, this book will go on to argue that boredom is the 'new' stress, and just as harmful.

The Upside of Downtime, however, ends on a positive note. Despite the gloom and doom of boredom, it has its upsides too. The antidote to boredom is humour and fun, both of which can be used to enrich society. Boredom also carries with it many useful functions, including being the catalyst for creativity, and my new research demonstrating this link is described here. The book offers the somewhat radical view that the solution to the 'boredom problem' is to harness boredom rather than trying to avoid it. As a society, we think we have failed if we are bored, but this book will argue that boredom can be a powerful, motivating force that instils creativity, intelligent thinking and reflection – if only we allow it back into our lives. Some people are already catching on to this, with signs that there is a movement away from wanting constant stimuli in our lives towards a desire for the real freedom that gadget- and connection-free time (e.g. on holiday) can provide. British journalist and broadcaster Mariella Frostrup's recent comments in *The Times*[1] about her 'downtime' holiday illustrate this trend: 'left to idle away a week with little phone signal and no technology was the greatest luxury we could hope for.' She is not alone in seeking time out from the demands of a 24/7 society as we are starting to tip more positively towards boredom. *The Upside of Downtime* aims to lead the way.

1

The Quest for Engagement:
What is Boredom?

'When I am bored, it feels frustrating, like I ought to be doing something useful, but I just can't motivate myself.'

'When I am bored, I can't be bothered to do anything.'

'I feel more bored when I am tired . . . and yet being bored makes me feel tired!'

'Being bored means my mind wanders. I can't concentrate on anything – at least nothing I'm meant to be thinking about. It's all just too much effort.'

'I just want to go to sleep when I am bored.'

'I get bored when there isn't enough to keep my mind active. I get bored in queues, or when reading the same book over and over to my kids. It feels like my brain cells are falling asleep.'

'I get depressed when I am bored.'

'When I am bored, I waste time.'

'Boredom is the feeling of having nothing to do.'

We all know what it is to feel bored. Which of us cannot relate to some or all of the comments above shared with me by participants in my own research? Some researchers believe that up to half of us 'often' feel bored[1] whilst one study claims that we typically spend six hours a week feeling 'completely and utterly bored with life'[2] (a finding that led one commentator to dryly observe '*only* six hours?').[3] Clearly then, most of us have an all too intimate knowledge of ennui, a condition that has been part and parcel of life probably since time began. Philosophers, scientists, journalists and religionists have contemplated boredom and its effects for centuries, mostly seeing it as a profoundly negative force. Researchers have even identified the most boring day in history (Monday, 11 April 1954, when, apparently, very little actually happened),[4] the most boring time of the year (January, according to both a poll of students[5] and my own 'straw' poll of people, of whom 44 per cent claimed that January is indeed the most tedious time of year) and the most boring museums in the world (see Box 1.1).

Box 1.1: The most boring museums in the world?

- The British Lawnmower Museum, Southport, Merseyside, UK
- The Dog Collar Museum, Leeds Castle, Maidstone, Kent, UK
- The Pencil Museum, Keswick, Cumbria, UK
- The Locksmith's House, Willenhall, West Midlands, UK
- York Quilt Museum and Gallery, York, UK
- The Bakelite Museum, Williton, Somerset, UK
- British Optical Association Museum, London, UK
- The Spam Museum, Austin, Minnesota, USA
- Cork Museum, Palafrugell, Girona, Spain
- Museum Cemento Rezola, (Cement Museum), San Sebastián, Spain
- The Salt and Pepper Shaker Museum, Gatlinburg, Tennessee, USA

- Musée du Papier Peint (Wallpaper Museum), Rixheim, France
- The Hair Museum of Avanos, Cappadocia, Turkey
- Paris Sewers Museum, Quai d'Orsay, Paris, France
- Soap Museum, Sidon, Lebanon
- The Japanese Sword Museum, Tokyo, Japan
- Ethnography Museum, Ankara, Turkey
- India Seashell Museum, Tamil Nadu, India

Work is, for many people, totally boring, whilst for others it is certain elements of their job that bore them, such as paperwork or attending meetings. Many people also spend a large portion of their non-working day in a state of boredom – on the train during the daily commute, at home listening to their spouse drone on about their day and at dull parties at the weekend. Our kids regularly complain they are bored – school is boring, family days out are boring (if they are teenagers), homework is boring ... the list is endless. Men and women have affairs because they are bored with their partner, people get hooked on internet poker sites or the shopping channel in order to combat boredom, and teenagers steal cars, smash bus shelters, take drugs, and perhaps even take part in organised riots – as happened in the UK in the summer of 2011 – all to relieve the tedium that is their lives. But, though we may know exactly what it is to be bored, when it comes to explaining this state, no one can quite come up with a definitive description.

In my own research,[6] which surveyed hundreds of people in the north-west of the UK, people reported that when they are bored they feel 'listless', 'demotivated', 'tired', as though they cannot 'concentrate', or that their 'mind wanders'. Respondents to my survey claimed that when bored, they 'have nothing to do' or, perhaps more pertinently, that what they are meant to be doing does not appeal or keep their attention. People do seem to be unclear as to whether they are bored because they have nothing to do, or because they are tired, distracted, demotivated, or whether, indeed, all these states are part of the boredom experience. Put simply, is boredom dependent on the task in hand (i.e. we are bored because the task itself is boring), or is it dependent on the individual (we are bored because we are boring people)? And, if it is the task that is boring, what is it about the task that makes it so? If it is we who are boring, what aspects of our personalities contribute to make us more prone to experience boredom? These questions will be addressed in more detail in later chapters.

Box 1.2: What does 'bored' look like?

© Wolfgang Kumm/DPA/Press Association Images

Harald G. Wallbott, a psychology professor at the University of Salzburg, Austria, showed that we can easily recognise when a person looks bored. Actors in his 1988 study who held a collapsed upper body (i.e. slumped), leant their heads backwards and who engaged in few bodily movements were recognised by participants as being bored.[7]

A Brief History of Boredom

According to the Oxford English Dictionary the word *'boredom'* first appeared in English in 1750, but it was not until 1852 that the first written record of the word appeared in literature: in the novel *Bleak House*, Charles Dickens refers to Lady Dedlock's state as a 'chronic malady'. The expression *'to be a bore'*, however, had already been in use in the sense of 'to be tiresome or dull' since 1768. Even before the use of the actual term, however, the concept had been well documented, with the word *'acedia'* (tedium) dominating ancient descriptions of monotony.

Box 1.3: How many words?

There are various words that can be used to describe boredom: tedium, ennui, monotony, dullness and possibly even listlessness.

Common expressions to emphasise a state of acute boredom include: bored to death, bored to tears, bored out of my mind and bored rigid.

It was not until the early 1920s, however, that researchers, usually psychologists, first began to study boredom, concentrating initially on bored workers in factories. One of the earliest studies of boredom in a laboratory setting was in the late 1930s, when Joseph Barmack of the City College of New York proposed that boredom was a 'sleeplike feeling'.[8] Barmack's study was fascinating, not only for what it revealed about boredom, but also for what it revealed about the lack of ethics in research in the 1930s; he gave participants drugs such as amphetamines to see if boredom could be reduced (it could). Such research would never pass muster with modern-day research ethics committees.

Since those early days many researchers have concluded that boredom is a distinct emotion. Cynthia Fisher, a workplace psychologist in the United States who was one of the first modern researchers of boredom (and someone I meet often on the 'boredom' circuit at international conferences), points out that 'boredom is an unpleasant, transient affective state in which the individual feels a pervasive lack of interest in and difficulty concentrating on the current activity [such that] it takes conscious effort to maintain or return attention to that activity'.[9] Thus, she says, boredom is an emotion, albeit an unpleasant one, akin perhaps to anxiety or sadness. In trying to understand boredom, then, we must first understand what emotions are and what roles they play in our lives.

What is an Emotion?

According to Abraham Maslow, the psychologist responsible for much of our understanding about motivation, emotion is the 'measure of humankind'.[10] That is, humans' experience of emotions is what distinguishes us from other lower-order animals. Whilst in modern times it is debatable to what extent other animals do experience emotions (and well beyond the scope of this book), it is highly unlikely that they experience quite the range of emotions that we humans do.

Many researchers believe that there are a number of distinct and universal emotions that all people, whatever their culture, exhibit and recognise; these include anger, fear, sadness, joy, disgust and surprise (but not boredom). They are sometimes termed 'primary emotions' and it is thought that they are innate – in other words, we do not need to learn to express or recognise these emotions, but are somehow born already wired with the ability to have these emotional experiences. If you need any proof of this, try feeding a tiny baby a new non-sweet food group; my own 6-month-old produced an expression that was clearly distinguishable as disgust – even his 6-year-old sister was able to recognise the emotion on his face (which greatly amused her). The reason for these innate, universal primary emotions is evolutionary, i.e. our very survival – a point that will be returned to shortly.

Most researchers believe that emotions consist of four distinct components and some believe that to truly experience an emotion, all four components must exist. These are:

- Our cognitions: i.e. what we think and our interpretation of events that produce the emotion. For example, thinking about a sad event such as bereavement induces sad emotions.

- Our feelings: we label the way we feel as being angry, sad, etc.

- Our physiological reactions: how our bodies react, e.g. sweating, raised heartbeat, etc. These include the bodily changes that we cannot see or notice, such as chemicals secreted from various glands during the experience of an emotion.

- Our behaviour: such as running away, hitting someone/something, hugging someone etc.

Thus, to experience the phenomenon of an emotion with which we are all so familiar, the emotional trigger or stimulus must penetrate our consciousness, there must be some kind of reaction in our body, we must produce some kind of behavioural change – and we label the whole thing as an 'emotion'.

It is important to remember that all emotions, arguably, are experienced for a reason – even boredom. That is, they are part of our evolutionary response, designed to help us adapt and survive in the world. Thus, for example, the function of anger is to prepare us for a response (such as fighting) against the person who has angered us – in addition, our angry faces indicate the strength of our feelings to our enemy and, with a bit of luck, they will run away before we have to get our hands dirty. Boredom, whilst not recognised as a 'primary' emotion (in other words, it is a more complex emotion), too, arguably, has similar adaptive purposes, and these will be discussed in more detail in Chapter 11.

What Produces an Emotion?

There is no clear-cut answer to this and psychologists and researchers have battled this one for years now. What is it that gives us the sensation of experiencing an emotion? How do we distinguish one emotion from another; how do we know we feel scared and not angry? Or bored and not just tired?

The earliest researchers into emotion in the nineteenth century, James and Lange,[11] thought that emotions are triggered by us noticing our physiological responses and identifying them as an emotion. For example, imagine that you are walking down a dark alley late at night. You hear footsteps behind you and you begin to tremble, your heart beats faster, and your breathing deepens. You notice these physiological changes (which are different from physiological changes that occur with, say, happiness or dismay) and recognise them as your body's preparation for a scary situation. You then experience fear. Thus, it is the feedback from our bodily reactions that allows us to experience an emotion – and different emotions produce different physical reactions in the body.

More recent explanations focus on the role played by our brains in interpreting physical sensations as emotions. It is not enough just to experience the physical reactions in our body; we must also have reason to interpret and label these changes as a particular emotion. It is now acknowledged that the actual physical changes we experience may be the same for every emotion; it is our interpretation of the environment, etc., that leads us to label these sensations as a particular emotion.

Imagine what might happen if you noticed that you were feeling hot and sweaty. The way you interpret these physical sensations will depend on what has happened before you noticed them:

- Scenario 1: Before feeling hot and sweaty, you had just sprinted 400 yards to catch a bus. You immediately assume that the physical sensations are due to your unaccustomed exercise (and you resolve to get fitter!).

- Scenario 2: A few minutes ago, you narrowly avoided being hit by a bus. You had been walking along, minding your own business, when the bus mounted the kerb, missing you by inches. You interpret the sweating and hot feelings as fear as you appreciate the danger you were in.

- Scenario 3: This time, you were at the bus stop in good time but the bus didn't stop and went sailing past. It wasn't even full! Here, you interpret your physical sensations as the emotion of anger.

So, our emotional experiences rely on us noticing physical changes in our bodies and giving them an appropriate emotional label. For some interesting studies illustrating this, see Box 1.4.

Box 1.4:

1. The Wobbly Bridge Study

© Design Pics Inc/REX Shutterstock

Psychologists Dutton and Aron[12] visited the Capilano Canyon in Canada, which is crossed by a number of bridges. One bridge was a rickety and apparently unstable suspension bridge that tends to sway, tilt and wobble, giving users the impression that they are likely to fall 70 metres (230 feet) into the canyon below. Another bridge is a solid wood one that is upstream and only 3 metres (10 feet) above a shallow part of the canyon below. People walking across the rickety bridge tend to be quite aroused with fear – their pulse rates quicken, they may sweat and their hearts pound. Indeed, this may be why they choose that bridge. No such arousal is likely on the lower, solid bridge.

The experimenters interviewed men crossing each of the two bridges and tested how attracted they were to a female confederate on the other side of the canyon. What they found was that those men on the rickety suspension bridge were more attracted to the woman than those on the sturdy bridge. The reason given by the psychologists was that the men on the scarier bridge experience a state of arousal, which, in the presence of a woman, they interpret as attraction for her. However, the men on the sturdy bridge have no such physical feelings to misinterpret.

The study shows why colleagues at work who have been through some emotional experience together (such as beating a tight deadline, winning a big contract, etc.) can end up in a romance – they misinterpret the emotions they are feeling as love!

2. The Adrenaline Study

Psychologists Schacter and Singer[13] carried out an intriguing (if ethically dubious by today's standards) study to show that our emotional experiences can be manipulated by altering the way we label the physical changes that accompany emotions.

They told subjects they were studying the effects of vitamins on performance. Half the participants were given an injection, not of a vitamin, but of an adrenaline-like substance. Adrenaline makes people feel hot and sweaty and causes their heart rate to rise. The other half were given a saline injection (the placebo).

The adrenaline participants were then told one of three things about how the injection might make them feel; one group were told that they would experience sweaty palms and racing heart (the correctly informed group). A second group were told that they would start to feel itchy (the incorrectly informed group) and a third group were told nothing at all (no information group). They were then left with a confederate who acted aggressive and irritating, with the aim of inducing anger in the experimental participants. So, which group would report feeling the most angry?

They found that those subjects given the adrenaline but the incorrect information were the angriest group. This is because they experienced physical sensations in their body that they could not attribute to the injection (unlike the correctly informed group). Instead, they concluded that their physical reactions must be caused by their experience of anger. The other groups had other explanations to hand (or did not experience the physical bodily changes at all, in the case of the placebo group) so did not label their arousal as anger.

These same misinterpretations can occur with the experience of boredom. Imagine you are doing something that isn't particularly engaging – maybe some paperwork or repetitive data entry. You glance at the clock every so often, hoping perhaps that it will soon be home time and you can do something more fun. But time seems to be moving so slowly – every time you look at the clock, it seems to have barely moved much at all. Gosh, you think, this task is *so* boring!

Now, imagine that you are in the same situation, but this time when you look at the clock, time seems to be flying by. This time you think, 'Wow, I must be having more fun than I thought with this data entry!'

This is what actually happened in a study performed in the 1970s[14] that showed how changing the environment can influence how bored people feel. The researchers showed that if a wall clock was fixed so as to move more slowly than it should, participants in an experiment reported feeling more bored doing tasks than did participants when the clock moved at a normal pace. They misinterpreted the apparent slow passage of time as boredom.

In another study, participants were given very dull, repetitive tasks to do. Some participants had to do this in noisy conditions and others in a quiet room. In the noisy conditions, they interpreted their inability to concentrate as due to the distracting effect of the noise, but in the quiet room they attributed their difficulty in concentrating to the boring nature of the task.[15]

These studies show how our experience of emotions like boredom is heavily dependent on our interpretation of events and environmental cues. In Chapters 4 and 5 we will examine a range of other factors that contribute to our experience of boredom (as well as discussing why some of us are more boredom prone than others).

Box 1.5: The most boring calendars in the world?

Why have an exciting calendar when you could have one of these on your wall?

- Post Boxes of Wales, 2015

- Fast Disappearing, Red . . . . . . Telephone Boxes of Wales, 2014

- Goats in Trees, 2012

- Round a bouts of Redditch, 2003 (which sold 100,000 copies worldwide)

- Highland Cattle, 2015

- Toilets Around the World, 2015

- North American Grain Elevators, 2015

- City Chickens & their Coops, 2014

- Dull Men of Great Britain, 2015

What is This Emotion of Boredom, Then?

Boredom, then, described as a 'plague of modern society',[16] is just one of a range of emotional states that we might experience. Contrary to popular opinion, boredom is not the result of having nothing to do, but rather of having nothing to do *that appeals* at that time. It is actually quite hard to think of situations where a person's options are so limited that s/he literally has nothing to do (with the probable exception of prisoners in solitary confinement) – although we can all think of those where of the range of available activities, there is actually nothing that we would *like* to do.

It is quite possible to find yourself with the same task or situation but that you only find yourself bored with it on some occasions and not others. That is, the same task, situation or even person, can appeal to us and engage us one day, but cause us utmost boredom the next. Clearly, boredom is not a uni-dimensional concept in that Task A is either boring or not; the elements of the task must somehow interplay and interact with the characteristics of the individual (hence, what is boring to one person is the epitome of excitement to another) and with the characteristics of the situation (thus, I may enjoy writing this book on Monday, but a bad night combined with the distraction of a sunny afternoon on Tuesday conspire to relegate the task to boring levels). All these elements will be explored in later chapters of this book.

Boredom, then, is partly independent of the task, situation or individual. It is described as an emotional state in 'which the level of stimulation is perceived as unsatisfactorily low'.[17] It is this lack of external stimulation that leads to increased neural arousal in search of variety – failure to satisfy this leads to the experience of boredom. In other words, for whatever reason, the task in hand fails to stimulate us. Whether this lack of stimulation is due to other competing distractions, or due to the nature of the task itself (perhaps it is repetitive or requires little mental effort – more on this in later chapters) – the point is that it is, in some way, unstimulating. We then engage in an effort to seek the missing stimulation – if we find it, all well and good. But seeking and failing to find that stimulation leads to the experience of the emotion that we label as 'boredom'. The more mental effort we have to put into trying to sustain our attention on something that is failing to provide adequate stimulation, the more bored we are likely to feel.

Thus the emotion of boredom is felt when:

1. There is not enough neural arousal or stimulation and either,
2. Effort is required to sustain attention to something that is not intrinsically captivating and/or,
3. Attempts are made to meet optimal arousal levels from other sources instead.
4. We are aware of the above and attribute the resulting negative experience as boredom.

Thus, boredom is a state of low arousal; you cannot be excited whilst at the same time bored. People prefer to be in their optimal level of arousal and this preferred level will be different for different people; some prefer a low level of arousal, with not much going on to stimulate them, whereas others like more of an all-singing, all-dancing atmosphere to keep them amused (this relates to the personality traits of extroversion/introversion, which will be discussed in Chapter 5). If arousal becomes higher than is comfortable (e.g. through information overload), the person will be motivated to do something to reduce that arousal (escape, etc.). Similarly, if the arousal is too low, then the person will take action to increase their level of arousal by seeking a less boring situation. In this way, boredom is often viewed as an avoidance emotion because it triggers a motivation to avoid or escape. Unfortunately, in many situations (dull meetings, boring job tasks, etc.), we cannot easily seek to increase our levels of arousal – though we try with techniques such as doodling, drawing boxes, writing our shopping lists, etc. Under other circumstances attempts to increase our levels of arousal can lead to risk-taking behaviours or unhealthy responses (such as drug use, 'joy' riding, gambling, etc.) – see Chapters 2 and 3 for more on this.

Boredom, then, is a negative or uncomfortable state to be in. As eminent boredom researchers William L. Mikulas and Stephen J. Vodanovich say, 'for it to be boredom, the person must not like it'.[18] You can be in a state of low arousal but be comfortable with that – you are relaxed and content, not bored. Similarly, some people enjoy being 'bored', relishing the sheer pleasure of having nothing to do: according to a report in the *Guardian* in 2007, the then US President, George W. Bush, was most looking forward to 'getting bored' once he stepped down from the Presidency in January 2009[19] (the fruits of his newfound leisure included his book *Decision Points* and a series of portraits of world leaders, dogs and himself in the bathtub). Again, this is not really boredom as the term has to imply a dissatisfaction with the status quo.

Boredom is thus an attentional phenomenon and the opposite of engagement or what happiness guru Mihály Csíkszentmihályi called 'flow',[20] which is when we are able to maintain attention without any difficulty at all. When we are in flow, we are totally immersed in what we are doing and unlikely to be bothered by distractions. Boredom is different too from disliking something or from other states of dissatisfaction, such as frustration. It is also an emotion unlike most others, for 'it doesn't have the short-lived intensity of more tangible feelings such as anger or fear'.[21] Indeed, whilst most emotions have been recognised throughout human history (anger, jealousy, disappointment, etc. are all mentioned, from the Bible through to Shakespeare), boredom appears to be a thoroughly modern emotion, with the noun itself only dating from the mid-nineteenth century. Boredom, it would seem, is the scourge of modernity, caused by our increased exposure to routine, repetitiveness, office work, bureaucracy, automation and regimentation (for more on the causes of boredom, see later chapters). However, that is not to say that boredom always has to have negative consequences: on the contrary, it will be argued in Chapter 11 that the seeking of arousal in order to reduce boredom can be a positive and motivating force.

Box 1.6: The world's most boring research study

© University of Queensland

When people hear that I study boredom, often they assume that this must be a boring occupation (it isn't!). There is research far more boring than boredom! For instance, in the world's longest-running scientific study, scientists have spent more than 85 years since 1927 watching pitch to try and spot rare drops of it falling in order to prove that the pitch, although appearing to be a solid, is in fact a liquid. (The study was set up by Thomas Parnell (1881–1948), a physics professor at the University of Queensland in Australia.) There have only been 8 drops in the past 75 years. The first drop fell in 1937, but it was another 10 years of observation before the next one fell in 1947. Since then, drops have fallen in 1954, 1962, 1970, 1979, 1988 and lastly in 2000. The study now has a webcam (http://smp.uq.edu.au/content/pitch-drop-experiment) so enthusiasts from all over the world can gaze at the pitch too, in the hope of spotting the next drop (which could be any time in the next 100 years). And they say the study of boredom is boring.

Other researchers who are surely close contenders for the honour of having carried out the world's most boring scientific study include:

- Henrietta Swan Leavitt: she was a researcher at Harvard College Observatory in Massachusetts and spent 20 years from 1895 scanning photographic plates to catalogue the brightness of stars.

- George Ungar: this eminent pharmacologist at the Baylor College of Medicine trained 17,000 goldfish in 1968 to distinguish colours so that he could then dissect each one to examine their brains.

Different Kinds of Boredom

Boredom does not always feel the same. In fact boredom researchers such as Richard Farmer and Norman Sundberg in 1986 (who developed the Boredom Proneness Scale that will be discussed in

Chapter 5) and Stephan Vodanovich in 2003[22] suggest there are two main kinds of boredom:

1. The type characterised by the desire to seek sensation, being restless and looking for arousal.
2. A more withdrawn kind characterised by negative affect and a withdrawal from the world.

Dull, boring and bland places to live

The town of Boring in the USA, near Portland, is named after its founder, William H. Boring, who began farming in the area in the 1870s. It recently twinned (unofficially – it is not large enough to have an official twinning) with the town of Dull in Scotland, which is 121 kilometres (75 miles) north of Glasgow. Both towns celebrate their twinning with road signs ('Welcome to Dull, paired with Boring' and vice versa) and an official Dull and Boring Day each year (the last one was 9 August 2015). The organisers are now hoping to link up with the Australian town of Bland too.

In 2014, Thomas Goetz of the University of Konstanz and colleagues from the Thurgau University of Teacher Education in Konstanz, Germany, expanded on this dichotomy. They collected real-time data from university and high-school students multiple times a day over a two-week period.[23] They had 63 university students and 80 high school students answer smartphone-based surveys about their activities and experiences and used the results to identify four different kinds of boredom (and later on, a fifth). Whilst some of us experience different types of boredom at different times, many people only ever really experience one kind in their lives.

Indifferent boredom: This is the most pleasant form of boredom, experienced as rather relaxing and even positive. In this kind of boredom, you just zone out and are happy to just let your mind wander without the need to deliberately seek stimulation.

Calibrating boredom: This is a less satisfying type of boredom that involves a casual search for ways to minimise the bored feelings. It involves a half-hearted search for stimulation but one that is never really satisfied – either because the bored individual doesn't quite know how to find that stimulation, or because it isn't there to be found (e.g. in a boring meeting when other, more exciting options are limited). In this state, people find their minds wandering but generally feel that they don't really know what they want to do. They are open to other options, but don't necessarily actively seek them out.

Searching boredom: People who experience searching boredom are far more motivated to find a more interesting activity than in the calibrating boredom state. Searching boredom feels more unpleasant too. This type of boredom can lead to innocuous behaviour like texting a friend, or doodling. It can also, of course, lead to the creative options that will be discussed in Chapter 11.

Reactant boredom: This is the most negative of all the boredom types. It is characterised by the individual who is restless and feeling wound up about being bored. They look for ways out of their bored state by reacting against the situation that they believe has led to the negative feelings they are experiencing. It is reactant boredom that can lead to hostile or aggressive behaviours, like vandalism or violence.

Apathetic boredom: This type of boredom was a later addition made by the researchers. Apathetic boredom is a very unpleasant form of boredom accompanied by a lack of motivation. It seems to be similar to depression or helplessness, and it may have more negative consequences than other types. Thirty-six per cent of the students in the original study were thought to experience apathetic boredom.

There is also a distinction between chronic (or existential) boredom and situational boredom. Situational boredom is what we experience in a dull meeting or when your friend shows you their extensive holiday album. Chronic boredom is when we are bored of life. It is often related to 'meaningfulness'; studies show that having 'life meaning' predicts levels of boredom, and that changing perceptions of life meaning can lead to changes in boredom levels.[24] Feeling that life has no purpose or meaning leads to an 'existential vacuum',[25] which manifests itself as chronic boredom characterised by apathy and indifference. As researcher J. M. Barbalet put it in a 1999 paper entitled 'Boredom and Social Meaning',[26] 'an absence of meaning in an activity or circumstance leads to an experience of boredom'. Later researchers go further, pointing out that perception of activities as meaningless is central to the experience of boredom.[27] Boredom thus leads us in a quest for meaning; researchers have shown that people who are frequently bored are much keener to search for meaning in life than those who are less bored.[28]

The concept of meaningfulness in relation to the experience of boredom will be returned to in later chapters.

How bored are you? A quiz*

Tick the answer that most applies to the following questions:

1. *When waiting in a queue at the supermarket, do you generally:*

   Enjoy time out from the rush (1).

   Feel impatient (4)

   Find yourself daydreaming (3)

   Occupy yourself by looking at the contents of other people's trolleys (2).

2. *During meetings at work do you generally:*

   Switch off (4).

   Concentrate and enjoy full involvement in what's going on (1).

   Find yourself doodling, colouring in the letters on your minutes, etc (2).

   Constantly look at your watch (3).

3. *On the commute to work do you:*

   Read the paper (2).

   Do some work (1).

   Gaze out of the window (3).

   Tap your fingers impatiently (4).

4. *When talking to people do you:*

   Listen attentively (1).

Tend to finish off their sentences (2).

Interrupt a lot (3).

Throw surreptitious glances at your watch/BlackBerry (4).

5. *On a workday morning do you:*

Look forward to the challenges of the day (1).

Want to go back to sleep (2).

Struggle to find anything to look forward to during the day (3).

Dread the day (4).

6. *When you read a newspaper do you:*

Read it from cover to cover (1).

Read the situations vacant ads first (2).

Skim read without absorbing much in depth (3).

Find little of interest to read (4).

7. *When your partner tells you about his/her day, do you:*

Switch off (4).

Ask relevant questions (1).

Do something else at the same time (3).

Try to stifle a yawn (2).

8. *If you were reading a bedtime story to a child, would you:*

Find that your mind wanders away from the plot (3).

Feel that you are totally involved in the story (1).

Enjoy being with the child (2).

Rush through it as quickly as possible (4).

9. *Do you generally feel . . .*

Lethargic (4).

Full of energy (1).

Demotivated (3).

Enthusiastic (2).

10. *I think boredom is:*

Something rare in my life (2).

Something to be avoided (4).

A good thing (1).

All too common in my life (3).

Now, count how many ones, twos, threes and fours there are.

Mostly ones

Boredom is not a significant problem for you. You tend to be quite good at finding enjoyment and pleasure in even the most mundane activities; finding things to interest you is a great skill to have. Use this book to hone those skills.

Mostly twos

Boredom is part of your life but you are pretty good at dealing with it. You generally look for ways to deal with any boredom you experience, perhaps by looking for interesting aspects to the situation, where possible.

Mostly threes

Boredom is a problem for you. Life is often boring, boring, *boring!* You struggle to find constructive ways to fill 'boring' time and often find it hard to concentrate on the task in hand. You need to learn better coping mechanisms for those boring episodes in your life – this book will lead the way!

Mostly fours

Oh dear, you *are* bored with life! Large swathes of your day are eaten by boredom. It is hard for you to find pleasure and interest in routine tasks and you spend a lot of time rushing through them, or watching the clock until the monotony passes. This book may not be able to take away all the boredom in your life, but it will help you reduce it by learning more useful coping strategies.

---

* *This quiz is not intended to be a diagnostic tool, but a fun way to help you start thinking about the way you deal with boredom.*

2

What Do We Do When We Are Bored? (Or, Why Boredom is Propping Up the Confectionery Industry)

Boredom, as shown in Chapter 1, is an unsatisfactory state. When we feel bored, we are motivated to 'unbore' ourselves; this drive, after all, is what boredom is. If we are not driven to increase the stimulation we receive then we wouldn't label that state as boredom, but as something else entirely (e.g. relaxation). How then can we 'unbore' ourselves? We attempt to do this by seeking out additional stimulation. There are really only two ways that we can achieve this; we can either:

(A) Refocus our attention and resources on the boring task or activity at hand and try to make it more stimulating or meaningful, or,

(B) Look for extra sources of stimulation that are not centred around the boring task at hand; these might be gleaned from other activities external to us, or from activities internal to us (i.e. within our own mind).

I have spent several years looking at what different populations of people do when they are bored, and believe that all the things that they do may be slotted into those two categories. For example, I asked 102 office workers* what they do when they are bored (at work).[1] The most common response (from over 60 per cent of respondents – see Table 2.1, below) was to drink something – usually coffee, tea, etc. This is clearly a Category B response, aimed at adding some extra sensory stimulation to otherwise dull proceedings. Taking a break was almost as popular – again, a Category B response, assuming that the break involved doing something more exciting than the current activity (even if it was just a bathroom visit). Almost as many people said they chatted to other people when they are bored, which is again a Category B response aimed at increasing the level of stimulation (by expecting others to stimulate them).

Forty-five per cent of people said they 'think' when they are bored. This could be a Category A response, if they are thinking about the task in hand and how to make it more interesting. If, however, they are merely deep in thought about a new recipe they want to try for dinner that night, or ideas about solving the Middle East crisis, then it would be a Category B.

Interestingly, over 40 per cent of people eat something when bored – usually chocolate or unhealthy snacks, which is why I titled a poster of my findings presented at a British Psychology Society Conference, 'A Mars A Day Keeps The Boredom Away (Or How Boredom is Propping Up the Confectionery Industry)'.[1] More on eating and boredom shortly.

* My later studies using larger samples are discussed in Chapter 9 and show similar findings to those presented in this chapter.

Table 2.1: What We Do When We are Bored; Study of 102 Office Workers	
Activity	Percentage of people in study claiming they did this when bored
Drink something, e.g. coffee	64
Chat to other people	60
Think	45
Eat something, e.g. chocolate	43
Daydream	33
Write shopping list (or similar)	29
Doodle	26
Play music	23
Take a break	6

Around a third of people daydream when bored – a Category B response that is internal, i.e. focused on seeking extra stimulation via thoughts and internal mental processes (more on daydreaming in Chapter 11). Writing shopping lists (29 per cent) and doodling (26 per cent) are both Category Bs, designed to provide extra stimulation to an otherwise boring existence, but playing music (23 per cent) could allow people to refocus their attention on a boring task (by providing the missing stimulation from a source external to the task), so could be a Category A.

The real Category A responses that would help make the task or activity more interesting were rarely mentioned by my respondents; these include things such as making the task more meaningful (perhaps by reminding oneself of its importance). As discussed in Chapter 1, it is thought that lack of meaning in tasks contributes to boredom so anything that increases meaningfulness might be a useful way to cope with boredom. The problem, of course, is that it can be very hard to make some tasks appear more meaningful, especially when they seem petty, repetitive, lack personal significance or are routine or undemanding. This will be explored more in Chapter 9.

Some of these responses to boredom will be discussed in more detail throughout the rest of this chapter.

Why Do We Eat When We Are Bored?

Although my research suggests that eating is one of the main things we do when we are bored, surprisingly, there is not a lot of other research on eating and boredom; whilst there is plenty of research on 'emotional eating', few studies have looked specifically at eating in relation to boredom. One of the earliest studies that did suggest a link between boredom and eating behaviour was in 1977, when psychologists found that participants ate more when they were given a boring task to do than when they were given a more interesting task.[2] A rather more recent survey carried out by the Priory Clinic in 2004[3] of 2,000 people found that 47 per cent of adolescents aged 16–24 and 40 per cent of those aged 35–44 claimed to eat because they were bored – figures remarkably close to that of my own research.

A study carried out in 2011 at Bowling Green State University[4] confirms how prevalent the boredom-eating link is. In that study, 139 young men and women were asked to report their eating habits using the Emotional Eating Scale, which is designed to assess how much emotions are a trigger for eating behaviours. The original scale grouped emotions into three subscales: (a) Depression, (b) Anxiety, and (c) Anger/Frustration, but this current study added an additional boredom subscale. The results suggested that eating out of boredom more than out of the other states of emotion such as anxiety or depression was linked to overindulging.

This reinforces the findings from an older study at California State University, back in 1977, which aimed to examine the differences in eating behaviours of obese and non-obese people. The researchers there fed obese and non-obese people until they were full, then gave them boring tasks to do. During the tasks, food was available and the researchers were interested to see how much food was consumed at this time. Results indicated that whilst the 30 obese participants consumed significantly more food than the non-obese, boredom markedly increased food consumption for both obese and non-obese.[5]

All of which suggests that eating must provide some sort of stimulation and thus is something we might do when we are lacking adequate levels of stimulation. But why does eating provide the extra stimulation sorely missing at that point in our lives? Scientists believe that the answer lies with a chemical called dopamine which, when released in our brain, gives us a stimulating buzz. Researchers have found that boredom is associated with reduced levels of dopamine in our brain[6] and our quest for boredom-busting stimulation is really a quest to increase our dopamine activity. Indeed, Peter Toohey, a professor at the Department of Greek and Roman Studies at the University of Calgary, argued in his book, *Boredom: A Lively History*, that 'boredom-prone individuals may have a naturally lower level of dopamine, which then requires from these individuals a heightened sense of novelty – to get the dopamine flowing'.[7]

There are, of course, various ways we can obtain that dopamine surge that we crave. Alcohol or drugs can do it, but these are not always socially acceptable to access in the middle of a working day. Food, however, is.

Dopamine production feels exciting and stimulating because it is, in evolutionary terms, in our interests for it to be something to crave. This is because dopamine is associated with those behaviours that are adaptive for us – i.e. designed to help us survive. Eating, of course, has a huge evolutionary benefit for us, so our bodies are designed to make us motivated to eat – hence the production of the feel-good dopamine when we eat.[8] And, more dopamine is released when we eat sugary or fatty foods, which were likely to increase our chances of survival for our hunger-prone ancestors (though of course, the opposite is true in the food-rich First World today); in fact, research has shown that eating junk food affects our dopamine production in much the same way as heroin does (though with less intensity).[8]

It is not just the dopamine-releasing properties of sugar and fat that keep us choosing chocolate when we are bored. New and novel things are, of course, exciting and stimulating (more on novelty later in the book), which is why we get bored of eating the same things. There are (probably) only so many healthy vegetables that we can eat but many, many varieties of junk food to satisfy our craving for both the hit from the food and the hit from the need for variety and novelty. In fact, research suggests a connection between having what scientists call a 'novelty-seeking personality' and being overweight. In a review from Washington University in St. Louis,[9] obese people were more likely than thinner folks to be novelty seekers; they also had greater trouble dropping pounds. One reason given for this is that being high in novelty-seeking can make you more likely to overeat as you are constantly looking for new ways to get that buzz from new sensations (see Chapter 5 for more on the novelty-seeking personality and Chapter 4 for more on the novelty and boredom link).

One way, then, to cut the boredom-food link would be to find other ways to introduce novelty and thrills into your life, other than from food.

A Skinny Boredom-busting Latte, Please

According to my research, drinking something is the most common thing that we do when we are bored – at least at work. Whilst the research did not ask people specifically what they drank, it is most likely that they turned to a drink containing caffeine, such as coffee, tea or cola; caffeine is, according to *New Scientist*, the planet's most popular 'psychoactive drug' with more than 90 per cent of adults in the United States using it every day.[10] The average adult in Finland, thought to be the world's most 'caffeinated country', consumes the equivalent of four or five cups of coffee a day.[11] And there would be good reason to expect this caffeine consumption to be at least partly as a result of boredom; a study in 1988 investigating the effects of caffeine intake on boredom levels amongst undergraduates found that caffeine decreased boredom (although it did increase tension and 'nervousness'),[12] suggesting that users consume it with these effects in mind (or at least to increase alertness, which is part of the same process).

What is interesting is how caffeine produces this effect of reducing boredom. As you might expect, caffeine works in the same way as food (i.e. through the dopamine effect), but via a slightly different mechanism. Boredom is the result of habituation processes – we get used to stimuli so that they are no longer stimulating for us, i.e. we habituate to them. Habituation is an adaptation process that allows us to be exposed to sensory information without 'old' stimuli distracting us by continuing to yield new signals to us. This allows us to stop attending to things that are the same, repeated or otherwise no longer worthy of using up valuable attentional resources. Imagine what life would be like if we never habituated to things: we would remain in a state of constant alertness and excitement over everything – our cornflakes, the rain, leaves falling, etc. It would be like being a perpetual toddler. Habituation allows us to screen out those things that we no longer need to pay attention to (for more on this, see Chapter 11).

Habituation, however, also works when we don't particularly want it to. For example, when doing something repetitive, we habituate, meaning that the task no longer excites us. That is why we become bored. The drug caffeine has the magical effect of slowing down the rate at which we habituate, and thus it takes longer until we become bored.

To understand how caffeine can do this, we need to understand a little about how it affects the brain. After drinking, it is absorbed into the bloodstream, levels peaking about 30 minutes after consumption. Caffeine then binds to receptors in the brain (especially in the hippocampus, cerebral cortex and cerebellum) called A1 receptors. These receptors normally work by inhibiting the release of dopamine (and other neurotransmitters) in the brain, so by binding to them, caffeine blocks this inhibition and thus increases dopamine activity in the brain. This results in increased arousal, vigilance and attention – and thus less boredom.[13]

Doodles, Bill Gates and Boredom

According to my research, around a quarter of us doodle when we are bored. And we are not alone; Microsoft's Bill Gates is apparently a prolific doodler, famously leaving behind pages of doodles at a world economic forum attended by the then-UK Prime Minister, Tony Blair.[14] To understand why Bill Gates and 26 per cent of the world's population doodle when bored, we need to look at what is happening in our brain when we are bored. A bored brain is not at rest, but constantly seeking stimulation. All the Category B things that we do when we are bored (see page 28) are ways to increase that stimulation in our brain – and doodling is one of them.

Doodling is actually a very clever strategy that our brains conjure up to allow us to get just the right level of extra stimulation we seek – but not too much that we are unable to keep an ear out for what is going on around us. It is thus the ideal tactic for when we are in a dull meeting or some other situation where we need to monitor what is going on, yet there is not enough exciting stuff happening to fully stimulate us. If we didn't doodle, we might meet our stimulation needs by drifting into daydreams or fantasies – which can be so stimulating and absorbing that we are no longer able to monitor the real world. Doodling does not take up as much cognitive resource as daydreaming and thus allows us to stay in the 'present' without letting boredom overwhelm us.

Box 2.1: The Doodle

Doodles may be shapes, patterns, drawings or scribbles – anything we produce whilst our attention is otherwise occupied. According to the Oxford English Dictionary, the word '*doodle*' first appeared in the early seventeenth century to mean a fool or simpleton, perhaps originating from a German word. This meaning 'fool, simpleton' is intended in the song title 'Yankee Doodle', originally sung by British colonial troops prior to the American Revolutionary War. It is also the origin of the early eighteenth-century verb to doodle, meaning 'to swindle or to make a fool of'. The modern meaning emerged in the 1930s either from this meaning or from the verb 'to dawdle', which since the seventeenth century has had the meaning of 'wasting time or being lazy'.

Common doodles include colouring in letters on a page, drawing boxes, making decorative edges to a page, faces, flowers and hearts. Some people believe that doodles reveal our unconscious selves because we do them whilst our conscious mind is otherwise engaged.[15]

Jackie Andrade, a cognitive psychologist at the University of Plymouth, UK, who recently published a study on doodling in the journal *Applied Cognitive Psychology*,[16] tested this theory by playing a lengthy and boring tape of a telephone message to a collection of people, half of whom had been given a doodling task to do during the experiment. After the tape ended, she quizzed them on what they had retained and found that the doodlers remembered 30 per cent more than the non-doodlers. Thus, in a boring situation, doodling can actually help us to concentrate by reducing the need to lapse into attention-absorbing daydreams.

They're Playing Our Song: Why Music Can Alleviate Boredom

Around a quarter of us play music when we are bored; music helps alleviates boredom by providing the additional stimulation we seek when bored, thus allowing us to concentrate on the task in hand without being distracted by our quest for stimulation. Sports psychologist Dr Costas Karageorghis and colleagues at Brunel University illustrate this point by suggesting that music can provide an athlete with an additional focus of attention that can relieve boredom and thus decrease the perception of effort; when we are bored, the task seems to demand more effort than when we are less bored – it is this perception of effort to attend to the stimuli that is interpreted as boredom. This effect even led Dr Karageorghis to refer to music as sport's 'legal drug' since we increase our effort when we are less bored (because we don't feel that effort as acutely so we feel we have more reserves to increase it) and thus perform better.[17] A similar effect was found in a study of driving behaviour; research published in the journal *Accident Analysis Prevention* suggested that listening to music whilst driving increased mental effort (because we perceive the effort we are putting in to be lowered and thus feel able to put more in).[18] Boredom, of course, involves a conflict between habituation and the effort needed to maintain the appropriate level of arousal in order to perform a task. If music can help maintain effort, then habituation from a monotonous activity (and hence boredom) can be overcome.

An alternative explanation as to why playing music facilitates the re-focusing of attention back to the task in hand (Category A, see also page 28) might be due to a *cognitive compensatory strategy* whereby the individual is aware that some cognitive capacity is taken up by listening to the music (thus fulfilling the purpose of fulfilling the quest for stimulation) so compensates by renewing their attention to the monotonous task in hand.

Box 2.2: Do we really yawn when we are bored?

It is a commonly held belief that we yawn when bored. Indeed, yawning whilst someone is talking to us or whilst they are delivering a speech is considered a major insult – signalling to the speaker that they are in danger of boring us to sleep. Such perceptions may be accurate, for there is research to suggest that we do yawn more when we are bored. Robert Provine, Professor of Psychology at the University of Maryland, asked volunteers to watch a dull television test-card for 30 minutes, and compared them to those watching rather more exciting music videos. His study found that the participants watching the test-card yawned a whopping 70 per cent more than those enjoying MTV.[19]

Bored Surfing

One of the things that people do when bored that is clearly missing from my office worker study is turning to electronic means of satisfying their thirst for stimulation. Surfing the net ('browsing'), accessing social media and texting are all activities in which we commonly engage to beat the ennui – you only have to glance around an airport lounge or train station to see how many people are tapping away on glowing mobile devices whilst they wait. One study led by Kansas State assistant professor Joseph Ugrin and Southern Illinois University associate professor John Pearson suggested that people spend a massive 60–80 per cent of their working day surfing the net.[20] The reason why these activities were not included in my office survey was that many employers who allowed me into their organisations to conduct the research refused to consider the possibility that staff were using work time for such activities. Many organisations proscribe the use of internet for non-work purposes (for good reason: one study estimated that lost productivity due to 'cyberslacking' is as high as 178 million dollars annually[21]) and thus it is likely that had I asked people if they engaged in these activities when bored (at work) they would have been reluctant to admit to doing so.

Students, however, have no such qualms and in a survey of 777 students at six colleges and universities in the US, more than 90 per cent of students admitted to using their devices for non-class activities during class times – and 55 per cent of them said they did this to combat boredom.[22]

Other research concurs with the view that we engage heavily in electronic-based activities when we are bored. Pew Internet & American Life Project is a research group based in the USA. In 2011 they asked 2,277 Americans how they use their phones: 42 per cent turn to their devices for entertainment as a cure for boredom.[23] Research published in the *Journal of Broadcasting and Electronic Media* in 2012, which surveyed 417 undergraduates, suggests that Americans spend eight hours a month on Facebook for the simple reason that they are bored.[24]

Box 2.3: Top boredom-busting internet sites

According to *Nerd's Magazine* in October 2014, these are some of the best sites to log onto when you are bored:

Literally Unbelievable: http://literallyunbelievable.org

People of Walmart: http://www.peopleofwalmart.com

Talking Animals: https://www.youtube.com/user/klaatu42

Autocorrect Failures: http://www.damnyouautocorrect.com

Smartphones have, of course, changed the way we view downtime and this will be discussed further in Chapter 6. We now have instant access to the internet, and can browse, message, update our status and tweet whenever any downtime should materialise, leading one commentator to lament that 'Between smartphones, tablets and e-readers, we're becoming a society that's ready to kill even a few seconds of boredom with a tap on a touchscreen'.[25] The downside of this will be addressed in Chapter 4.

Other Things We Do When We Are Bored

In a later (as yet unpublished) piece of research, I asked 310 people what they do when they have suffered an extensive period of boredom, such as after a really dull day at work. Whilst this will be discussed in greater detail in Chapter 9, some of these things (and others) will be discussed briefly below.

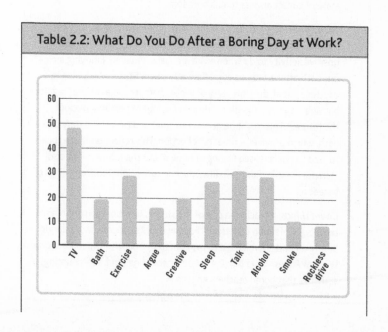

Table 2.2: What Do You Do After a Boring Day at Work?

- *Watch TV*: this is the most popular thing to do after a boring day and it is easy to see why. TV is a passive medium that provides entertainment and escapism – both of which meet the need for more neural stimulation caused by a dull day; as one researcher put it, 'television provides much-needed stimulation to compensate for the dull routine that characterises daily life'.[26] TV as a medium of entertainment will be discussed in more detail in Chapter 6.

- *Sleep*: Almost a third of respondents in the above study claimed that they are likely to sleep after a boring day – and for some this might be on the commute home. This might be harmless if they are taking the train but not so if they are driving. According to the National Sleep Foundation, 37 per cent of Americans fell asleep whilst driving (in itself a boring, monotonous task)[27] in the past year, whilst the figure in the UK is nearer 7 per cent.[28] We are more likely to feel sleepy when we are bored due to the inability of the environment to sustain our attention. A study in 1977 found that people who completed a boring task were sleepier and felt more tired than those completing a more interesting task.[2] Choosing to go to sleep (rather than it being unintended) is also a way of escaping the unbearable state of consciousness that is boredom.

- *Take a bath*: this provides sensory stimulation (which is a slight paradox, as a warm bath is considered relaxing) so can thus be a positive activity to do when extra arousal is required. Enjoying a nice hot bath after a tedious day offers other benefits too. Neil Morris, a psychologist at the University of Wolverhampton, claims that regular bathing leads to a significant drop in feelings of pessimism about the future.[29] This might be due to the quiet and peaceful nature of a bath, which provides a time for reflection. This reflection that appears to lead to an increased feeling of hope about the future might also increase meaningfulness in life, which in turn might reduce feelings of boredom.

- *Count things*: a teacher in one of my studies into boredom within the teaching profession confessed that she counts window panes during boring meetings, which led to my conference paper entitled *Counting Window Panes* [30]: see Box 2.4 for other counting (and non-counting) activities that bored teachers engage in.

Box 2.4: What exam invigilators do when they are bored

© David Davies/PA Archive/Press Association Images

Most of us have encountered the sheer terror of sitting in an austere exam hall, the required space away from our neighbour's desk, attempting to complete an exam at school or college. But have you ever stopped to wonder how boring it must be for the invigilator who must undertake a rather tedious vigilance task involving walking up and down the aisles for hours at a time, checking that no one is peering at someone else's work, reading crib notes scrawled on their arm or exhibiting any other suspicious activity?

Comments posted on the *Times Educational Supplement*'s web chatroom and a BBC website[31] reveal exactly what these bored teachers do when the tedium gets too much. Activities include:

- Games of 'spot the ugliest pupil/student'.

- Running slowed-down 'races' around the hall.

- Translating exam papers into foreign languages.

- Counting things like the number of bricks in the wall, the number of left-handed pupils, the number of coughs, etc.

- Making figures out of Blu-Tack.

- Running bets on the people asking to use the bathroom.

- Practising belly-dance moves.

- Racing to the student with their hand raised.

- Calculating things, such as the length of the floorboards or columns used in the exam room.

- Playing I-Spy with a colleague.

- Texting colleagues.

- **Drive recklessly**: This concurs with a 2011 UK study which surveyed motorists and found that the drivers who were most prone to boredom whilst on the road were more likely to engage in driving habits that put them at high risk for accidents and crashes – like tailgating, speeding, driving whilst sleepy, or daydreaming behind the wheel – perhaps in an attempt to make the drive more exciting.[32]

- **Drink alcohol**: This will be addressed in the next chapter.

- **Shop**: Shopping can be a way of introducing the novel stimuli we seek (as we buy new stuff), but this is less likely to be a hit for men; according to a study commissioned by Quidco. com, men get bored after just 26 minutes of shopping (women take 2 hours before the tedium kicks in).[33] With internet shopping, this strategy can be one that is constantly accessible.

- **Chat**: Over 30 per cent of people turn to others to provide much-needed extra stimulation in the form of chat and gossip. Chatting to others enlightens an otherwise dull day or task – and gossip probably fulfils this role more than any other form of chat. Gossip has been shown to play an important role in providing stimulation in monotonous jobs that have little variety or challenge and thus is important in reducing boredom in such situations.[34] This is why a call centre magazine points out that 'malignant gossip is frequently the result of boredom', and thus to reduce gossip, managers need to reduce boredom.[35] Could this even explain the mighty success of celebrity-gossip magazines – perhaps the boredom of our own lives leads us to seek gossip about other people?

- *Argue*: This item referred specifically to arguing with a spouse or partner at the end of a boring day; something more than 15 per cent of us claim to do. It is likely to be due to the restless, arousal-seeking type of boredom discussed in Chapter 1 that leads bored people to pick fights, bicker or complain about possibly minor issues.

- *Exercise*: A surprisingly popular response to boredom, with almost 30 per cent of respondents claiming that they turn to exercise after a dull day at work. This is a very positive way to cope with the restless and agitated sense of energy that being bored leaves. Many people find themselves fidgeting or drumming their fingers/jiggling their legs when bored, as if they have a mass of energy that they simply cannot unleash; going for a run clearly allows that energy to be dissipated. This 'energising' theory of boredom is in contrast to the sleep approach (that explains why some people feel sleepier when bored, not more energised) but the two different reactions are explained by the different types of boredom as discussed in Chapter 1 (pages 18–20).

- *Be more creative*: Some 20 per cent of people believe that boredom has positive and not negative consequences; being more creative is something that will be returned to in Chapter 11.

Box 2.5: How far would you go to relieve your boredom?

All of the activities discussed so far seem reasonable ways to attempt to combat boredom, but a recent study published in the prestigious journal *Science* suggests that many of us would take far more extreme measures to beat the boredom. Led by Professor Timothy Wilson, the research at the University of Virginia, USA, involved asking students to sit in an unstimulating environment with nothing but their own thoughts to entertain them. They were then offered the chance to give themselves an electric shock, one they had previously experienced and indicated that they found unpleasant. The findings suggested that people were more likely to shock themselves when bored than when they were not. It is speculated that they were perhaps attempting to shock themselves out of their boredom, or just preferred any stimulation (even a painful one) to none at all.[36]

Drugs, Truancy and Riots:
What Boredom Does to Us

On a sunny August day in 2013, 23-year-old Australian exchange student Christopher Lane, who was on a baseball scholarship at East Central University in Ada, Oklahoma, was taking an afternoon jog near his girlfriend's home. Chancey Allen Luna, 16, shot him dead with a handgun and escaped in a car driven by another teen, Michael Dewayne Jones, 17. Fifteen-year-old James Edwards was also a passenger. After they were arrested, Jones confessed that they shot Lane 'because they were bored.'[1] They explained, *'We were bored and didn't have anything to do, so we decided to kill somebody.'*[2]

Sadly, so-called 'thrill-kills' are not that rare. Sheer boredom has been cited as a reason for murder on a number of occasions in recent times.[3]

- In Connecticut in 2010, six teenagers fatally stabbed 25-year-old pizza chef Mathew Chew, telling authorities they did it because they were bored.[4]
- In 2008, 22-year-old Jeromie Cancel suffocated a university student, Kevin Pravia, in the victim's Manhattan apartment by wrapping a plastic bag around his head; prosecutors said Cancel told them he murdered Pravia because he was bored.[3]
- In 2006, in the United Kingdom, 19-year-old Stuart Harling fatally stabbed nurse Cheryl Moss; a prison guard later testified that Harling had said he'd committed the murder out of boredom.[3]

- In 2014, 16-year-old Marcell Dockery started a fire that killed one NYPD officer and critically injured another – because he was 'bored'.[5]
- Everardo Campos, 23, was standing outside his home in Greenville County, S.C., in 2014 when he was shot and killed by Conrad Allen, 17, and Dameion Robinson, 18. Their motive was that 'they had apparently been bored and wanted to do something'.[6]

Not all such boredom-induced acts of violence are carried out by young people, however. Consider the case of an unnamed truck driver in Portland, Victoria, who had been asked to attend the docks in 2012 to take cargo from a ship. The ship failed to arrive on time and the worker, and two of his colleagues, were subject to an 18-hour wait. During that time there was very little for the men, all of whom were over 50, to do and at some point the truck driver attacked one of his colleagues; he did not kill the man but did cause severe injuries. All the men blamed being bored for the attack – so much so that the injured man brought a legal claim against the company, blaming it for the boredom that led to his being attacked (a claim rejected by the Supreme Court, who insisted that the company could not be held responsible for the crime, even if it was induced by work-related boredom).[7]

The cases above illustrate the dark side of boredom, an emotion that we are so motivated to eliminate that it can apparently drive some of us to carry out terrible deeds. Of course it would be disingenuous to suggest that boredom causes people to commit murder (or even grievous bodily harm). After all, most of us are bored at some point, even chronically bored, yet do not take such drastic measures to eliminate our ennui. However, as this chapter will illustrate, the dark side of boredom, whilst rarely including murder, is never very far away.

Were the British Riots of 2011 Caused By Bored Teens?

On 4 August 2011 a police officer shot and killed 29-year-old Mark Duggan during a traffic stop on the Ferry Lane bridge, next to Tottenham Hale station, in the UK. The explanation given by the police as to why they had killed this young black man proved unsatisfactory for many and it led to protests and demonstrations about the way black people were treated by the police. Several violent clashes with police ensued, along with the destruction of police vehicles, a magistrates' court, a double-decker bus, and many civilian homes and businesses, thus rapidly gaining attention from the media. Overnight, looting took place in Tottenhale Hale Retail Park and nearby Wood Green. The following days saw similar scenes in other parts of London, with the most rioting taking place in Hackney, Brixton, Walthamstow, Peckham, Enfield, Battersea, Croydon, Ealing, Barking, Woolwich, Lewisham and East Ham. From Monday 8th until Wednesday 10 August, other cities in England, including Birmingham, Bristol and Manchester, along with several towns, saw what was described by the media as 'copycat violence'. I vividly remember the horror of seeing a local library in my home town of Salford, Greater Manchester, being burned by rioting youths and of visiting Bradford, a town near Leeds, with my children for a day out in the school holidays – and being anxious about returning before nightfall when the riots seemed likely to resume.

© Darren Staples/Reuters Images

By 15 August, about 3,100 people had been arrested, of whom more than 1,000 had been charged. There were a total 3,443 crimes across London and an estimated £200 million worth of property damage was incurred. Five people died and at least 16 others were injured as a direct result of related violent acts.[8]

Following the riots, commentators and researchers began to look at the reasons why the violence and destruction escalated in such a dramatic way. Many felt that young people who were unconnected with the original protests about the shooting of Duggan joined in simply because they were bored during school or college summer holidays; 'profound boredom was cited by rioters as one of their principal motivations,' screamed the *Daily Mail* in their analysis of the riots one year on in 2012[9], whilst the *Daily Telegraph* claimed that rioting teenagers 'were bored in (the) long summer holiday'.[10]

The suggestion is that young people with nothing much to do saw looting and arson as an exciting way to bring missing stimulation back into their lives. Kids who had no knowledge of or interest in Mark Duggan went looting shops, stealing designer clothes, burning buildings and committing arson simply to fill a void caused by an under-stimulating environment. Quite why teenagers are so bored today is the subject of another chapter later on, but for now, let us content ourselves with accepting that boredom can be a very destructive force.

The idea that boredom can lead to anti-social behaviour is not a new one and was around long before the British riots of 2011. A Fox News report in 2001 blamed a spate of serious wildfires on boredom: 'arson suspects tell investigators nearly the same story each time — they were bored'.[11] A BBC report in 2008 on the increase of arson attacks in Leicestershire in the UK suggested that bored teens were to blame.[12] In 2009, police in the Tampa Bay area of America claimed boredom was the reason why five 'good' teens (two of whom were A-grade students) were motivated to embark on a wild arson spree using homemade Molotov cocktails – a mixture of petrol and sodas – to set fire to 14 vehicles and one house.[13] In 2011, parents in Coley Park in the UK said the reason for groups of youths attacking buses in the area was because they were bored and had nothing better to do.[14]

And so it goes on. Google 'arson' and 'boredom' and pages and pages of stories come up. But arson is only the start of what being bored can induce us to do.

Box 3.1: Bored man lasers helicopter – and gets two years in prison

According to a report in the *Washington Post*, a 26-year-old Californian man pointed two high-power laser beams at a police helicopter in 2014, causing temporary blindness to the pilots. He told police officers on his arrest that he did it because he was bored.[15]

Gambling on Being Bored

According to a research paper published in the journal *International Gambling Studies* in 2010, 'boredom is reported to be an important factor in problematic gambling behaviour'.[16] The researchers, who include fellow boredom expert John Eastwood from York University in Canada, cite correlational data that has consistently demonstrated a link between people who have gambling problems and their self-report measures of boredom. One study, for example, found that having a low tolerance for boredom seemed to be a factor in developing gambling problems, whilst another found that the more bored gamblers were, the more games they played.[16]

Indeed, when gamblers in a number of studies were asked what they felt were the primary reasons for their engaging in gambling activities, they cited boredom as their main motivator. For example, a study in 1984 suggested that gamblers in Las Vegas cited the quest for 'boredom and excitement' as the primary motivation for playing the odds,[17] whilst a study of older adults in 2002 found that 30 per cent of them claimed that they gambled in order to relieve their boredom.[18] The research is borne out by anecdotal evidence too; for example, England footballer Wayne Rooney claimed in his 2006 autobiography, *My Story*, that he developed a gambling problem due to being bored – 'Basically, I did it out of boredom,' he wrote.[19]

The gambling-boredom link is clearly to do with the stimulation and sensation provided by risk-taking as well as that from winning. People who may have low tolerance for boredom (are boredom-prone – see Chapter 5), or have chronically under-stimulating lives, may turn to gambling to increase the level of stimulation to more acceptable levels. Research indeed suggests that bored people gamble to increase their level of arousal (rather than simply to provide an escape from the unpleasant negative feeling that boredom is).[16]

There are, of course, other ways to meet that craving for arousal and chemically-induced stimulation is equally of concern.

Drug and Alcohol Abuse

Several sources suggest that boredom is a major factor in the abuse of drugs and that drug abusers are more likely to use drugs when they are bored.[20] A UK survey by the charity Drinkwise in 2009 found that 29 per cent of teenagers had turned to alcohol as a means to relieve boredom.[21] Teenagers who are 'frequently bored' increase their chances for substance abuse by 50 per cent, according to a study by the National Center on Addiction and Substance Abuse (CASA) at Columbia University in the US.[22] Drugs and alcohol can both be mind-altering substances so it is easy to see how people might be tempted to use these to relieve the state of boredom in their brain. It can sometimes be easier to turn to such strategies than to try to address the underlying causes of boredom and do something about it (e.g. take up new challenges, hobbies, etc.). Once individuals try drugs or alcohol, unless the causes for their boredom are addressed, it is easy to become addicted; in one study of 365 addicts who had completed a treatment programme, boredom was the number one reason given for re-using drugs or alcohol (followed by anxiety, loneliness and anger).[22] This is illustrated by the case of another (former) England footballer Paul Gascoigne, who famously attributed his relapse into alcoholism in 2013 to the fact that, 'I was just bored.' [23] He spent a month in a rehab clinic in Phoenix, Arizona, USA, to tackle this latest relapse.

Box 3.2: Drug addict who craved prison because he was so bored

Thirty-year-old drug addict Lee Price was so bored of life in a quiet market town in Shropshire, UK, that in March 2014 he rang the police and begged them to send him to prison. The police, naturally, turned down his request, telling him that he would have to commit a crime to be imprisoned; he duly did so. He went on to steal £128 worth of goods from a local supermarket and achieved his goal; he was sentenced to 12 weeks in prison.[24]

There are other ways, apart from chemical, that we might obtain stimulation when levels are low, risky or thrill-seeking activities being one such avenue.

Why Boredom Leads to Risk-taking

People who are bored are, as we know from Chapter 1, under-aroused. They are motivated to reconcile this by seeking sensation or stimulation, but sometimes this drive for sensation overrides concerns for personal safety. These people might engage in unsafe sex, drive recklessly and indulge in drug abuse (see above). People who engage in such risky behaviours when they are bored are likely to be high on the sensation-seeker personality trait. High sensation-seekers have a strong need for novelty, thrill and adventure-seeking and are easily bored in situations where there is not enough stimulation for them.

The brains of high sensation-seekers might even be wired differently from low-sensation seekers. In a recent study using functional MRI scans at the University of Kentucky,[25] researchers found that different brain areas are activated in high- vs. low-sensation seekers in response to strongly arousing stimuli (in this case, pictures that they viewed). Regardless of whether the pictures they saw were pleasant (e.g. mild erotica) or unpleasant (e.g. a snake poised to strike), the high-sensation seekers showed early and strong activation of an area of the brain called the insula. The insula receives and interprets signals from the body so it makes sense that it would be more active when people are aroused.

The low-sensation seekers did not show the same activity in their insula when they viewed the arousing pictures. Rather, there was strong activity in a different part of the brain called the anterior cingulate, which is linked to the regulation of emotions; this did not happen as strongly in the high-sensation seekers. This suggests that the low-sensation seekers may have emotional inhibitors that dampen down their quest for arousal and allow them the control to avoid dangerous arousal-seeking activities that the high-sensation seekers may lack.

The dopamine hypothesis, discussed in relation to over-eating in Chapter 2 (see page 30), may also be relevant here. Dopamine, as you may recall, is the primary neurotransmitter involved in pleasure and reward. Some studies have found that people with higher levels of a specific type of dopamine receptor (the D4 receptor) have greater sensation-seeking tendencies.[25] Thrills and novelty send a rush of dopamine to these receptors, which is very motivating. But, like most things, we habituate or get used to the dopamine rush, which explains why high sensation-seekers need to try ever more thrilling (and more dangerous) activities to get the same feelings. Such a quest for that dopamine rush may override any fear that they may ordinarily get from risky behaviours.

Box 3.3: The rise of extreme sports

Extreme sports appear to be gaining in popularity year on year. The number of Americans who skateboard, for example, has grown by nearly 50 per cent since 1999. Today, more than 14 million skate on a regular basis.[26] Between 2000 and 2011, around 4 million injuries in the US were thought to be caused by extreme sports such as surfing, mountain biking, motocross, skateboarding, snowmobiling, snowboarding and skiing.[26]

Could this rise in popularity of these activities be due to sensation and thrill-seeking – caused by increasing boredom in modern life? Thrill-seeking involves our old friend, dopamine, which is released when we are exposed to new, exciting experiences. As we have seen, the dopamine hit is particularly rewarding, especially for those who do not get that hit (or enough of it) from other means. Risk taking has indeed been linked to levels of dopamine; research conducted by Dr Ernest Noble of the University of California links the D2 and D4 dopamine receptor genes to risk-taking behaviour. After his 1998 study, Noble estimated that 20 per cent of people are born with the D2 dopamine receptor, while 30 per cent are born with both the D2 and the D4 dopamine receptors.[27]

© Dave Bunnell

Caves are inherently dangerous environments
and caving is considered a risky activity.

All of which suggests that those who pursue extreme sports crave that dopamine rush, either because they have a high need for such a hit (sensation-seeking individuals) or because the levels in their own lives are unsatisfactorily low. Such people are sometimes called Type T personalities for thrill-seeking, and 'they often bore easily'.[28] If there is a rise in such personality types, as the rise in extreme sport participation would suggest, could this be due to the development of a more boredom-prone society today? (see Chapter 4 for discussion of why society is more boredom-prone today).

Boredom Behind Bars

If boredom can have such drastic impacts on 'ordinary' people who have a wealth of activities available 24/7 to entertain and stimulate them (see Chapter 4 for more on this), then what about its effects on those who are far more limited in their ability to reach the optimal levels of arousal needed to avoid ennui? Boredom in prisons might not be a top concern for many of us, but it perhaps should be; if being bored can turn 'ordinary' folk into anti-social thugs, what might it do to hardened criminals – and how might this impact on society?

If life outside is considered so boring by so many of us (see Chapter 1, pages 1–2), imagine how dull life inside must be. According to a report in the *New York Post* in 2010, celebrity prisoner O.J. Simpson claimed to be 'bored out of his mind' at Lovelock Correctional Center in Nevada, where he is currently serving 33 years for armed robbery.[29] And it's not just celebrity prisoners for whom boredom is a problem: according to a report by Brigadier Hugh Monro, the Chief Inspector of Prisons in 2012, boredom amongst prisoners is a concern at Scotland's only open jail; 'except for the gymnasium,' he noted, 'there is very little for prisoners to do'.[30] Prisoner 'Ben', in his blog of 2010, put it succinctly when he wrote that, *'The secret burden of imprisonment is that it is a mindlessly boring existence'.*[31]

Does any of this matter? Indeed it should. Anyone who is bored will look for ways to drag themselves out of their ennui and bored criminals should be a major concern. On 14 February 2013, Gary Smith, 48, and Lee Newell, 44, two prisoners at a Long Lartin high-security prison in the UK, followed fellow convict Subhan Anwar into his cell, armed with weapons fashioned out of a pen and a toothbrush before binding his ankles with tape and strangling him with his own tracksuit bottoms. And the reason given by one of the killers immediately after the murder? 'I'm bored, it was something to do.'[32]

Whilst few prisoners resort to murder to alleviate their ennui, many do turn to drugs. A report on drug abuse in prisons in Scotland's *The Herald* pointed out that 'drugs are a time-killer – an antidote to boredom – and if anything characterises today's prisons it is boredom'. [33] Violence is another antidote, as the above case illustrates. According to a report published in 2011, about Pentonville Prison in Islington, UK, life for prisoners there is a 'grim regime of boredom, violence and drug-taking' with most sitting around 'doing nothing'. [34] This boredom has been blamed for a number of dangerous prison riots, including one that involved 400 inmates at low-security prison HMP Ashwell, near Oakham in Leicestershire, UK, in 2009. Lack of investment in facilities to occupy prisoners was one of the explanations for the riots put forward by Colin Moses, national chairman of the Prison Officers Association, which led to what he described as 'unhappy and bored prisoners'.[35] And boredom in prisons looks set to increase, not decrease, as resources and budgets continue to be stretched to accommodate burgeoning prison populations.

The problem of boredom is not only in the things it might make us do in an effort to overcome it, but also that it affects our very health and well-being. And this matters if you are subject to a great deal of boredom – whether that be due to being incarcerated in a prison, or in a boring workplace.

Box 3.4: Bored Computer-hackers

Have you ever wondered what motivates people to hack into computers or commit other cybercrimes? Various anecdotal reports suggest that boredom is to blame. Jake Davis, a 20-year-old from the Shetlands, for example, masterminded the world's biggest hacking scandal when he hacked the CIA, the UK's Serious Organised Crime Agency, the Arizona police force and a website affiliated with the FBI. He blamed boredom for his crimes.[36] Another hacker, Australian Anthony Scott Harrison, who developed a malicious Trojan virus capable of stealing internet banking credit card details, was described as 'unemployed, bored and obsessed with computers'. [37] And in 2012 a bored teenager in Darlington risked being arrested by MI5 after trying to break into a north-east police force's computer system during his school summer holidays.[38]

Such anecdotal reports that boredom is a contributory factor for cybercrime are backed up by scientists such as sociologists Paul Taylor in 2009[39] and David Dittrich and Kenneth Himma, in their 2006 essay, 'Hackers, Crackers and Computer Criminals'.[40]

Is Boredom the New Stress?

I have been quoted in a range of media across the globe, from the *Daily Mail* in the UK to CNN in the USA, as asserting that boredom is the new stress.[41] The reason I made these claims is partly because vast numbers of participants in my research suggested that being bored is stressful (see Box 3.5), and partly because of the comparisons with the way stress has been regarded over the past couple of decades. Stress used to be seen as something rather shameful to admit to, a sign of weakness. It was often felt that mentally strong people should be able to cope with daily stressors and when they couldn't cope and ended up ill or missing work, they often pretended they were ill with more 'acceptable' complaints, such as back pain or flu, rather than admit to being stressed.

Box 3.5: Boredom and stress

Findings from various studies that I have conducted suggest that boredom and stress are linked. For example, 21 per cent of teachers claimed that boredom leads to them feeling stressed.[42] Similar numbers of students claimed the same.[43] Forty-four per cent of supermarket employees who were bored often or most of the time also claimed that being bored led to them feeling stressed.[44]

The reason why boredom is considered stressful is that boredom is typically the result of attempts to increase effort to engage with something that is not arousing enough. This results in irritation that itself leads to mental strain and anxiety; boredom has been found to lead to increased levels of the 'stress' hormone cortisol and increased heart rate, just like when we are stressed.[45]

The tide has turned somewhat and whilst there are still some who are reluctant to admit to being stressed, stress is now seen as something understandable and even acceptable to suffer from. Organisations have a legal responsibility to ensure the health and safety of their employees, and ensuring that they are not exposed to too much stress is considered part of this remit. Stress management programmes abound in organisational life and being stressed is rarely seen as something to be ashamed of anymore. In fact, I would go so far as to suggest that being stressed is almost a badge of honour; if you are not stressed, you are almost considered not busy enough, or important enough. Stress has become quite competitive.

I would argue that boredom is now where stress used to be. It is regarded as something shameful to admit to, suggesting some failing or lacking on the part of the bored. Whenever I deliver presentations on the subject of boredom, 99 per cent of the audience will admit that they are sometimes (if not often) bored. But there is always one person who raises their hand and asserts proudly that they are NEVER bored. They insist that their lives are so full and their minds so active that they never experience boredom. Whether this is true or not (I suspect that they simply have excellent coping mechanisms for boredom rather than never experiencing it), the implication for everyone else is clear: only the inactive, lazy and feeble-minded get bored.

When I conducted my research into workplace boredom, I struggled to get access to many organisations. And the reason? They refused to contemplate the idea that any of their staff were ever bored. One CEO told me, 'My staff are never bored – they don't have time.' Such people are in denial. Boredom is part of life and I hope that over the next few years, it becomes as acceptable to admit to boredom as it does to admitting to being stressed – and that organisations will take steps to reduce boredom for employees in their organisations just as they are obliged to do so now for stress.

Being Bored is So Depressing

Not only is boredom stressful but it is depressing too. Boredom is not the same as depression, but people who are bored may be more prone to depression,[46] possibly because of the link with life meaning discussed in Chapter 1. A study reported in 2012 to examine risk-behaviours of 845 drug-users revealed that those experiencing high boredom were almost five times as likely to report high depressive symptoms.[47] This sort of boredom is likely to be the apathetic boredom mentioned in Chapter 1 and is characterised by a lack of interest in the environment, a lack of feeling, and a lack of connection with life itself and towards other people. These, of course, are very similar symptoms to depression.

Depression, of course, carries the risk of suicide, but this is not the only mortal risk that being bored can bring.

Bored to Death

People talk of being 'bored to death', probably because the idea of being so mind-numbingly bored may mean that we (jokingly) suggest that death would be preferable, or that we are so under-aroused that we may actually stop being motivated to breathe. But researchers have recently found that the concept of being bored to death may not be anything to joke about. It seems that people who complain of being bored are indeed more likely to die young – and that those who experience a lot of boredom are more than twice as likely to die (from heart disease) than those who are not bored. Researchers from the Department of Epidemiology and Public Health at University College London followed up more than 7,000 civil servants in the UK aged 35–55 over a 25-year period.[48] These civil servants had been interviewed between 1985 and 1988 about their levels of boredom and those who claimed to suffer from boredom were nearly 40 per cent more likely to have died by the end of the study (in 2009) than those who did not.

This is the first study to link heart disease to boredom, although care should be taken before we start accusing our school maths teacher or tedious colleague of culpable manslaughter. What is not known is whether it is boredom per se that is leading to heart problems – or whether it is the things that bored people do to overcome their ennui that are unhealthy. Indeed, this chapter and the previous one have shown many of the things that we do when bored which could contribute to long-term adverse health outcomes (such as over-eating, drinking alcohol, etc.).

One way that good health outcomes can be achieved is through the maintenance of strong and supportive relationships – the most significant of which is surely with our long-term partner. And yet, the whole concept of 'long-term' can simply mean 'boring' to many, so what happens when it is our partner who bores us?

Bored of Each Other: Relationship Boredom

One of the most significant consequences of boredom is also one of the least researched: couple or relationship boredom. Boredom is probably responsible for much of marital and relationship breakdown and is part of what some authors refer to as the 'stagnation stage' of a relationship, when couples stop engaging in new and arousing activities together (such as going out together or sometimes even just talking). According to a 2003 study in which researchers in the US and Europe surveyed 1,761 people who had been married more than 15 years, this often happens after only two years of marriage.[49]

Box 3.6: Bored, not unloved

A survey presented at the 109th Annual American Sociological Association conference in San Francisco, USA, in 2014, suggests that women who cheat on their husbands are happily married but just 'bored' in the bedroom.[50]

One of the few studies on relationship boredom involves an American study published in 2010. The authors asked participants who were in relationships (including married or just dating) to think of times when they felt bored and then questioned them about those experiences.[51] They found some of the most frequent causes of boredom to be 'doing the same things', 'not going out', 'no communication' and 'partner doing things without them'. These all reflect lack of novelty and stimulation and a lack of quality time spent together. Relationship boredom seems to stem from the lack of something positive (e.g. stimulation or meaningfulness), but also from the human tendency to habituate, or adapt to stimuli, so that however fantastic our partner might be, we simply get so used to them that they no longer excite.

The participants in the American study coped with their relationship boredom in a number of ways, including attempting to talk to their partner more and trying new things together. Interestingly, nearly half of the married participants coped by engaging in more solo activities, such as exercise, personal hobbies and focusing on their career. According to US social psychologist Arthur Aron this is a mistake: what bored couples should be doing is engaging in fun activities together, not solo. And these activities should be exciting and not merely pleasant. Aron conducted an experiment whereby some long-term couples took part in 'pleasant' activities together (such as cooking, seeing friends, watching films) and others engaged in more 'exciting' activities (such as skiing, dancing, concerts). After 10 weeks, the couples who did the more exciting activities reported being more satisfied with each other than those who did the merely pleasant ones. [49] The reason for this could be due to the misattribution of arousal discussed in Chapter 1 (see the Wobbly Bridge study, page 10).

Box 3.7: How to fix a bored marriage: advice from India

An article in *The Times of India*[52] in 2014 offers the following advice for spicing up a dull marriage or long-term relationship:

- Go on a spontaneous 'date' with your partner.

- Share new experiences – e.g. go to a restaurant or venue that you haven't been to before.

- Try something new in bed.

- Do solo activities too, allowing the chance to miss each other.

- Have a laugh with each other.

- Encourage your partner in their endeavours.

Other negative impacts of boredom are discussed elsewhere in this book, e.g. over-eating (Chapter 2) or counter-productive work behaviours (Chapter 9) and truancy (Chapter 8).

How Modern Society Fosters Boredom: The Causes of Boredom

Terry Waite, the Church of England envoy kidnapped in Lebanon in 1987, spent nearly five years captive, much of it in solitary confinement. He later described the mind-numbing boredom he had to endure '*in a dark room with no books and papers for a long, long time and no communication with anyone or with the outside world*'.[1] It is easy to understand how bored he must have been, but thankfully, few of us ever get to experience the extremes of sensory deprivation that Terry Waite had to sustain, and certainly not for any length of time. Indeed, most of us experience sensory overload rather than underload on a continual basis. So why are we, with all that we have to entertain us today, so bored?

Why Are We All So Bored These Days?

Boredom researcher Lars Svendsen (and author of *A Philosophy of Boredom*) laments, '*it is a disturbing aspect of our western culture that, whilst we are presented with an unprecedented range of opportunities to satisfy our desires, people now appear to be more susceptible to boredom than ever before*'.[2] Internet, DVDs, iPods, Xboxes, PlayStations, 24-hour supermarkets, multiple TV channels, multi-screen cinemas, bowling, retail parks, on-line chatrooms, Facebook, Twitter, MSN, Instagram, Pinterest, texting, Whatsapp – today we have so many varied ways to spend our leisure time that we should all surely never know what boredom feels like. Yet, the more we have to stimulate us, the more stimulation we seem to crave. Our world is a fast-paced, ever-changing montage of novel stimuli assaulting all our senses and as a consequence of this, we seem to be losing the ability to cope when faced with routine, repetition and lack of excitement. Increasingly intolerant of lower levels of stimulation, we experience this discomfort as boredom. We are driven to cure this boredom but this simply leads us on a never-ending quest for stimulation because, like a drug, the more we have, the more we need.

The likely reasons for our increasing ennui with life (actually we don't know if we are more bored now than in times gone by as there is no data available to compare with, but what we do know is that we *shouldn't* often be bored now at all, given the wealth of avenues to stimulate us in the information and technological age) include the following:

1. Repetition and routine breeds boredom

Although we seem to live in a varied and exciting world with a plethora of entertainment at our fingertips, this is actually the problem; many sources of our stimulation are obtained in remarkably similar ways – via our fingertips. Think about it: we spend much of our day now in an office-environment – tapping away at our keyboards. We then look for entertainment via the internet or our phone – more tapping. We are becoming surgically attached to a keyboard, which is removing the means to access stimulation in different ways.

Not only that, but we are living our lives vicariously (and repetitively) via a screen. We watch movies, read books, catch the news, interact with friends – all via a glowing screen (and tap-tapping away on its keyboard). On the train we avoid eye contact because we are too busy staring at the screen on our lap. We even view real life through a screen; go to any school concert or big event and you will see most of the audience gazing at the stage via the confines of an iPad or smartphone screen. Even taking part in real-life can rarely happen without being drawn to that screen; out to lunch or coffee with friends we cannot resist the lure of updating our status or tweeting a picture of the food (one French restaurant has reacted to this obsession with tweeting images of meals by banning cameras, claiming that the preoccupation with photographing meals ruins the experience of the food).[3]

All this is simply becoming boring. We are stuck in a rut of trying to satisfy our need for neural stimulation via exactly the same methods. Instead of using varied activities that engage different neural systems (sport, knitting, painting, cooking, etc.) to relieve our boredom, we are falling back on the same screen-tapping schema for much of our day. Life becomes monotonous, repetitive and routine when it revolves

© AFP/Stringer/Getty Images

around a flickering screen and a glowing keyboard. The irony is that in trying to avoid a single dull moment, we fill in every spare minute by engaging in routine and repetitive tasks. On the one hand, our mobile devices should ensure that we should be able to plug every boring moment with stimuli, but on the other hand, our means of obtaining that stimulation has become so repetitive and routine that it could be a source of boredom in itself.

Our constant tapping and gazing, of course, also prevents us from finding other more productive means of beating the ennui, such as mind-wandering, daydreaming and reflection, the benefits of which are discussed in Chapter 11.

2. Increased expectation of ever-changing novelty

Our brains are hard-wired to seek novelty in favour of the old. We even have a 'novelty-centre' in our midbrains called the *substantia nigra/ventral tegmental area (SN/VTA)* that responds to novel stimuli. Several years ago, researchers Nico Bunzeck and Emrah Düzel at University College London and Otto von Guericke University used functional imaging techniques to look at what happens in the brain when we see a novel stimulus. In a paper reported in the journal *Neuron*,[4] they noted that the SN/VTA area 'lights up' when a person was shown a new picture. The researchers hypothesise that when these novelty centres light up, they cause a surge of dopamine to be released. You will recall from Chapter 2 (page 31) that dopamine is associated with pleasure – and thus this would suggest that there is something very motivating about novelty; we are programmed to seek novelty and are rewarded with a feeling of pleasure when we find it. Novelty seeking is of evolutionary benefit to us as it encourages us to explore our environment and perhaps discover new resources or new and better ways to do things. The drive for novelty also means that we are able to ignore stuff that doesn't change much in favour of alerting our attention to changes in our environment that might be important to us (signally danger or access to new resources, for example). This is why we get 'bored' or habituate to routine and repetitive stimuli but are attracted to new and novel things.

However, what Bunzeck and Düzel found is that the novelty centre of the brain only responds to totally new stimuli. As soon as a new stimulus is noticed, it is no longer new and after a while becomes background noise – something to be ignored. It bores us. In order to get that same dopamine hit that is so pleasurable, we thus need to seek new stimuli. And, dopamine is thought to be addictive – the more we have, the more we crave.

We are constantly bombarded with novel stimuli throughout our day, mainly via electronic means. Yet it all becomes 'samey' and we need new stimuli to keep up that dopamine rush we are so used to. This explains why Facebook, once the exciting and new kid on the block, is now regarded as 'boring' by a third of users.[5] In fact, Christopher Mimms, writing for *MIT Technology Review*, lamented that the entire internet was now 'boring'. Boring? All that access to movies, news, books, information, shopping . . . all dismissed as boring! But, as Mimms explains, 'the novelty has worn off'.[6]

And yet, we have become used to the constant buzz of novelty streaming down our electronic devices. If it's boring, then we must crave even newer things. This is why Dr Peter Whybrow, a British-born psychiatrist who runs the Semel Institute for Neuroscience and Human Behavior at UCLA, brilliantly referred to our smartphones, computers and devices as 'electronic cocaine'; 'with technology,' he explains, 'novelty is the reward. You essentially become addicted to novelty.'[7] The more we get, the more we crave. And the less these cravings are satisfied, the more we interpret that feeling as boredom (more on the novelty-seeking personality in Chapter 5).

3. Rise in amount of leisure time

Until the beginning of the twentieth century, it is likely that there wasn't time to be bored. Journalist Lucy Scholes points out that *'our modern concept of boredom was born at the same time as that of the invention of leisure'*.[8] Day-to-day life then was consumed with the business of survival: earning a living, obtaining and preparing food and maintaining shelter and warmth. Any spare time will have been spent in godly pursuits: attending church or other religious outlets. The Industrial Revolution brought with it an increasing amount of leisure as our lives were no longer dominated by work, survival and religion. People began to spend time in new pursuits such as visiting coffee houses, the seaside, parks and other venues. As national 'bank' holidays were introduced, along with weekends, working time directives and labour-saving devices, people began to look for ways to fill their increasing amount of leisure time.

Even in the past fifty years or so, the amount of leisure time has increased dramatically. Between 1965 and 2003, leisure for men increased by 6–8 hours per week (driven by a decline in working hours) and for women by 4–8 hours per week (driven by a decline in time spent on housework).[9] The peak for the amount of leisure time was probably around 1995, prior to the electronic communication explosion that has resulted in work creeping more and more into our leisure time. However, even in today's climate of blurred work/home boundaries, where leisure time may seem like a luxury for some (80 per cent of workers surveyed by Direct Line Insurance in the UK in 2013[10] said their leisure time was eroded by the constant need to be connected to work through emails and smartphones – with our free time shrinking to, on average, just two hours and 45 minutes a day), it is likely to still be far more than it was a century ago. Certainly, the value of leisure is well recognised; even 'workaholics' are urged to take time off, since the role of adequate leisure as a means of achieving well-being and good health is widely acknowledged.

The problem with increased leisure is twofold; until relatively recently there simply wasn't enough to do to occupy people during this leisure time, especially for those with limited financial resources. Then came the technological age when the range of activities available to fill this increasing leisure time began to include more and more (cheaply available) passive pursuits that became more appealing than the more active ones of days gone by (of which more below). For example, the average American today spends more of their leisure time passively watching TV than anything else; of the 5.26 hours per day Americans had for leisure time on average in 2013, they spent 166 minutes of it watching TV (compared with 43 minutes socialising, 26 minutes playing computer games, 19 minutes reading, 18 minutes engaged in sporting activities, 18 minutes thinking and 5 minutes in arts pursuits[11] (more on TV soon).

Despite this rise in ways to fill our leisure time, we are increasingly bored, with one study across 36 countries suggesting that around a third of us are affected by 'leisure boredom'.[12] Part of the problem, according to a Taiwan-based study published in 2012, is that people don't always have 'leisure skills' – the ability to manage their leisure time.[13] Such skills include goal setting, evaluating priorities, organising activities in advance and being flexible, if planned activities need to be changed at the last minute. People who lack some or all of these skills are more likely to be bored during their leisure time.[13]

Box 4.1: A life spent scrolling and tapping

Mary Meeker (an internet analyst at Morgan Stanley) found that on average we spend six to seven hours in front of our phone, tablet, computer and TV screens every day.[14] This means that we spend around 40 per cent of our waking life gazing and tapping. No wonder we are so bored!

Table 4.1: Leisure boredom by country	
Country	Percentage of people experiencing leisure boredom very often/often/sometimes
Continental West Europe	
Switzerland	11
Netherlands	19
Germany	20
France	27
Scandinavia	
Denmark	22
Norway	29
Finland	38
Sweden	43
English-speaking countries	
Ireland	33
New Zealand	35
Australia	38

USA	40
UK	42
Eastern Europe	
Hungary	17
Slovakia	24
Czech Republic	28
Croatia	34
Poland	46
Latin America	
Argentina	38
Mexico	56
East Asia	
Japan	40
Taiwan	40
Korea	49
Others	
Israel	48
South Africa	63
Philippines	70

Adapted from Haller, Hadler and Kaup, 2013, who suggest a range of possible explanations for the differences between countries, ranging from income, number of children to welfare state model of each country (see [12] for review).

Other researchers suggest it is what people do in their leisure time that is the source of boredom rather than how they manage it. For example a lack of meaningful involvement in leisure activities might be a key trigger for leisure boredom. Meaningful activities might be creative ones such as baking, cooking, sewing, woodwork, etc., or activities that enhance the quality of life such as exercise. One researcher suggested that engaging in nostalgic activities can be a way to inject meaningfulness into one's life since nostalgic reverie 'bolsters perceptions of life as meaningful ([15] p.450). It is also suggested that having the income with which to take part in meaningful activities is also a protector against leisure boredom[12] – but of course, not everyone has such an income.

4. Expectation of passive rather than active stimulation

As long ago as his 1987 book, *Amusing Ourselves to Death*, Neil Postman pointed out that as we moved from a culture revolving around the static printed word to one that revolves around rapidly moving and constantly changing images (often accompanied by loud music), we have become high users of passive stimulation. As one commentator put it, '*as TV invaded our front rooms, our definition of entertainment moved from the active to the passive.*'[16] Talking, reading, exercise, crafts, exploration of new places, public meetings and gatherings, etc. are the things we used to do in our leisure time, but many of these active pastimes have been replaced by activities that require little physical or cognitive input. Of course, not all 'modern' pastimes are passive (you can interact with others via electronic media, etc.), but much of what we do in our spare time today requires little from us, other than scrolling and occasional clicking. A study in 2010 suggested that Canadians, for example, spend 2.2 hours per day in passive leisure activities.[16] Passive activities include watching TV or films, listening to music and scrolling social media.

Box 4.2: TV viewing around the globe

In 2005, NOP World, a market research organisation, interviewed more than 30,000 people in 30 countries and reported that the United States was one of the highest TV-viewing nations. [17] This concurs with previous research by NationMaster.com, in 2002, who found that the United States and the United Kingdom were the highest-viewing nations at 28 hours per week, with the lowest-viewing nations being Finland, Norway and Sweden at 18 hours per week. [18]

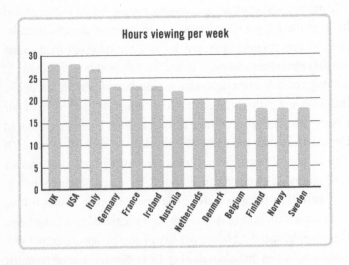

Research shows that the more TV (the ultimate passive medium), including online viewing, we watch, the more passive we become. This is why in 1992, *Newsweek* [19] reported that prisons are relying more and more on TV to 'sedate' inmates: 'faced with severe overcrowding and limited budgets for rehabilitation and counseling, more and more prison officials are using TV to keep inmates quiet'.

Researchers have shown that when we watch TV, our brainwaves slow down, causing us to feel more relaxed and less active. It doesn't matter what we are watching, our brains still slow down (incidentally, this brainwave slowing does not happen when we are reading). The effect of this reduced brainwave activity is to make us less alert, less responsive and less actively engaged with the world. After all, we are viewing someone else's representation of the world rather than finding it out for ourselves. And this 'sedation' effect continues for a while, even when we have stopped watching,[17] which makes it easy to understand why TV is such a powerful tool for prison officers. Bruce E. Levine, a clinical psychologist and author of *Get Up, Stand Up: Uniting Populists, Energizing the Defeated, and Battling the Corporate Elite*, puts it succinctly when he says, 'viewing television puts one in a brain state that makes it difficult to think critically, and it quiets and subdues a population.'[17] TV viewers, after all, need not communicate, respond or even think.

Not only is being passive inherently more boring than being active, but the expectation that our boredom can be solved through passive means that simply confounds the problem. As my own research has shown in Chapter 2 (page 40), we use TV as a means to escape boredom, little realising that such a technique is unlikely to have the desired effect. That is not to say that small bursts of passive entertainment are not worthwhile; TV is relaxing (as shown above) and fills our brains with some form of stimulation after all. The problem is that over-reliance on passive media means that we become passive recipients of stimulation and are unable to go out and get our own stimulants. We become chronically bored, lack curiosity (which involves an alert and active brain) and unable to 'cure' our own ennui.

It is not just TV that is passive; our use of the internet is passive too. Studies show that people spend, on average, far more time passively scrolling through newsfeeds than they do actively engaging with content.[20] This is because we have so many demands on our time that we become passive users, mindlessly scrolling and swiping without thinking about the material we are accessing – and, as we now know, 'passive experiences, no matter the medium, translate to feelings of disconnection and boredom'.[20]

5. Increased distractions

Attentional theories of boredom emphasise that boredom is felt when we are unable to attend to a task (that we are expected to attend to) due to it not providing enough stimulating cues to sustain our interest. It would make sense to consider that we will be less able to maintain our attention to cues if there are other stimuli competing for our attention. If these other stimuli are more exciting, then it will be harder to sustain our attention to the less exciting stimuli – and the effort required in doing so will be perceived as reflecting boredom with that task.

Distractions, then, play an important role in the experience of boredom. An intriguing study in 1989[21] showed how even being exposed to subtle distraction can make us feel more bored. Psychologists asked participants to listen to someone reading an article that was mildly interesting. During the task, a TV in an adjoining room was playing either loudly, softly or muted. Participants were then asked how boring they found the article. Those who were exposed to the low TV sound in the background claimed that they found the article more boring than those in either the very loud or muted conditions. This suggests that subtle distractors can be more insidious in our experience of boredom than none at all or even very prominent distractors; it could be that when we are aware of prominent distractors (loud noise, etc.), we compensate by making more effort to sustain attention. We also blame our distractibility on the prominence of the distractors rather than assuming that the task itself must be boring (see Chapter 1). With low levels of distraction, however, we are barely aware of it and thus do not make such efforts to attend to the task – and this low awareness means we cannot readily blame our lack of concentration on the background distractors (so instead assume our difficulty in sustaining attention must be because we are bored). However, clearly, these low levels of background noise can be more of a distractor than we realise.

Life in the twenty-first century is rife with subtle (and less subtle) distractions. We seem to live life to the beat of background noise, whether the TV is on whilst we are doing something else, our smartphone bleeping with emails or our tablet pinging with updates. These more subtle distractions (as opposed to the more prominent ones of phones ringing, etc.) seem likely to make it harder for us to sustain attention on tasks – and this effort is noted and perceived as boredom (if it is hard for me to concentrate, the task must be boring).

Of course, life has always had its distractions. The quest for food, warmth and shelter must have been disrupted by a range of on-going distractions that stole focus from the tasks of our ancestors – illness, other people, insects, predators, weather, etc. But surely distractions have never been as constant, varied and intrusive as they are now, in what one commenter has referred to as 'the Age of Distraction'?[22] As I write this on the computer, I have an iPad at my side and a smartphone on my desk. In the time it took to write that sentence, all three devices pinged or bleeped to alert me to input demanding my attention. I have a Facebook notification (someone who wants me to play Candy Crush), a direct Facebook message, three emails to my private account and two to my work email address. As I wrote that sentence, a Twitter notification pinged – I have three separate Twitter accounts. I also have LinkedIn, with updates arriving from there regularly. My mobile phone also 'whistles' with text or Whatsapp messages and of course it rings every so often too. Then there is my landline, which can also interrupt my flow. And, if I'm working from home, the postman might ring to ask me to sign for something, or the window-cleaner might knock, asking for money. At work, students or colleagues knock on my door with disturbing regularity. And those are only the intrusive distractions. There is also a range of distractions sitting around me, enticing me away from my work with the practised air of a skilled seductress. Social media to scroll (I wonder what's happening out there?), newspapers to read, washing to do, tidying up, ironing, meals to shop for and cook ... it's a wonder I manage to get anything done at all!

This description of my life is probably fairly typical. I sometimes feel I am drowning in a whirlpool of distraction that is trying to suck me in, and toss me around so much that I have forgotten not only my current goals, but even my life goals. The blurring between work life and home life that so many of us experience now only adds to the number of distractions we face. And I find that all these distractions have a stronger hold when I am tired or when I am not intrinsically engaged in the task. In both cases, my ability to sustain attention is compromised, for the distractors seem to offer more stimulation than the task in hand (even the ironing can seem more appealing than marking the twentieth undergraduate psychology essay on the same topic).

Box 4.3: Our reduced attention span

According to Nicholas Carr in his book, *The Shallows: What The Internet Is Doing To Our Brains*, the average amount of time we could stay focused on one task without our mind wandering to something new in 2000 was 12 seconds. In 2010, it was 8 seconds.

6. High expectations of self-actualisation

Another important reason that I believe can account for the rise in boredom today is in our increased expectation of self-actualisation, fulfilment and meaningfulness. We believe that we deserve to be entertained and expect to lead exciting lives, as we see on TV, Facebook and other media. If our lives are perceived as anything less than extraordinary, we feel dissatisfied and unfulfilled.

As discussed earlier in this book, many researchers see boredom as highly connected with meaningfulness. According to this view, we get bored when events lack meaning and this boredom motivates us to seek out events that are meaningful to us.[23] Being bored then 'entails a sense of purposelessness'[23] because we view our activities as lacking value.

Having purpose to our life, living fulfilled lives and expecting every moment to be thrilling and exciting is a relatively new phenomenon. I distinctly remember a conversation with my grandfather, who was bemused by my having career aspirations that would fulfil and stimulate me – and that these concerns overrode potential financial reward; 'You go to work to earn a living, not to be fulfilled,' he commented. For him and his generation, work was what men did to support their families and the idea of taking a less-paid job in order to be more fulfilled was anathema. How times have changed! When I was employed as Dr Work, a workplace agony aunt for the *Guardian*'s internet site, one of the most common issues that people used to write in about was to do with dissatisfaction with their current job and the quest for a more 'fulfilling' career. We no longer go to work purely for the money; purpose, meaning and self-actualisation are just as (if not more) important.

Box 4.4: Man who quit high-paying job to pursue his dream

Investment banker Sam Stephens is the embodiment of today's generation that value self-actualisation above financial reward. He enjoyed a steady pay cheque, paid vacations and health insurance, yet gave it all up to pursue his dream of opening a restaurant based entirely on one food: oatmeal. OatMeals in the West Village of NYC, USA, opened in 2012 and is going from strength to strength.[24]

The Information Age must surely play a role in encouraging this need for meaning in life. Tales such as that about Sam Stephens above serve to inspire others to follow their own dreams. Social and mass media allow us to see what meaning and value others have in their lives, and cause us to reflect on how meaningless our own lives are in comparison. Compared to other people, our own lives might seem boring, empty and lacking in meaning. Facebook, for example, allows social comparisons to take place with ordinary people on a scale never seen before. It used to be that we would compare ourselves with those in our own social group or those who lived near us – and who, in all likelihood, lived similar lives to us. Now, our circles are so much wider and we regularly see the highlighted and edited lives of a much wider range of people. We learn about their achievements, their holidays and their successes and suddenly, our own lives can seem dull in comparison. According to new research in 2014 by disability charity Scope nearly two-thirds of social media users say that sites such as Facebook and Twitter make them feel inadequate about their own lives and achievements.[25]

Retirement: The Problem of Enforced Downtime

Boredom amongst children and in the workplace will be discussed in separate chapters, but what happens when we get to that stage in our lives when downtime is foisted upon us? Retirement from work is a relatively new concept; indeed, living long enough to be 'old' is a modern phenomenon. Until the nineteenth century, you worked until you dropped; it was only in 1889 that German Chancellor Otto von Bismarck introduced the concept of modern pensions that allowed workers to stop work. In those days, of course, retirement lasted a few years if you were lucky; nowadays we can probably hope for twenty or thirty years to enjoy our downtime.

The problem is that adjusting from a hectic, packed and busy schedule of juggling work and play to play alone is one many senior citizens are struggling with. To put it baldly, we are so used to uptime that we cannot cope with downtime. This difficulty adjusting to a slowed pace of life is illustrated starkly by the problem that many working people have in switching off from work when on vacation, so much so that one British newspaper commented wryly that most of us seem to take so much of the office with us that we now go on 'working holidays'.[26] As many as 86 per cent of us cannot go on vacation without taking a *work* mobile

© TDway/Shutterstock

with us, whilst 90 per cent of us check work emails in the evenings on holiday.

If we cannot cope with downtime on holiday then it should come as no surprise that permanent downtime can be such a daunting prospect. According to a survey conducted by the Skipton Building Society in the UK in 2013, the novelty of retirement wears off for 40 per cent of retirees after just 10 months ... when boredom kicks in.[27]

Box 4.5: The great-grandmother who blamed her crimes on being bored

A 76-year-old great-grandmother from Cheshire in the UK embarked on a 4-year shoplifting spree because she was 'bored of being old'. The elderly woman stole goods, many of which she would never use (including a breast pump), and hid them in her shopping trolley. She blamed her crimes on being bored and lonely.[28]

It seems that modern society has fostered such a novelty-driven and fast-paced way of life that we just can't cope any more without that constant stimulation. So much so that there is even a growing trend for 'encore careers' or second careers that start up post-retirement to help seniors cope with the sudden lack of stimulation in their lives. There is even a handbook to help retirees establish their new careers (*The Encore Career Handbook* by Marci Alboher) – and an annual conference dedicated to their needs (the Encore Conference in 2014 was held in Tempe, Arizona, USA). People with encore careers are referred to as 'Boomers', and, interestingly in the context of boredom, what Boomers search for most with their new careers is 'purpose'.[27] The website Encore.org stresses the need for Boomers to find jobs and occupations that give their lives 'personal meaning', which reflects the view that boredom is highly connected with the need to find meaning in our lives. This suggests that it is not simply random stimulation that Boomers crave, but meaningful, purposeful stimulation. Many Boomers do not go back to their old pre-retirement professions but get involved in new enterprises that contribute to the greater good of society and thus give purpose to their lives. All of which goes some way to suggest that the antidote to boredom is not stimulation per se, but stimulation with meaning.

Box 4.6: The 100-year-old 'boomer' who found retirement boring

Jim Clements, from Essex, UK, grew so bored of retirement that at the age of 66, he started a new job working two mornings a week for an organisation called Active Security. Thirty-four years later, at the age of 100, he was still there. He claimed in a report in 2013 that his job kept his mind 'active' and he had no plans to give it up.[29]

The Boredom-Prone Personality: Why Some People Get More Bored Than Others

Some people are clearly more susceptible to boredom than others. As discussed in other chapters of this book, boredom is an interaction between a task, the environment and the individual. I personally would find stacking shelves in a supermarket for six hours mind-numbingly dull but someone else might appreciate the repetitive nature of the task and how it fits in with the rest of their life. They might only enjoy it, however, on days when they are not tired or distracted – on those days the task might be boring to them too. Similarly, the supermarket shelf stacker might balk at the idea of writing an entire book on boredom and consider mine the most boring occupation in the world, yet I find it engaging and stimulating; although admittedly, when I am sleep-deprived, or when the sun is shining (which doesn't happen that much in Manchester, UK), then I too might be a tad bored.

Clearly, there are differences in our propensity to be bored in a given situation. Even with the same task and the same environmental circumstances, not everyone will experience the same amount of boredom. Psychologists have long been interested in what makes some people more prone or susceptible to being bored than others; this chapter explores the psychological profile of the bored individual.

Are Extroverts More Likely to Get Bored?

The idea that extroverts might have high stimulation needs has led many to postulate that they would be more likely to experience boredom than introverts. The brain attempts to balance its need for just the right amount of arousal using a system known as the 'Ascending Reticular Activation System', or ARAS. It is thought that introverts have an ARAS more sensitive to sensory stimuli, and thus relatively low levels of stimulation provide them with high levels of arousal. Extroverts, on the other hand, are thought to have a less sensitive ARAS, which leaves them without enough arousal to satisfy them. They are thus driven to seek out other forms of sensory stimulation in the form of outward-focused behaviours. Introverts have enough arousal already so tend to avoid situations that are likely to provide even more.

This is illustrated by a study carried out in 1984 by Russell G. Geen, a psychology professor at the University of Missouri, who asked 70 extroverts and 70 introverts to select the noise levels that they most preferred whilst performing a task. The extroverts chose significantly louder music than the introverts, which is consistent with the idea that they seek more sensory stimulation. When working under the sound level they had chosen, both groups performed well. Geen then switched the levels of noise across the groups, so that the introverts now had the louder music and vice versa; at this point, the extroverts became bored, the introverts became upset, and the performance on the task worsened in both groups.[1]

Thus, it would seem that extroverts require higher levels of stimulation to maintain their interest than introverts. The study also explains why some people work better with music or the TV on in the background, whilst others find it too distracting – and perhaps why I sought music to listen to during the boring cytology screening work I described in the Introduction to this book (and why my supervisor felt it would be too distracting).

This suggests then that extroverts should get bored more easily than introverts as they need more stimulation to reach their optimal arousal levels. Some studies have indeed shown that extroverts are more susceptible to boredom[2] but others have not confirmed any such link. This suggests that extroversion/introversion cannot be the only influence on susceptibility to boredom; there must be some other factor that is important for mediating individual differences in the experience of how bored we feel in a given situation.

Are More Intelligent People More Likely to Get Bored?

The evidence for the impact on intelligence on the experience of boredom is mixed. Anecdotally, many people seem to think that more intelligent people are more likely to be bored because they will need more cognitive challenge to meet optimal arousal levels. Certainly it would seem likely that situations of low cognitive arousal would be more boring for more intelligent people than for less. Indeed, a study in 1978 showed that the more intelligent participants in a task were, the more bored they found that task.[3] A study of long-distance truck drivers in 1982 used educational level and participation in 'intellectual' leisure activities to measure intelligence and found that subjective boredom when driving down monotonous and familiar stretches of road was somewhat greater for men of higher intellectual abilities.[4] This effect is also shown in the literature on education, which frequently suggests that if brighter children are not given appropriate stimulation, they will bore easily[5] (see also Chapter 8 for more on gifted children and boredom). However, not all research points to such a strong link between boredom and intelligence. In fact, there is a counter argument that suggests that more intelligent people have the cognitive ability to offset boredom and thus cope with it better. Intelligent people might be able to manage their boredom by playing cognitive mind games, or by using their imagination, problem-solving abilities, etc., which less intelligent individuals might struggle with. Indeed, two studies of women in low-skill jobs with little variety found no relationship between intelligence and boredom ([6] and [7]).

It's All About Me . . . Yawn

Several researchers suggest that narcissism (a personality trait that involves excessive preoccupation with oneself) is strongly related to boredom,[8] such that narcissism actually leads to boredom. This could be because narcissistic traits inspire certain goals but the person may lack the capability to match these aspirations. For example, narcissistic people might aspire to be famous, to be widely admired and to be a great success but their abilities may not be compatible with such unrealistic and unattainable (for them) goals. Lack of achievement, then, of these goals, might leave them feeling their life lacks meaning – and thus they feel bored. Even if they do attain their goal of, for example, gaining the attention and approval they crave from some people, they can become bored quite quickly and start to need the same from different people to avoid boredom.

The Boredom-Prone Personality

In 1986 psychologists Norman Sundberg and Richard Farmer, both professors at the University of Oregon, developed the concept of the boredom-prone personality. Boredom – proneness, they claimed, is a tendency to 'experience tedium and lack of personal involvement and enthusiasm in one's life surroundings'.[9] Building on an existing idea of 'boredom susceptibility', they developed a 28-item questionnaire, the Boredom Proneness Scale (BPS), which could be used to identify those people who were most boredom prone. The Scale is thought to be made up of five dimensions:[10]

1. Need for external stimulation, which includes the need for excitement and novelty.
2. Internal ability to keep oneself stimulated and entertained.
3. Affective responses to boring situations; how one feels about them.
4. Perception of the passage of time.
5. Reactions to feeling constrained or unable to do things that they might want to do at that time.

Box 5.1: Norman Sundberg, 1922–2014

Professor Emeritus Norman Dale Sundberg, who was a keen supporter of my boredom research, sadly died during the writing of this book. He was born on 15 September 1922 in Aurora, Nebraska, graduated from the University of Nebraska, served in the US Army in Germany, and received his Ph.D. in psychology from the University of Minnesota before joining the University of Oregon in 1952. Over the years he co-authored several books on clinical psychology and personality assessment and is best known in the boredom research world for his Boredom Proneness Scale (BPS) of 1986.

Using the measure, researchers have since been able to investigate the boredom-prone personality and find out more about those of us who are most prone to being bored. For example, one study found that men scored significantly higher on aspects of the BPS concerning external stimulation (which assesses need for challenge, excitement and variety) than women did; this was interpreted to mean that environments lacking in external stimulation, such as repetitive ones, are more likely to bore men than women .[11] They also found that men were more likely to attribute feelings associated with boredom to external sources (the task is boring) than women, who tended to attribute them more to internal causes (e.g. it is my fault this is boring – I am not intelligent enough, etc.).[10]

Boredom-prone people might be that way because they need more stimulation than most to reach their optimal arousal levels – and may be unable to obtain that stimulation from within (e.g. by using their imagination). They may find it harder to refocus attention on the task or to seek it in constructive ways elsewhere. As one source puts it, 'highly bored individuals tend to lack the ability to entertain themselves'.[12] This could be why they are more likely to turn to unrelated sources to gain the stimulation they crave, such as drugs[13] or gambling, which can be viewed as simple ways of easing their boredom.[14]

This is borne out by my own research. Together with a research student of mine, Andrew Robinson, we wanted to see what students do when they are bored in lectures or classes. Using the BPS we classified the 211 students into low or high boredom-prone categories and found roughly a quarter in each category (with the rest falling into a mid-category of BP). Students who scored highly on the Boredom Proneness Scale rated more time in lectures as boring and missed more lectures (because bored students tend to skip lectures, as will be shown in Chapter 8) than participants with low boredom-proneness scores. In addition, students who scored highly on the Boredom Proneness Scale employed significantly more stimulation-seeking strategies in lecture time than those with low boredom proneness scores. Thus, they were more likely to entertain themselves by playing games on their mobile phones, sending text messages during lecture time, making shopping lists, 'switching off', doodling, writing notes to the person next to them and daydreaming than the less boredom-prone.[15]

This suggests that boredom-prone people tend to entertain themselves in ways unconnected to the task in order to reach their optimal arousal levels. Part of this search for neural stimulation may be connected with the search for novelty discussed in Chapter 4 (see pages 65–67). Novelty seeking, or neophilia, is a personality type that might be connected with boredom proneness, as well as sensation seeking. Boredom-prone individuals may be in higher need of novelty, a genetic trait that might have conferred an evolutionary advantage in the past. After all, seeking out new ways of obtaining or using resources might have made the difference between death and survival for our ancestors (as discussed in Chapter 4, see page 69). Being high on the novelty-seeking scale has been linked to high dopaminergic activity stimulated by sensation and thrill seeking.

Boredom proneness has been linked to a number of other attributes. A study of French adults in 2000 found that high BP people were also prone to introspectiveness. They were more likely to pay attention to feelings and thoughts about themselves than those who were low in BP.[16] Boredom-prone individuals are also more likely to experience lapses in attention, which can cause everyday errors.[17]

Those who are more prone to boredom have also been shown to be angrier than low BP individuals. A study by boredom researchers Deborah Rupp and Stephen Vodanovich at the University of West Florida in 1997[18] found that those who scored highly on the BPS also reported that they got angrier more frequently and even that they were more aggressive than those low on the BPS. It is thus suggested that not only do boredom-prone people get angrier but that they also have less ability to control and manage that anger. Some believe that the reason for this is that boredom is actually a manifestation of inner anger, whilst others suggest that the findings are to do with boredom-prone people having less impulse control than those who are less prone to boredom. These findings might go some way to explaining the reports in Chapter 3 about bored individuals committing violent acts (see page 46); if bored people feel more anger and hostility and have poorer impulse control, we can see what might result in terms of violence and aggression towards others.

A range of other links have been found with the boredom-prone personality, including lower educational achievement, higher truancy rate and poorer work performance,[19] depression, anxiety, hopelessness, loneliness, impulsiveness and procrastination,[9] lower motivation, lacking of goals, ambition, sense of meaning/purpose.[11] In fact, it seems there are very few symptoms that cannot be blamed on being boredom-prone (they even report more physical ill-health, according to one study[19]), but perhaps there is another reason why boredom-prone people would appear to have such poor psychological and physical health. Boredom researcher Stephen Vodanovich suggests that it is not necessarily that boredom-prone people are more ill then less boredom-prone, it is just that boredom-prone people may be more likely to notice symptoms (see discussion of introspection above) than their less boredom-prone friends. This idea has received credence from many authors who believe that boredom-prone people tend to dwell on themselves in a narcissistic way.[19] In fact, high BPS have been found to be related to high narcissism scores.[19] It is this inner focus that could lead to high BP individuals reporting more symptomology.

Research suggests, however, that not all highly boredom-prone individuals are the same and there may in fact be two types of boredom-prone people.[17] One type is the 'apathetic' BP personality who is bored but not very motivated to do anything about it. In contrast, the 'agitated' BP individual is far more motivated to relieve their boredom and restless in their attempts to do so. This typology can be compared with the categories of boredom identified in Chapter 1 (see page 19). As mentioned earlier, research suggests that boredom-prone people are more likely to suffer attentional lapses and errors, but it is actually the apathetic type who is more likely to experience this rather than the agitated type. This could be due to the agitated BP individual making more of an effort to sustain interest and attention than the apathetic type.

Box 5.2: Time really does fly when we're having fun

Time really may fly when we are less bored – or at least a recent study suggests it slows when we are bored. Psychologists James Danckert and Ava-Ann Allman at the University of Waterloo in Canada gave the BPS to over 400 students and used this to select the 20 most and the 20 least boredom-prone individuals. They then had the students watch a series of illusory motion displays that showed a dot appearing to move around in a circle, and in each case they had to say how long the movement had lasted. The boredom-prone individuals were significantly less accurate at judging how many seconds the illusory motion lasted, particularly tending to overestimate its length.[20]

Quiz: How Predisposed to Boredom Are You?

Indicate on a scale of 1–7 how much you agree with the following statements:

1	2	3	4	5	6	7
Agree						Disagree

1. I generally find it easy to concentrate on my work or the tasks that I have to do.

2. When trying to do something, I get easily distracted.

3. Often I find my mind wandering to matters unrelated to the task at hand.

4. I have to work on tasks or activities in short bursts rather than sustained periods.

5. I think I get more easily bored than other people.

6. If I have nothing to do, I can usually find something quite easily.

7. The idea of having nothing to do does not bother me.

8. I get agitated when there is nothing to do.

9. Life is generally repetitive and monotonous.

10. The internet doesn't hold much of interest for me.

11. Most of social media, e.g. Facebook, Twitter, bores me.

12. I wake up each morning excited about the day ahead.

13. I get restless if I have to wait in a line.

14. Life does not offer me enough challenge.

15. I am always looking for new ideas or new things to do.

16. I am happy with the way things are.

17. Often I am the first to embrace new technology, e.g. new mobile phone, etc.

18. When bored, I can usually entertain myself without external input (e.g. phone, computer, other people, etc.).

19. I like to have lots of variety in my life.

20. Too much variety stresses me out.

How to score

Reverse score items 1, 6, 7, 12, 16, 18 and 20 (i.e. scores of 1 would be given 7, 2 = 6 etc.). Add the scores – the lower the score, the more boredom prone you are likely to be.

Note: This is a 'ballpark' measure of how predisposed you might be to boredom and not a diagnostic tool.

Bored: The New Cool?

Far from boredom proneness being seen as a liability, for many sections of society today being bored is the new cool. This is reflected in clothing items now available in mainstream stores that proclaim the wearer to be bored. These clothes, usually aimed at teenagers or even children, suggest a bored, blasé attitude to life is far cooler than the enthusiasm and interest showed by younger children. As one source puts it, '*Holding back your enthusiasm has to be one of the worst side-effects of cool behavior.*'[21]

Clothing from Primark

Clothing from Matalan

It is not just kids who are too cool for school these days, though. Models sneer at us from the pages of magazines, for all the world looking as if life is just too boring to get out of bed for. We are meant to be cool to potential suitors, lest our interest and enthusiasm scare them off. We should be cool and seemingly uninterested too when viewing a house or a car, lest our obvious delight should drive up the price. In short, these days it's just not cool to be excited by things.

It is perhaps understandable that teenagers feel obliged to affect a look of calm disinterest at all times. Excitement and enthusiasm are seen as childish emotions to portray. Toddlers are perpetually curious and delighted by the most mundane things, so to distinguish themselves from their former childish states and to show the world that they have definitely grown up, teenagers must distance themselves from such emotional displays. The bored teenager is thus almost de rigueur but that does not explain why adults must curb their enthusiasm for life too. We seem to be living in a culture where zest for life is not cool. As one commentator puts it, 'unfortunately, the era we are currently living in is not one where happiness or contentment is seen as chic'.[22] Instead, it is fashionable to look perpetually discontent, bored and uninterested – which is reflected in the iconic fashion images glaring at us from billboards and magazines. Indeed, models standing tall is no longer considered cool as it was in the past; now it is all about the 'slouch', which, according to an article in the *Wall Street Journal*, conveys the 'perfect attitude' – 'I'm so beautiful, so rich, so bored'.[23]

6

'Mum, I'm Bored': How We Are Growing a Nation of Bored Kids

Why are we all so bored these days? This is a theme throughout this book and earlier chapters have addressed some of the reasons for this. But could it be that we, as a society, are bored, despite having so much to occupy us because we are being raised in an increasingly boredom-averse world? It is not merely that we scroll, swipe and tap every threat of boredom from our lives, but we are bringing up our kids in a world that shuns boredom.

Parents today seem so afraid of letting their kids get bored. They seem to view childish boredom as a personal slight on their parenting ability. Modern parents hothouse their children, rushing them from activity to activity to ensure that their lives are constantly enriched with stimulation as an antidote to the terrors of ennui. The downside of this is that kids today don't know how to create their own stimulation and are becoming passively reliant on external suppliers of entertainment and engagement. This chapter will argue that if we want to enrich our children's lives then we need to embrace boredom and allow it back into their lives. The possible long-term consequences of not doing so, in terms of what becomes of these children when they become adults, are explored.

From Womb to (Nursery) Room

Our 'first world' obsessive fear of our children being bored is driven by a strong motivation to stimulate them in order to boost their brain power. New parents are bombarded with messages from the media and advertising that we must stimulate our offspring if we want them to reach the dizzy heights we surely aspire for them. If we don't provide a suitably enriching (i.e. not boring) environment for their developing brains, we have failed them – and failed as parents. And that is something few parents dare contemplate these days.

This pressure to stimulate our offspring begins even before birth. When I googled 'how to stimulate baby in the womb', over 300,000 pages popped up, suggesting this is becoming a fairly mainstream aspiration of new mums who want to give their progeny a head start. Of course an appropriate foetal environment is important and it is indeed well recognised that 'compromised foetal development may have effects on health and cognition'.[1] But whilst until recently this has meant the gestating mum eating healthily, avoiding alcohol, drugs and certain food types, mums are now being advised to play music, massage their bump and even read to their unborn child.[2]

Box 6.1: The Mozart Effect

The concept of the 'Mozart Effect' was first described by French researcher Dr Alfred A. Tomatis in his 1991 book, *Pourquoi Mozart?* (Why Mozart?). He used Mozart's music as the listening stimulus in his work, attempting to cure a variety of disorders. This was followed by a study by Rauscher, Shaw and Ky, published in the esteemed journal *Nature* in 1993,[3] which investigated the effect of listening to music by Mozart on spatial reasoning. They found a temporary enhancement of spatial reasoning but the study made no mention of an increase in IQ in general (because IQ was never measured). Despite this, the results were popularly interpreted as an increase in general IQ. This misconception, and the fact that the music used in the study was by Mozart, led to the wide reporting of the so-called 'Mozart Effect'. However, it was the 1997 book by Don Campbell, *The Mozart Effect: Tapping the Power of Music to Heal the Body, Strengthen the Mind and Unlock the Creative Spirit*, that really popularised the Mozart Effect. In the book, Campbell discusses the theory that listening to Mozart may temporarily increase one's IQ and produce many other beneficial effects on mental function. Campbell recommended playing specially selected classical music to infants in the expectation that it will benefit their mental development.

After *The Mozart Effect*, Campbell wrote a follow-up book, *The Mozart Effect For Children*, and created related products such as CDs and manuals. In 1998, Zell Miller, the Governor of the state of Georgia in the US, even requested funds to be set aside in the state budget so that every newborn could be sent a CD of classical music. There is now a huge industry in products capitalising on the so-called Mozart Effect (to see how many products are out there, just google 'Baby Mozart' or 'Baby Einstein') despite the fact that the underlying theories are controversial; the relationship of sound and music (both played and listened to) for cognitive function and various physiological metrics has been explored in various later studies with no definitive results.[4]

And why not? It is well known that babies can hear in the womb. By week 18 of gestation, the ear and brain of the foetus are able to hear the mother's heartbeat. At 24 weeks, the ear is fully formed, and as early as week 25, we know that babies are able to hear voices and sounds from the external environment. We also know that music and stories, etc. can greatly benefit children from an early age, so why not get a head start and begin stimulating them before they are born? Several sources even suggest that since foetuses can detect light and taste, mums could stimulate them even more by passing torches across their bumps and by eating a variety of foods to stimulate their taste buds.

Is all this really necessary or are we simply at risk of turning the peaceful, quiet and tranquil environment of the womb into an over-stimulating classroom? Could this quest to stimulate our unborn children create a novelty-seeking, sensation-seeking baby, who is born with a low-boredom threshold because s/he has become accustomed to so much stimulation – before s/he is even born?

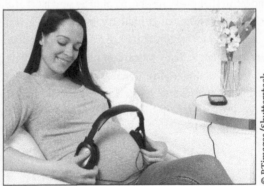

© RTimages/Shutterstock

Box 6.2: The 'Lullabelly'

For those mums anxious for their unborn child not to miss out on the stimulation that music can provide, an innovative product called the Lullabelly is available from the United States (http://www.lullabelly.com/index.html). This is a prenatal music belt that can be strapped to mum's tummy to provide music on the go for the unborn child. The website does urge caution, however, and it has a pre-set maximum volume that does not allow the music to become louder than normal speech. Lullabelly also sensibly recommend its use for no more than one hour at a time and limited to two to three times per day – 'prenatal music stimulation should be practiced in moderation'. At least there is some acknowledgement with this responsible company that too much pre-natal stimulation might be harmful.

http://www.lullabelly.com/index.html

Of course once Baby has emerged from the relatively low-stimulation world of the womb (at least if we allow it to be), then our Quest to Stimulate really turns up a notch. As soon as Baby is born, new parents are urged to choose 'stimulating' toys. An American website, for example, called geniusbabies (http://www.genius-babies.com/preninstim.html) sells hundreds of toys designed to stimulate every sense, from Infant Stimulation Baby Crib Sets to Infant Stimulation Clip Along Flash Cards. There are products for babies and toddlers using brand names such as Baby Einstein, Baby IQ, and BrightMinds, all apparently designed to stimulate the developing brain. Popular pre-school toys seem to be overloaded with functionality to teach children that everyday objects on their own are simply not exciting enough; see, for example, the

Fisher-Price Smart Stages Chair (with light-up remote shape and number buttons, electronic story book, magic ABC seat and over 50 tunes and phrases), the VTech Kidizoom 8-in-1 Smartwatch (with camera, alarm, voice recording and more) and the Fisher-Price Laugh and Learn Magical Musical Mirror (where your little one can learn ABC, colours and greetings through song and more). Are ordinary chairs, watches and mirrors not exciting enough for toddlers? They might have been for the last generation of children, but apparently not for today's kids.

Then there are the kiddy versions of grown-up gadgets, designed to allow children to copy Mum and Dad but in so doing introduce them early on to the concept of the real thing: for example, VTech Baby's First Smartphone or My First Tablet allow them to get into the screen habit from very early on.

Even traditional toys have gone high tech; the old-fashioned shape sorter, for example, is no longer considered stimulating enough so has to have lights and sounds too (e.g. the VTech Baby Sort & Soar Rocket) and the old-fashioned baby walker, which toddlers push along like a child-sized Zimmer frame, is now multi-functional, with songs, stories, sounds and lights to amuse them (in case walking upright is not thrilling enough for crawling babies).

Then, lest these inspiring toys are simply not proving enough stimulation for our offspring, we are expected to seek out special baby classes and enrichment programmes. In my hometown of Manchester, UK, for example, I could take my baby to any or all of the following classes:

- Adventure Babies
- Baby Funtime
- Colouryou Happy on a Saturday
- Creative Explorers
- Brighter Sounds
- Busy Bodies
- Mother and baby choir
- Dancing Dots

- Happy Makers
- Kids Creationz
- Lankys Arts and crafts
  (from birth)
- Little Art Bugs
- Little Strikers (football)
- Mini Makers (art class)
- Baby Explorers (for
  non-walking babies)
- Baby Sensory (from birth)
- Drama 4 Tots
- Happy Hands (baby
  sign classes)
- Jittabugs Baby Move and
  Groove
- Kidsology Baby Rock and Roll
- Rhyme and Sign
- Rhythm Time
- Sing and Sign
- Tiny Talk Baby Signing
- Baby Ballet
- Baby Boogie
- Babywinks
- Boogie Bat
- Boogie Tots
- Baby Massage
- Baby Yoga
- Baby Reflexology
- Mini and Me Yoga
- Mini Massage
- Big Cook, Little Cook Group
- Crafty Cooks
- Aquanauts
- Little Stars Ballet
- Diddi Dance
- Jabberjacks
- Jacappella Music
- Jo Jingles
- JoJos Music
- Kiddiewinks
- KidsRock
- Little Groovers
- Mini Maestros
- Baby Boppers
- Music Babies
- Musical Monkeys
- Suzuki Violin Group
- Enjoy-a-ball
- Let's Play Baby
- Little Kickers
- Little Superstars
- Physi-ball
- Play Gym
- Rugby Tots
- Tennis Tykes
- Tiny Tots Ramblers
- Tumble Tots
- Tiny Tykes
- Kiddy Cook
- Dutch Singing
- La Jolie Ronde
- Little Amigos Language Club
- Los Patitos Language Classes
- Mandarin Rhyme
- Maskarade French Clubs
- Talking Tots

- Swim City Tots
- Just Swim
- Little Bubbles
- Puddle Ducks
- Splish Splosh
- Swim Baby Swim
- Train2Swim

- Baby Splash
- Aqua Babies
- Messy Church
- See and Know
- Water Babies
- Afro Tots

Most of these are available from birth or around six months and most are also franchised groups across the UK and beyond. If a new mum (or dad) in Manchester was to take their child to even a fraction of these classes then between those and the stimulating toys, s/he can be sure that the little one is never bored for a moment. But, in case s/he is still worried, s/he can always turn to the many museums and art galleries in the city. Where once these were serene places for reflection for adults, they now seem dedicated to providing even more stimulation for our already highly stimulated babies and toddlers. Here is a taste of what is on offer from the cultural hotspots of Manchester:

- A football museum offering 'training' for babies from 0–12 months.
- An art gallery providing both art and dance classes for the under-5s.
- A museum holding weekly storytime sessions and sensory play for under-4s.
- A Tudor hall with storytime sessions for pre-schoolers.
- Another art gallery offering two art clubs; one for babies who are not yet walking and another for older toddlers.
- A science museum providing creative activity sessions with science-based themes for pre-schoolers.

Then, of course, there are libraries. Most libraries now run weekly singing, story and rhyme sessions for babies and toddlers. In fact, the idea of a library as a peaceful place for quiet reflection and a refuge from the stimulating fast-paced outside world is long gone. So much so that many older users have complained that libraries in the UK are being turned into noisy children's playgrounds.[5]

Box 6.3: Café culture

© Alexandralaw 1977/Shutterstock

As I write this, I have just come back from a Christmas Eve visit to a local chocolate-themed café for a hot chocolate treat with my kids. Whilst my own children fidgeted and squabbled whilst waiting for our order, I noticed another mum arrive and sit down at the table next to ours with her young baby, who looked to be under the age of one. The mum plonked her little one in a high chair, then pulled out an iPad and set up a series of *Peppa Pig* shows. Mesmerised, the child gazed intently at the screen for the entire time, leaving her mum free to chat away happily with her companions.

Now I don't blame the mum for using the iPad as an instant entertainer to give her a bit of a break (and indeed, I felt slightly envious as my own kids squabbled and fidgeted some more), but I couldn't help wondering at what cost she had earned her hour of peace that day. True, the baby, whilst in the enthral of *Peppa Pig*, did not fidget, bang her spoon, cry, scream, flick chocolate at other tables or engage in any other anti-social behaviour, but neither did she engage in any active learning or discovery. She did not learn to amuse herself, to interact with others; she did not learn what socially acceptable behaviour is, or that actions have consequences. Nor did she learn to entertain herself, or to use her curiosity to discover the world around her. True, she was not bored that day, but by the time her mum is once more child-free and able to enjoy coffee in peace, will her daughter have developed a potentially damaging low tolerance for boredom?

All of which means that before a child has even started school the chances are that s/he has been exposed to a constant barrage of stimulation that leaves them, arguably, unable to entertain themselves and with low tolerance for low-stimulating environments. The more stimulation we give them, the more they want and expect. By providing this constant stimulation, we are creating a nation of bored kids – and future adults too.

Box 6.4: Then and now: compare

Chloe, at 29, is mum to Jacob, who is 18 months old. This is what she says:

'I think it is really important to ensure that he has the right stimu-lation to develop his brain. There is no way I would want him just whiling away the time – these are his most valuable months, when his brain is developing so fast. I want every minute to count. Our schedule is pretty busy and I try to give him a variety of different experiences to stimulate different senses and areas of his brain and physical and

social development. We tend to have an activity in the morning and afternoon in the week; on Monday it is music play session in the morning, then football training in the afternoon. Tuesday is swim class in the morning, then his French class in the afternoon. Wednesday, we go to storytime at the local library and squeeze in a baby art class at the art gallery. After lunch it is Jo Jingles, his music group. Thursday morning is Gym for Babies and in the afternoon he goes to the soft play, where they have different activities each week. Friday morning is the local playgroup and in the afternoon a group of mums and tots meet up, either at someone's house or the park, if it's nice. Jacob has a nap in the afternoon and he watches CBeebies in the early evening whilst I cook. At the weekend we go on day trips to farms or museums and also do the shopping – which I try to make into an educating experience for him too.

Jacob also has masses of electronic educational toys, including toy laptops, iPads and music makers. I swap these toys regularly so he doesn't get bored of them – I'll put them away and get another lot out so he has lots of novelty.'

Jill is 70, and remembers what it was like for her when she had her two children in the late sixties and early seventies:

'I don't remember doing anything specifically child-centred with them, really. I did get together with other young mums every so often but that was it. The rest of the time the kids would come with me to the shops, watch me clean the house, "help" me cook, or play in their rooms or the garden. The toys they had weren't the noisy interactive things my grandchildren have now. They were more sedate but still educational – shape sorters and jigsaws, dolls and action figures. They played with pans and cardboard tubes, anything really. We did go on outings if it was a nice day in the summer but these tended to be things we adults enjoyed, like walks around a village, rather than activities geared to the kids.'

Whilst Chloe's children will come to expect constant stimulation and novelty before they even start school, Jill's kids grew up with a lower need for new sensations and thus a higher tolerance for boredom. It is probable that they will have learnt to entertain themselves too, in a way that Chloe's kids will never have had the need to. Without that practice, this sort of 'self-stimulation' is a skill that is likely to be lost for today's generation.

The Daycare Generation

All the above assumes that the baby or toddler is at home 24/7 with their primary carer, which is highly unlikely these days. Many working parents rely increasingly on day nurseries – and if we think attending pre-school classes and clubs is over-stimulating, they have nothing on day nurseries! Look up any day nursery on the internet and you will undoubtedly see it proudly proclaiming itself to offer a 'stimulating' environment. For example, a nursery in Bradford, UK, talks about making the most of 'stimulating environments', one in Essex, UK, states that they provide 'safe, secure and stimulating' care, whilst a daycare facility in Dartford, UK, offers an 'innovative, stimulating and inspiring' environment, and so on. There is nothing intrinsically wrong with this – and no parent would want a nursery that failed to stimulate their child, that left them bored and uninspired. The problem is that day nurseries, by their very nature, are over-stimulating places, with lots of children and staff, bright walls, continually changing activities and novel stimuli. They typically have art and craft projects, storytime, singing sessions, sandboxes, water-play, outdoor time, home corners, dress-up boxes, building areas and dance sessions and many even have structured language, swimming or music classes too. Day nurseries offer a far more stimulating environment than most parents could ever provide at home; indeed, this is one of their attractions to parents. This, of course, is how it should be – the problem is that kids who are in these environments for too long can easily get accustomed to the constant stimulation that these environments provide.

It is estimated that around half of pre-schoolers in America are in daycare – and most are in daycare for at least 40 hours each week.[6] A study published in *Child Development* journal showed that children in full-time daycare were close to three times more likely to show behavioural problems than those cared for by their mothers at home. Part of the problem was the demand for excessive attention from their care-givers.[6] Whilst many studies have looked at the problems of excessive daycare on children it is true that few have attributed the explanation for any ill effects on over-stimulation. Indeed, the fact that excessive daycare results in stress for the child[7] may be due to other factors rather than too much stimulation, but I contend that giving kids a constantly changing, novel, fast-paced environment in the form of stimulating day nurseries is causing longer-term problems, which are less easy to measure. Children are growing up on a diet of novelty and as a result seek more and more sensation and stimulation.

Could over-reliance on daycare nurseries take some of the blame for creating our bored nation?

Switching, Scrolling and Swiping

One of the main stimulants that a child is exposed to in the Western world is, of course, the television. Parents in fact tend to encourage their toddlers to watch TV, partly because they believe the programmes to be stimulating and educational and partly to entertain and occupy them whilst they are busy doing other things (see Box 6.5, below). Pre-school TV may well be educational, but it does get children into the habit of watching TV, which as we have shown in Chapter 4 (see pages 74–5) is a passive activity. It come as no surprise then to learn that children aged 2–5 spend 32 hours a week in front of a TV – watching television, DVDs, DVR and videos, or using a game console.[8] This is almost the equivalent of a full-time job.

What about older kids? Seventy-one per cent of 8–18-year-olds now have a TV in their bedroom.[8] Media technology now offers more ways to access TV content, such as on the internet, cell phones and iPods. This has led to an increase in time spent viewing TV, even as TV-set viewing has declined. Forty-one per cent of TV-viewing is now online, time-shifted, DVD or mobile.[9]

Box 6.5: Why do kids these days watch so much TV?

Clearly there are a range of reasons to explain the rise in television viewing for children across time. One is the increased amount of TV programmes being aired: more channels mean more viewing choice. There are also dedicated TV channels now for kids whereas in the past there may have only been an hour a day of scheduled children's programming. Society is more affluent and it is the norm for a household to own several TV sets, including those in children's rooms. And of course, no one needs an actual TV set to view programmes anymore; such material is more readily available on other devices.

There are other, cultural reasons for the increase in kids' TV viewing, such as a reluctance on the part of parents to allow their children to entertain themselves outside, as would have happened in the past. According to research by Play England

and its counterparts in Wales, Scotland and Northern Ireland in 2013, whilst half of adults played outside at least seven times a week when they were growing up, less than a quarter of children are allowed such freedom today.[10] Around half of the 3,000 parents surveyed blamed their reluctance on letting children out of their sight on the danger posed by traffic, while 40 per cent give the reason as 'stranger danger'. Around a quarter of parents also fear if they let their kids play outside unsupervised, neighbours might make negative judgements about their parenting capabilities. Parents also worry about the noise their kids might make. Lack of suitable outside places to play is also a factor in discouraging such freedoms. The whole idea of going outside to play is becoming outdated and kids need alternatives to fill their leisure time; TV seems to fill the gap perfectly.

Another factor is parents' lifestyle today: they are often too busy to actively engage with their offspring. More couples are working and sharing the household chores, so they are just too busy or tired to play with their children. Sitting them down in front of the 'telesitter' is far more appealing. A survey of 1,000 parents in the UK in 2011 suggested that a quarter of them admit to using the TV as an electronic babysitter for their young children.[11]

This TV viewing is likely to be replacing active pastimes that kids might otherwise have been involved in, such as reading, sport, social interaction or craft hobbies. TV is not just watched but often simply on in the background, providing a background noise of stimulation; in about two-thirds of households, the TV is 'usually' on during meals. In 51 per cent of households, the TV is on 'most' of the time. [7] By the time of high school graduation, children will have spent more time watching television than they have in the classroom.[12]

The effects of all this TV viewing are well documented, but we will concern ourselves here solely with issues relating to boredom. Many commentators are of the view that constant bombardment of images from TVs, computers and other electronic devices means that children are growing up in a fast-paced, high-intensity world characterised by change and novelty. This limits their ability to attend to stimuli once they lose their novelty factor, as they learn to constantly seek novelty (see also Chapters 4 and 5, pages 82 and 90). Nearly three quarters of the 685 public and private teachers surveyed in an online poll commissioned by Common Sense Media believe that students' use of entertainment media (including TV, video games, texting and social networking) 'has hurt students' attention spans a lot or somewhat'.[13] This is because children are simply not used to concentrating on things that are not new, novel and constantly changing. They grow bored and look for something more stimulating (i.e. novel) – they scroll to the next page, flick to the next video clip, check their emails during a slower part of a programme, comment on Twitter about what they have seen or done, or update their Facebook status. They are simply used to being bombarded by a range of fast-moving stimuli that change at such a pace that no effort is required to sustain attention.

Another online survey concurs with this view. This one, by Pew Research Center's Internet & American Life Project, polled 2,462 middle and high school teachers and found that 87 per cent report that these technologies are creating 'an easily distracted generation with short attention spans'.[14]

These surveys back up more scientific findings, which have consistently found that television seems to reduce youngsters' attention spans. For example, 1,278 children at age 1 and 1,345 children at age 3 were followed until the age of 7 in a longitudinal study reported in 2004. The study found that early television exposure is associated with attentional problems at age 7.[15] A later study in 2010 found similar results; researchers in Iowa and Minnesota studied 1,323 children over 13 months, with their exposure to TV and video games reported by both parents and the children themselves. Any attention difficulties (as described by teachers) were also noted. They also examined a sample of 210 college students in late adolescence or early adulthood, who also provided self-reports of TV exposure, video game play and perceived attention problems. The results suggested that exposure to TV and video games was linked to greater attention problems.[16] The reasons for such findings could be tied in with comments from previous researchers that 'most television shows are so exciting that children who frequently watch television have more difficulty paying attention to less exciting tasks'[15] and that 'because most television programs involve rapid changes in focus, frequent exposure to television may harm children's abilities to sustain focus on tasks that are not inherently attention-grabbing'.[17]

Box 6.6: Campaign against toy deemed 'ultimate electronic babysitter'

The Campaign for a Commercial-Free Childhood (CCFC) took issue in 2013 with a Fisher-Price product called Newborn-to-Toddler Apptivity Seat for iPad devices. The toy gives infants from birth the ability to sit in a bouncy seat and be entertained via an iPad device and has been branded 'morally irresponsible' by parents signing a petition calling for the toy to be banned.[18] According to Fisher-Price's website, the toy 'provides another way to stimulate and engage baby'. The petition to have it recalled gained over 11,000 signatures but at the time of writing, this product is still available in the US – although the Apps do at least time out after 10–12 minutes to limit viewing.

But it is not just increased TV watching that is contributing to attentional problems of children. The use of social media via smartphones and other electronic devices is now commonplace. According to a 2011 poll, 22 per cent of teenagers log on to their favourite social media site more than 10 times a day, and more than half of adolescents log on to a social media site more than once a day.[19] Seventy-five per cent of teenagers now own cell phones, and 25 per cent use them for social media, 54 per cent use them for texting and 24 per cent use them for instant messaging.[19] And such activities start young; around 59 per cent of children have already used a social network by the time they are 10, even though official age limits for accessing such sites are usually much older (e.g. age 13 for Facebook and Snapchat and 16 for Whatsapp).[20] Even more shocking is the finding that 72 per cent of kids under the age of 8 have used mobile devices – and 38 per cent of children under age 2.[21]

The effects of TV, computers, social media and electronic games then on children is two-fold; on the one hand, kids become used to and crave the novelty that these constantly changing media bring. And, going hand in hand with that thirst for constant stimulation is the reduced ability to meet those needs internally; children who are used to meeting those stimulation needs by switching, scrolling and swiping lose the ability to meet their quest for neural stimulation through processes that require imagination, creativity and problem-solving.

Box 6.7: Smartphones: the new babysitter App

Almost half of the top 100-selling education apps in the iTunes App Store in 2009 were for preschool or elementary-aged children, according to a content analysis by the Joan Ganz Cooney

Center.[22] The reason for this is thought to be that parents are using their devices as mobile entertainment centres to occupy their young children when they get bored; waiting in a supermarket line, in a restaurant, when travelling or in the doctor's waiting room. Three quarters of parents surveyed in a 2013 study agreed that their tablet is a useful tool for entertaining and educating their offspring.[23] Where once kids might have had to amuse themselves with crayons or even their own imagination, now, before they can even whine 'I'm bored', they have a constant and ever changing supply of fast-paced, novel stimuli at their fingertips (see also Café Culture, my earlier tale, page 105).

At the time of going to press, of the top 20 best-selling paid educational apps available on Amazon, 13 were clearly aimed at pre-schoolers.

After-school Activities

The over-stimulation provided by the modern school environment will be discussed in Chapter 8, but for now let us consider what children do after school – when they are not engaged in their on-going screen activities (TV, computers, social media, etc.). Parents keen to give their kids the 'edge' and a head start in an increasingly competitive world schedule 'educational' classes and 'developmental' activities for them to the extent that modern youngsters simply don't get a chance to be bored. When school is out, they are rushed from activity to activity, all designed to provide even more stimulation for kids already over-stimulated by school (of which more in Chapter 8), and novelty-rich screen time.

Box 6.8: Dubai parents urged to see after-school activities as 'antidote to boredom'

On its website the Math Learning Center in UAE urges parents to recognise that after-school maths lessons can be an antidote to boredom for their kids. The Center points out that children who engage in traditional after-school activities, such as watching TV, simply 'pass away the time', whereas after-school maths offers 'better, more stimulating options' for Dubai's youngsters.

Of course, the Math Learning Center may well be right; maths lessons are probably superior forms of time filling than TV. But hopefully parents in Dubai will not be urged to fill their child's every spare moment with structured activities – and allow them time to be bored too.[24]

A survey in 2014 found that primary school children in London, UK, engaged in an average of 3.2 activities per week, whilst for secondary school aged kids this decreases to an average of 1.7.[25] This probably means that half of children under the age of 11 are attending after-school classes every night. This leads to over-scheduled kids, who are too busy to get bored as they rush from one stimulating class to the next. The problems of over-scheduling have been well documented in a flurry of books such as *The Over-Scheduled Child*, *The Pressured Child*, *Pressured Parents*, *Stressed-Out Kids* and *Hyper-Parenting: Are You Hurting Your Child By Trying Too Hard?*, with psychologists and commentators arguing that kids need downtime too – time to be bored. It is this over-scheduling that led Richard Harman, who led the UK Headmasters' and Headmistresses' Conference in 2014, to beg middle-class parents to 'refrain from programming their (child's) every waking hour'.[26]

Michael C. Nagel, author of *Nurturing A Healthy Mind*, warns about the dangers of over-stimulating our kids, whilst Julie Robinson, education and training director of the Independent Association of Prep Schools (IAPS), believes that too much stimulation caused by too many after-school activities can lead to 'generations of manic' individuals.[27] Too many structured and scheduled activities ensure that children get little time to reflect, think and be inventive and creative. Not only that, but the constant stimulation of activities, classes and social events means that we are raising kids who expect a diet of constant excitement. As Dr Mary Bousted, general secretary of the Association of Teachers and Lecturers, said in an article in the *Guardian* in 2014, 'expecting life to be a roller-coaster of constant entertainment is not a good preparation for the adult world'.[27]

Box 6.9: What after-school activities?

According to a survey of over 1,000 London-based parents by online tuition provider MathsDoctor [25] in 2014, the most popular after-school activities for primary-aged children (up to age 11) were:

1. Swimming lessons.

2. Musical instrument tuition.

3. Drama clubs.

4. Dance.

5. Guides/Scouts.

The most popular activities amongst secondary school children (aged 11–18) were:

1. Sport clubs.

2. Musical instrument tuition.

3. Dance.

4. Driving lessons.

5. Guides/Scouts.

Not only is over-scheduling of kids creating a nation of boredom-prone adults, but we also risk children growing bored of the very activities we are trying to hothouse them in. When you do something too long, it becomes repetitive, routine *and* boring, so youngsters who have been learning the violin since the age of 5 are far more likely to quit than those who pick it up at a later age. Research shows that by the age of 13, three quarters of children who participated for several years in organised activities have given them up because they have grown bored of them.[28] Kids who are constantly offered new and novel challenges simply don't have the staying power to persevere with something that no longer offers that buzz of the new. They prefer to drop the violin in favour of something new – and parents are often only too happy to indulge them in pursuing their new interests, reasoning that as long as they are doing something stimulating, it matters little what it is; thus their lives become a haphazard mix of starting a hobby, stopping and then taking up a new one.

Box 6.10: Hot-housing and Tiger Mothers

Hothousing is a controversial form of parenting, which involves exposing children to intensive after-school and extra-curricular activities in order to stimulate their minds. It is likened to the hothousing of crops that are grown under intensive farming conditions in order to encourage faster growth. Hothousing has been associated with the Tiger Mom concept, espoused in *Battle Hymn of the Tiger Mother*, a book by Amy Chua published in 2011. In the book, the Chinese mother appears to advocate very strict 'hothousing' principles such as forcing her daughters to practise their musical instruments for hours each day. Whilst the book led to fierce debate about parenting, hothousing and Chinese versus Western parenting styles, it also led to a wide debate about how much parents should encourage extra-curricular and scheduled activities for their children.

Let Them be Bored!

Why then are parents today so afraid to allow their kids to be bored? We have seen why they don't let their kids play out, why kids might watch too much TV, use the computer for entertainment and why parents might over-schedule them. The reasons for all these boredom-minimising activities are varied, as has been discussed – from lack of parental time to 'stranger danger'. But none of these reasons addresses the real issues: they are all about wanting our kids to get a competitive advantage, and to do well in life – but what about the more deep-seated fear that parents today seem to have, of allowing their kids to be bored?

Parents today view boredom so negatively that they will do almost anything to prevent it. Boredom equals under-stimulation, and as we have seen, stimulation is seen as something as important to provide our kids with as food and love. Indeed, stimulation has become the zeitgeist of the twenty-first century and as such, its polar opposite – boredom – has become the pariah. If we fail to stimulate enough, from birth and even before, we are failing in our duty as a parent, and fear of failure is a very real concern for today's parent. When our child is bored, instead of telling them to go and find something to do (as my mum always used to say), we see this as a personal attack on our parenting abilities. Many parents today already feel guilty – time-poor mums and dads who are juggling work and home life want to compensate by ensuring their offspring have the best educational developmental advantages. A complaint of being bored then can easily feel like a deeply cutting accusation. Yet many argue, as I do, that we have got it wrong. In trying to combat and even pre-empt our children's boredom, by filling every waking moment with stimulation, we are failing them. We are so caught up with the quest for stimulation, with filling their time with meaningful, worthy activities, that we have forgotten how beneficial downtime can be.

Some parenting experts have begun to realise this and are starting to call for parents to embrace, not fear boredom. Dr Teresa Belton, senior researcher at the University of East Anglia's School of Education and Lifelong Learning, interviewed a number of authors, artists and scientists in her exploration of the effects of boredom. Her findings, published in 2013, urged parents to allow their children to be bored so that they can develop their creativity. She points out that author Meera Syal began to keep a diary complete with poems and stories – her first experience of writing – out of boredom. Belton urges kids to have time to 'stand and stare', to get bored and to have downtime so as to learn to entertain themselves and be forced into other creative outlets.[29]

In 2014, Julie Robinson, the education and training director of the Independent Association of Prep Schools (IAPS) told the IAPS magazine that boredom prepares children for the reality of adulthood when life is not constantly exciting and fun. Quiet, calm and reflection, she urged, should be considered as important as any structured class or 'stimulating' activity.[30] And commentator Edward Collier[31] wrote an inspiring article in the *Guardian* in 2010, in which he lamented the rise of what he called 'boil-in-the-bag entertainment' that parents seem hell-bent on supplying for their kids. Boredom, Collier insists, 'opens channels' that can lead to using writing, poetry, music composition and all manner of other pastimes that draw on resources from within, rather than from without.

What should we do then to embrace boredom in our children's lives? These are my suggestions:

- Start young: don't bother with in-womb stimulation devices – all their needs are met in the womb and we have to assume (until proven otherwise) that this includes the need for stimulation too.
- Forget the 'whizzy-whizzy-bang-bang' toys that dominate the baby and toddler marketplace. Young children don't need lights AND music AND movement AND actions all at once! Go back to basics with simple toys that allow infants to develop their own skills (e.g. shape sorting) without so many distractions.
- Provide the basic building blocks to beat boredom creatively: paper, colouring materials, pens and crafty bits and pieces.
- Avoid too much background noise; turn the TV on only to watch specific, carefully chosen programmes.
- Limit time spent in day nurseries. There is nothing wrong with such childcare provisions but too much time spent there can be over-stimulating.

- Limit screen time for all children. This includes TV, computers, smartphones, etc.
- Let your children gain stimulation from the real world: nature, watching the washing machine go round, banging pans, etc. There is plenty of stimulation around us, they don't need to learn to expect more.
- Don't over-schedule kids. Some classes and activities are great, but make sure, whatever their age, they have downtime too.
- Rejoice when they say 'I'm bored'. See this as a reflection of your superior parenting skills rather than a slight on them.
- Finally, don't bring an iPad to entertain them in a café. Instead bring crayons and encourage them to look around and interact with their environment (warning: this might involve interacting with them).

Box 6.11: Small children were bored during the making of this book

The plaintive cry of 'I'm bored' has reverberated around my own house with alarming (for some) frequency during the writing of this book, which largely took place at weekends or during the evening. My 7-year-old son soon learned that my standard response to his complaint was 'Great!' Although at times I did resort to the tele-sitter, I tried very hard to resist, even though his cries were, at times, heart-rending. So, am I a cruel, neglectful mum, putting my career before the needs of my child? You tell me, but first, here are some of the things that my little boy eventually came up with to do whilst he was 'bored' during the writing of this book:

- He made a card factory; he created different greeting cards for different occasions and created a stand to display them. He then attempted to persuade members of the family to buy them.

- He wrote several newspapers and magazines.

- He created a whole fantasy world called 'Canchowie' with fictional places and destinations.

- He conducted a long experiment in 'chain reactions' by making devices that roll a can in such a way that it would hit another object and push that onto something else until he had a whole chain reaction of events.

- He created his own 'office' in his bedroom in imitation of mine (which I duly spent time admiring).

- A model 3D 'shop' was crafted using just paper and sticky tape. He even put in paper clothes to 'buy'.

- He came up with a new invention of a three-in-one pencil. Again using craft materials, he put together a contraption that included pencil, sharpener and eraser in one.

- He made a fancy dress outfit.

- New songs were composed, including one entitled 'The Coolest Man on Earth' and another 'There's a Robber in the House'.

- A game was produced, complete with 3D board, paper money and game pieces. The game was called Backdrop Town and I am not entirely sure what the objectives were (it might need some refining before it reaches mass production stage!).

Boredom and the Rise of ADHD and Autistic Spectrum Disorder

Boredom is characterised by a search for stimulation and manifests itself in restless, sensation-seeking behaviour such as fidgeting, difficulty maintaining attention and inability to concentrate (on things that require sustained effort). Coincidentally, this perfectly describes a person with ADHD (Attention Deficit Hyperactivity Disorder). The question might be asked, then, whether there is a distinction between ADHD and the boredom-prone personality and whether some (or even all) of the children being diagnosed today with ADHD are, in fact, simply bored; the products of a culture that increasingly fosters a drive towards novelty and stimulation and an intolerance of slower-paced stimuli requiring sustained attention (like homework).

The Rise of ADHD

The fidgety, inattentive, bored child is not a modern phenomenon; indeed in 1845 German poet Heinrich Hoffmann crafted a story about 'Fidgety Philip', a boy so restless that he is begged by his irate father to sit at the table nicely 'for once'. In a description that will be recognised by parents worldwide today, Philip is unable to comply, and his wriggling and jiggling sees him swinging back and forth in his chair with such force that he falls back, grabs the tablecloth in a desperate attempt to support himself and brings the tableware down on top of him. Poor Philip is 'in 'disgrace' at his actions, yet nowadays most likely to have a diagnosis of ADHD and a prescription for Ritalin slapped on him.

'Fidgety' children most likely always existed, but the label of ADHD is undoubtedly on the rise. It was first recognised as a condition in 1902 by British paediatrician, George Frederic Still. Since Still's day, the disorder has been called by various names, such as Hyperkinetic Syndrome, Attention-Deficit Disorder (ADD) and now ADHD. The American Psychiatric Association's Diagnostic Manual, the *DSM-5* (the 'bible' for diagnosing all mental health conditions), outlines indicators for ADHD that include: inattention (a child is easily distracted), hyperactivity (he or she may fidget a lot, for example), and impulsivity (the child may blurt out answers too quickly). All of which seem to be exactly the same symptoms that a bored child (or even adult) might display.

ADHD is indeed a rather controversial condition. There is no sure-fire way of diagnosing it and the phenomenal rise in children being given this label has led many to believe that it is being diagnosed far too readily; a survey in 2005 by psychologists Jill Norvilitis of the University at Buffalo, S.U.N.Y., and Ping Fang of Capital Normal University in Beijing revealed that in the US, 82 per cent of teachers agreed that 'ADHD is overdiagnosed today'.[1] Certainly the statistics suggest a massive increase in people with the condition; the Centers for Disease Control and Prevention's national survey of Children's Health in the US reported an 830 per cent increase in youngsters diagnosed with ADD or ADHD from 1985 to 2011.[2] An article in *The New York Times* in 2013 reported that in the span of 24 years, the number of children on medication for ADHD in America has soared from 600,000 to 3.5 million.[3] This means that nearly one in five high-school age boys in the United States and 11 per cent of school-age children overall have received a medical diagnosis of Attention Deficit Hyperactivity Disorder.[4]

The disorder is now the second most frequent long-term diagnosis made in children, narrowly trailing asthma.[3]

Reasons given for this massive rise include misdiagnosis, as well as greater awareness on the part of teachers and clinicians. There are many who feel that normal boredom or boredom-proneness is simply being medicalised; either way, it does seem (as previously outlined in Chapter 6, page 118) that we are growing a nation of bored, fidgety, restless kids – who are being diagnosed (correctly or otherwise) as having ADHD.

Dr Dimitri Christakis, a paediatric researcher at Children's Hospital and Regional Medical Center in Seattle, appears to share my view that it is our fast-paced, novelty-seeking society that is leading to a burgeoning in ADHD; he particularly credits the rise in TV watching as a possible link. Back in 2004, he published a journal article (referred to in Chapter 6, see page 113) in the journal *Pediatrics*, in which he found that TV viewing in very young children contributes to attention problems later in life.[5] Specifically, he blamed the overstimulation of TV programmes for this in the ways I have outlined in Chapter 6. Kids who are conditioned to expect a fast-paced, novelty-infused world are simply unable to sustain attention for very long to slower-moving stimuli. Thus, all those things that require sustained attention (such as reading, maths, comprehension, homework, etc.) become boring as the child struggles to maintain their concentration. Is it any wonder more and more kids are labelled with ADHD?

That is not to say that watching too much TV (or other screen time) *causes* ADHD, since most studies do suggest a genetic aetiology too. However, it could be that for those pre-disposed to boredom proneness, the fast-paced society we live in is driving them over the edge from being merely boredom-prone to being diagnosed with attention-deficit disorders. There could also be an over-enthusiasm to label bored and inattentive kids, brought up on a diet of high-intensity action that does not match the reality of everyday life, with the condition; this enthusiasm is driven partly by parents who want an 'easy' answer to explain their child's difficulties, a pharmaceutical industry keen to push its range of ADHD treatments, and teachers who can often receive more funding and help for a child diagnosed with 'special needs'. For more on this, see Box 7.1, below.

Box 7.1: Parents who push for diagnosis of ADHD

There is a growing trend in Western society for middle-class parents to push for an ADHD diagnosis for their 'difficult' child. Professor Sir Simon Wessely, head of the Royal College of Psychiatrists in the UK, laments what he calls 'medicating normal traits in children'.[6] One motivation of such parents is that it may be preferable for them to have a child with the label of ADHD, than for others to blame their troublesome behaviour on poor parenting.

Ambitious parents are also keen for medication that will help their child concentrate and thus perform better at school. Schools often collaborate with this over-diagnosis because of the extra funding they can receive for each 'special needs' child and the shifting of responsibility from their own teaching methods being at fault to the child being the one with the problem.

One expert, paediatric neurologist Dr Richard Saul, based in Chicago, USA, goes further, claiming that ADHD does not exist at all, and that adults like the label in preference to admitting that they are 'stuck in a boring rut'.[6] In other words, we would prefer to be labelled as having ADHD than to admit we are simply bored and unable to sustain attention to things (usually intellectual pursuits) that do not offer enough stimulation. Middle-class parents of under-achieving children who are bored and restless in numeracy and literacy classes would much rather the world thought their child had a medical condition than that they might be considered lacking in intelligence. There is also the issue of financial reward for families; in the UK at least at the time of going to press, the condition is classified as a disability, and as such the family of an ADHD child can be entitled to a raft of welfare benefits, including carers' allowances and disabled child tax credit. It is estimated that there are currently around 43,000 claimant families in the UK receiving benefits for ADHD, compared with just 800 in 2001. Some are even given a taxpayer-funded car; according to a study in 2011, 3,200 households with an occupant who has an ADHD diagnosis have been provided with a vehicle under the Government's £1.5 billion 'Motability' scheme.[7]

This enthusiasm for diagnosis of ADHD is undoubtedly aided and abetted by the pharmaceutical industry. Over the past 20 years, the worldwide value of the market for ADHD drugs has risen from £11 million to no less than £11 billion.[7] In the US, where drug advertising is permitted, the pressure on parents to obtain such an apparently magical cure for their child's inattention or concentration difficulties (which might simply be due to boredom) is huge. What was once regarded as normal – a child being unable to sit still at his desk during a tedious maths lesson – is now being medicalised as something to be treated with powerful drugs that can improve drive, focus and attention – and thus becomes a 'short-cut to better grades'.[4]

The Link Between ADHD and Boredom Proneness

The physiological link between ADHD and boredom proneness is demonstrated by neuroscience research. For example, it has been shown that people with ADHD are actually hard-wired for novelty seeking such that they are more likely to find everyday life dull and lacking stimulation; they have a higher need for novelty and new stimuli than the rest of us. This was shown in a study that examined the brains of people with ADHD using PET scans. Dr Nora D. Volkow, a scientist from the National Institute on Drug Abuse (NIDA), compared the number of dopamine receptors in the brains of a group of unmedicated adults with ADHD with a group of healthy controls. The adults with ADHD had significantly fewer D2 and D3 receptors (two specific subtypes of dopamine receptors) in their reward circuits than did healthy controls. Furthermore, the lower the level of dopamine receptors was, the greater the subject's symptoms of inattention. These findings suggest that people with ADHD have reward circuits that are less sensitive than those of the rest of us, which makes normally interesting activities seem dull – leaving them to crave novelty and exciting new stimuli.[8]

Box 7.2: Why French children are less likely to have ADHD

In France, the percentage of children diagnosed and medicated for ADHD is less than 0.5 per cent, far lower than in the US or the UK. The reason for this is that in France, ADHD, whilst still regarded as a medical condition, is viewed as one with psycho-social and situational causes, requiring not medication but treatment with regards to a child's social context (e.g. psychotherapy). So successful are French doctors at finding and repairing what has gone wrong in the child's social context (including expectations, food intake, lifestyle) that fewer children there qualify for an ADHD diagnosis.[9]

Whilst this craving for novelty may have yielded an evolutionary benefit in the past, it is now an irritating relic that hinders us in a world where academic achievement generally conveys the most advantages in life. People with ADHD are thus drawn towards risk, excitement and sensation seeking – and away from routine, sitting still, repetition and sustained attention. Therefore they have a low tolerance for boredom, but I can't help wondering if this predisposition might have been attenuated had they not been fed such high levels of constant stimulation from an early age. Can people with ADHD, a real condition (in my view), be helped by having a calmer upbringing in which their expectations of excitement are lowered somewhat? My suggestion of 'downtime therapy' (discussed next) for children from birth might not eliminate ADHD (of course not), but it could reduce its severity and frequency.

Box 7.3: A culture where ADHD is an advantage

In our evolutionary past, having ADHD would have been advantageous. As hunters, we needed to be able to quickly scan the environment, be easily distracted by novel stimuli and able to switch our attention quickly between events – all of which would have helped us locate the next meal (whilst not becoming it for someone else!). In the Western world today, such skills are less needed and the ability to sustain concentration on repetitive and dull stimuli without getting bored tends to yield more rewards (at least in the long term).

However, there is a nomadic tribe today in Kenya called the Ariaal, with a subgroup who have settled in agriculture-flourishing areas. This has allowed Dan T. A. Eisenberg, an anthropologist at the University of Washington, to compare the nomadic and settler groups of the Ariaal in terms of their frequency of a dopamine type-four receptor called DRD4 7R. This DRD4 7R makes the dopamine receptor less responsive than normal and is specifically linked with ADHD. Dr Eisenberg found that the nomadic men who had the DRD4 7R variant were better nourished than the nomadic men who lacked it. So, if you live a nomadic lifestyle, having a brain structure that promotes ADHD-like behaviour confers a considerable advantage, just as it would have done for our hunter-gatherer ancestors. In those circumstances, to be able to concentrate for long periods on the same stimulus is not an advantage, but being distracted by anything novel (and either dangerous or edible) is likely to be. Sadly, for most ADHD sufferers, today's more settled lifestyle that most of us live in, is not best suited for ADHD behaviours.[10]

Downtime Therapy

If, as I propose, ADHD is caused in part by our increasingly over-stimulated culture, then perhaps it might be possible to treat ADHD with 'downtime therapy'. This would involve introducing significant amounts of 'downtime' to children as a way of reducing their dependency on novelty and constant stimulation. It is treating stimulation as an addiction, suggesting that many people have become so dependent on it that they need help in reducing their cravings.

Downtime Therapy could consist of mindfulness, relaxation therapy, meditation and digital, screen-free scheduling. The idea of using mindfulness techniques on those with ADHD is not new and has been shown to be very effective; one study reported in *Clinical Neurophysiology* in 2014 suggested that adults with ADHD could benefit from mindfulness training combined with cognitive therapy to such an extent that their improvements in mental performance were comparable to those achieved by ADHD participants taking stimulant medications.[11] A study in 2012 found similar effects with children.[12]

Mindfulness, a relatively recent construct in Western psychology, with an over 2,500-year history in Eastern traditions, predominantly Buddhism, would seem to work because it gets to the core of the attention issues that people with ADHD have. It is a technique that involves paying close attention to inner thoughts, feelings and emotions – in the 'here and now' (rather than flitting around, looking for the next thing to happen). Mindfulness helps people pay attention to what they are paying attention to and involves silent periods of reflection, in which thoughts and cognitions are addressed inwards. It is the opposite of sensation and novelty seeking – instead of looking for new stimuli, it helps decrease arousal and concentrates attention on appreciating and acknowledging already existing stimulation.

Box 7.4: How to do 'mindfulness'

According to Lidia Zylowska, M.D, a psychiatrist and author of *The Mindfulness Prescription for Adult ADHD*, mindfulness involves three main stages: (1) focusing attention towards an 'attentional anchor' (often this is the process of breathing in and out), (2) noticing when distraction occurs and trying to tune out that distraction, and (3) refocusing or reorienting attention back to the 'attentional anchor'. In her book, however, Zylowska talks of an 8-step programme, which includes practices such as sitting meditation, body awareness, thoughtful speaking and listening, development of self-acceptance, mindful self-coaching and more.

Meditation could also be used as part of this proposed 'down-time therapy' and indeed is already included in some ADHD programmes. It is a mental training skill that can help regulate attention as mindfulness can. Recent research has demonstrated that mindfulness meditation training can actually modify attentional networks, change neural activity and alter dopamine levels (for review, see [13]), all of which are implicated in both boredom-proneness and ADHD. This might seem odd since many people with ADHD may feel that they simply would be unable to concentrate long enough to practise meditation. Yet it seems to work: a random-assignment controlled study published in *Mind & Brain* found decreased symptoms of attention-deficit/hyperactivity disorder in students practising the Transcendental Meditation® (TM) technique.[14] An earlier study, published in *Current Issues in Education*, followed a group of school pupils with ADHD, who meditated (again, using TM) twice a day in school. After three months, researchers found over 50 per cent reductions in ADHD symptoms.[15] TM was used in these studies because it does not require intense concentration, controlling the mind or a disciplined focus, which are difficult for those with ADHD.

The power of all of these downtime therapies shows that countering the over-stimulating world we live in with reduced stimuli can benefit the ADHD sufferer and re-condition them to start coping with lowered amounts of novelty and sensation in their lives. The implication of this is that if we reduce the stimulation that our kids get from such an early age, we might be able to stem the tide of burgeoning ADHD diagnoses in many parts of the Western world.

Are 'Boring' People Actually Autistic?

Chapter 10 turns to a different take on boredom by examining not what makes someone bored, but what makes them boring. Boring people are everywhere, and are often the bane of the lives of other (presumably not-boring) people. Whilst Chapter 10 discusses in great detail what makes someone boring, here we continue the theme of the relationship of special needs with boredom by asking whether those people we class as boring in fact might not be so much boring as autistic. In other words, if boredom proneness is a 'special need', ADHD, maybe being boring is too (Autism).

Box 7.5: What is ASD (Autistic Spectrum Disorder)?

The National Autistic Society in the UK estimates 11 in 1,000 people (1.1 per cent of the population) have autism spectrum disorders. Sometimes referred to as autism or Asperger's Syndrome (for those who have it more mildly, or who are described as 'high functioning'), the condition is characterised by three main groups of impairments: impaired ability to engage in reciprocal social interactions, impairment of social communication and difficulties with social imagination. A great deal of the autistic syndrome then is connected with social difficulties. Many people on the spectrum (for it is a spectrum, rather than an all-or-nothing condition) find it difficult to maintain social interactions either because they cannot read the emotions of others, cannot express their emotions appropriately, react inappropriately with others (e.g. taking things too literally or talking about one subject too much), or prefer repetitive interactions that other people might quickly grow bored with.

It should be noted that ASD affects people in different ways, but most of those with the condition do experience difficulties in two main areas:

- Problems with social interaction and communication – including problems understanding and being aware of other people's emotions and feelings.

- Restricted and repetitive patterns of thought, interests and physical behaviours – including making repetitive physical movements, such as hand tapping or twisting, and becoming upset if these set routines are disrupted.

In 1994 an intriguing paper was published in *Clinical Social Work Journal* called 'Only Sane: Autistic Barriers in "Boring" Patients',[16] in which the authors refer to patients who are 'bored and boring'. Such people show little emotion and are lacking in imagination. Because their thinking is so concrete and literal, their speech lacks depth and richness, leading to them to be considered boring by others. The authors suggest that being boring is not simply a personality trait, but a condition – even an illness. They quote British child psychoanalyst D. W. Winnicott, who in 1971 claimed that someone who bores you is 'sick' and in need of 'psychiatric treatment'.

It is an interesting argument that suggests it is inappropriate that 'boring' people be subject to ridicule or possibly criticism (as indeed they often are), as they should be regarded as having some form of mental disorder. I suspect that nowadays, Dr Winnicott would have recognised boring people as being not sick, but on the autistic spectrum. Indeed, the link between being boring and being autistic is furthered by the development of a new device, reported in *New Scientist* in 2006,[17] that can pick up on people's emotions and alert a user if the person they are talking to starts showing signs of getting bored. The device, termed the 'Emotional Social Intelligence Prosthetic', was developed by El Kaliouby, along with MIT colleagues, Rosalind Picard and Alea Teeters, and is intended to help autistic people whose difficulty in picking up on social cues means that they are unable to recognise when they are boring another person.

Box 7.6: The perfect job for autistic people?

© Elan Images/Alamy

The Transportation Security Administration baggage screeners at airports have to constantly monitor hundreds of X-rayed bags, trying to pick out dangerous objects. It is boring, routine and repetitive work, and most employees find that their minds wander very quickly, which is potentially dangerous, but some autistic people might be perfectly suited to this work.

A study published in 2013 by researchers at Carnegie Mellon University, the University of Pittsburgh and the University of Minnesota, USA, found that high-functioning autistic men were just as accurate and almost as fast as non-autistic people in finding weapons in X-ray images of baggage. More importantly, their performance improved as time went on, rather than deteriorated, suggesting they did not get distracted, unlike the non-autistic workers.[18.]

A later study, published in 2014 in *Frontiers in Neuroinformatics*,[19] might explain this finding. Here, researchers scanned the 'resting' brains of autistic and non-autistic children using magnetoencephalography (MEG), a non-invasive (and quiet) technique. The results suggested that in the same dull situation, those with autism process more information than their neurotypical peers. They may thus be able to more easily detect small differences than their non-autistic peers. This could be especially so with visual information, as shown by another study, published this time in *The Journal of Neuroscience*.[19] This study found that the visual cortex of the participants with autism responds more strongly to visual stimulation than that of controls, which could make their sensory experience more intense.

In Chapter 10, I will outline the 30 habits of boring people. Many of these also happen to be traits of autistic people. For example, those on the autistic spectrum tend to have narrow hobbies or interests, which they like to talk about (and which they may talk about obsessively), can be emotionally flat, can also be very focused on detail and find it hard to understand the point of view of others. They may find it hard to maintain eye contact, may not make or understand jokes (taking things literally) and may not understand the social cues that suggest someone else wants to speak or is bored. Thus, a 'high functioning' ASD individual may be regarded as boring but these traits could simply be tied in with their condition.

Interestingly, the incidence of ASD has also risen dramatically over the years. In the 1970s and 1980s about one out of every 2,000 children had autism. Today, the Centers for Disease Control and Prevention estimates one in 150 of 8-year-olds in the US has an autism spectrum disorder, or ASD.[20] One reason for the apparent increase could be greater recognition of the condition and also greater inclusivity of criteria to be diagnosed. It could well be then that the sort of children simply labelled as odd or socially aloof in the past are now being diagnosed as autistic. Because these changes have meant that it is easier for kids today to be diagnosed than in the past, there are likely to be many adults walking around who could be on the spectrum, but were never labelled at school due to lower awareness of the condition and only the most severe children being included in the diagnostic criteria. According to the UK's National Autistic Society (NAS), one in 100 adults has some form of autism and most of them are unaware of this.[21]

I would thus contend that there are thousands of adults out there who, as they talk endlessly about their obscure hobbies, without much emotion or awareness of the other person's feelings on the subject, or who talk about themselves but fail to ask questions of their audience, or who talk in a dull, flat monotone, might be described as boring – when they are, in fact, undiagnosed autistic.

The Plague of Interactive Whiteboards: Why Boredom in Schools and Further Education is Booming

Despite the fact that teaching methods seem to be more exciting, interactive and fast-paced than ever before, our kids seem to be as bored as ever. The latest large-scale research available suggests that 66 per cent of students are bored on at least a daily basis in school, with 17 per cent reporting that they are bored in every single class.[1] It seems that the more stimulation that is available, the more we seek (an argument made in previous chapters of this book). This chapter argues that modern teaching methods and the increasingly child-focused society we live in (as discussed in Chapter 6) are leading to a new generation who expect all aspects of life to be stimulating and exciting – and who feel bored when their demands for stimulation are not met (e.g. in later life at work). In other words, the more 'exciting', fast-paced and attention-seeking teaching methods become, the more we contribute to the creation of a low-boredom threshold society.

Interactive White-'bored'?

'You know a class is boring when you've wasted 40% of your battery in it ...'

When Gallup asked American teenagers in 2004 to choose three words that best described their typical feelings in school from a list of 14 adjectives, 'bored' was chosen most often – by half of students.[2] In another survey, in 2006, of 467 American high-school dropouts, nearly half said boredom was a major factor in their decision to quit school.[3] Indiana University's High School Survey of Student Engagement (HSSSE) reached more than 81,000 students in 110 high schools across 26 states in 2007. Two out of three high-school students in this survey said they are bored in class every single day.[4]

Boredom in school is not restricted to the US, though. According to a survey in 2001 (the most recent available), across 31 countries nearly half of 15-year-olds said they often felt bored at school; Table 8.1 below shows that Ireland fared worst of all, with 67 per cent of teenagers reporting frequent boredom, with the least bored in Portugal at 24 per cent.[5]

Table 8.1: Which countries have the most bored pupils?	
Country	Percentage of teenagers who 'often' feel bored at school
Ireland	67
Spain	66
Greece	66
United States	61
Australia	60
New Zealand	60
Finland	60
Sweden	58

Norway	58
Canada	58
United Kingdom	54
Italy	54
Luxemburg	50
Austria	49
Germany	49
Liechtenstein	47
Czech Republic	47
Belgium	46
Korea	46
Denmark	41
Switzerland	38
Poland	38
France	32
Japan	32
Latvia	31
Iceland	30
Brazil	30
Hungary	29
Mexico	28
Russian Federation	27
Portugal	24

Adapted from the OECD Programme for International Student Assessment (PISA) Database 2001[5]

Box 8.1: Bored in Japan

Despite the country's low boredom position, a newspaper article in Japan in 2000 suggested that boredom was the main reason for a new phenomenon of exodus to private schools that was being observed there. It seems that a new policy of a 'lighter curriculum' introduced to Japan in 2000 (perhaps after the above research was carried out in Table 8.1) meant that students in state schools were becoming 'paralyzed with boredom'.[6]

Lest all these studies pre-date the massive rise in the use of technology in the classroom (of which more later), which we might expect to 'cure' student boredom, I have tried to find as much recent data on student boredom as possible. Although there is surprisingly little hard evidence in the last few years (see Box 8.3, page 144), there is plenty of anecdotal evidence that despite the all-singing, all-dancing education that schoolchildren now receive (see Box 8.2), they are still bored. A study in 2010 found that 44.3 per cent of pupils 'partly to strongly' agreed that they frequently experienced boredom in maths classes[7] and a 2011 report by Youth United for Change found that boredom was one of the greatest factors driving students in Philadelphia to drop out of school.[8]

Box 8.2: Drumming and dancing

According to Ofsted (the UK Government-run Office for Standards in Education, Children's Services and Skills) in 2010, pupils were so bored that schools were found to be resorting to ever-more extreme methods such as drama, role-play, music and dance to engage them. One secondary school used drums to highlight the relationship between numbers in a maths lesson – pupils created drumming routines to accompany the multiplication table. Another school employed dance routines to develop pupils' understanding of chemical bonding in a science lesson.[9]

Box 8.3: Why is classroom boredom so under-researched?

As German and Swiss researchers Preckel, Gotz and Frenzel lamented in a 2010 paper published in the *British Journal of Educational Psychology*,[10] there is a dearth of research on boredom in the classroom. The reason for this, they explain, could be that boredom is perceived as a rather benign 'silent' emotion that does not attract anywhere near as much attention as other 'louder' emotions like anger or anxiety. Classroom boredom is seen as something merely unpleasant rather than destructive, despite the wealth of evidence linking it to a range of very negative outcomes (see page 161). In fact, boredom should by rights be the focus of as much educational attention as other 'academic' emotions such as anxiety, which directly relate to learning outcomes.[11]

We only have to look at Twitter to learn just how bored at school kids today remain. Boredom rush hour seems to happen around 10 or 11 a.m. Eastern time in the US, by which time school bells have rung all over the country and the Tweets begin to proliferate. At the time of writing, there are 13 Tweeters using the names Bored At School, including:

@Boredatschool

@BoredAtSchool

@BoredAtSchool

@BoredAtSchool2

@BoredAt_School

@bored_school

@Soboredatschool

AND. . . @MrBoredAtSchool (is this a teacher?)

Box 8.4: Bored tweets – a sample

Nov 20 2014 #boredatschool I need help get me out of school.!!!!!!!!! Sitting in class typing behind the teachers back.

Nov 19 so bored in school #boredatschool

Nov 19 School is so boring #boredatschool

Nov 17 Study hall is soo freaking boring! Someone entertain me please #entertain #boredatschool

Nov 17 I don't wanna be here at school.#boredatschool

19 Sep 2013 Halfway through the school day and I'm at 10% battery. . . It's just one of those days. . . #BoredAtSchool

23 Apr 2013 Dear math, go away from meeeeeeee. #BoredAtSchool

17 Jan 2012 I just want to play basketball at the church right now #boredatschool

Apr 11 Today's date (4/11/14) is the same forward as it is backward. Man I need a life.. #boredinclass

Apr 10 I look at the clock, and then look back and I swear that time went in reverse. #BoredInClass

Mar 23 I wouldn't hate school so much if I was taking classes that were actually going to help me with my future #bored-inclass #pointless

But why are pupils so bored in school? This boredom epidemic seems at odds with the obsession that educators have in the twenty-first century to stimulate and engage young minds when compared with the old style of 'chalk and talk'. School used to be a place to sit and listen, to recite by rote, to memorise and regurgitate knowledge. Now, the interactive whiteboard generation (of which more later in this chapter) can expect a range of teaching styles designed to encourage active learning, participation and, above all, engagement. What is going wrong?

The problem is the same as I have identified throughout this book: the more stimulation there is, the more we crave. School is fast becoming a place not just of learning but over-stimulation too, as teachers compete to introduce ever-more 'engaging' methods into their material (such as the drumming and dance routines described earlier). Technology in schools is certainly providing the more exciting world, visually, aurally and via other senses, that children have come to expect. There is no question that schools are more exciting than they were in the 'chalk and talk' days, yet look at the data on student boredom.

Consider a 4-year-old (the age when most children start formal education in the UK) and the range of exciting formats and events s/he will encounter during a typical school day. This is what my 4-year-old son enjoyed a couple of years ago in his 'reception' class:

- Interactive white board based learning (of which more later)
- Special assemblies
- Regular school trips
- Regular 'dress up' days (dress up as a Victorian, a book character, a World War I character, etc.)
- Computer-based sessions
- iPad-based learning
- Visitors to school to talk about special events (e.g. World War I, different professions)
- Concerts and plays to prepare for and showcase
- Cookery and baking sessions
- Art-based work
- Canteen-style lunches where they can choose their food from a range of options
- 'Busy' and frequently changing visual displays in classrooms
- Sports days
- Generation lunches (where parents can join their kids in school for lunch)
- Phonics bingo events
- Sponsored walks
- Trips to museums

That is a lot going on for a young child, who is also having to cope with a range of new people, both peers and teaching/auxiliary staff. Even too much stimulation via one sense can be overwhelming, never mind when all the senses are constantly bombarded with novel and exciting stimuli. Researchers at Carnegie Mellon University conducted a fascinating experiment in 2014, in which they taught an identical series of science lessons to kindergarteners in two different classrooms; one classroom was extensively decorated with colourful posters and pictures whilst the other classroom was left bare and dull. They found that children were more distracted by the highly visual environment and spent more time off-task than in the plainer classrooms.[12] Too much stimulation led to difficulty sustaining attention on a task, which sounds a lot like boredom. This is reinforced by a report in *Education Week* in 2012, which pointed out too much aural stimulation as might be found in a noisy classroom can 'sap students' attention and contribute to their boredom'.[13]

Box 8.5: The interactive whiteboard

Almost every classroom, from pre-school to senior high, now has an interactive whiteboard (IWB) in place of the old-style blackboard/chalkboard. An interactive whiteboard is a large, multi-media interactive display that connects to a computer. A projector projects the computer's desktop onto the board's surface, where users control the computer with a pen, finger, stylus or other device. Many companies now focus on creating supplemental instructional materials specifically designed for interactive whiteboards. The IWB thus acts as an overhead projector, television, DVD player, photo album, computer, and much more.

Some manufacturers also provide classroom response systems as an integrated part of their interactive whiteboard products. Handheld 'clickers' operating via infrared or radio signals, for example, offer basic multiple choice and polling options. More sophisticated clickers offer text and numeric responses and can export an analysis of student performance for subsequent review.

All of which is a long way from the old static chalkboard; now teachers can present film clips, animation, pictures, interactive quizzes, sound and much, much more at the click of a button. This allows a faster teaching pace, with the ability to constantly change the stimuli in order to retain pupils' attention.

In 2004, 26 per cent of British primary classrooms had interactive whiteboards,[14] and by 2011, 80 per cent of schools had at least one IWB.[15] Today, there are few schools without them.

Of course, classrooms need to be engaging places, and I am not advocating a return to the austere Victorian schoolroom. Kids today have higher expectations of stimulation and if they are used to iPads, Xboxes and computers at home, they will find the low-level stimulus of a textbook, for example, boring (see Box 8.6, below). IWBs provide what I refer to as a 'whizzy whizzy bang bang' environment where there is noise, bright visuals, moving images and interaction – a far cry from the dull blackboard of yesteryear. According to Professor Michael Fullan, a University of Toronto academic who has advised education authorities in the US, Canada and the UK, 'kids nowadays have an attention span of three seconds'[16] and thus grow bored very quickly if things are not changing at a fast enough pace. But our quest for 'engagement' might come at a price – lowered tolerance for quieter, slower-paced, low-action environments. This means that we need to provide ever-more exciting environments to keep the attention, and also that there is thus increased susceptibility to boredom. As one (anonymous) teacher explained in a BBC report on the increased use of technology in schools, 'Children's worlds are so electronic already – schools should be a relative place of peace away from all those electronic goods.'[17] John D. Eastman, an expert in boredom and professor of psychology at York

University in Toronto, put it clearly when he said, 'If someone is bored, the worst thing you can do is respond to it by over-stimulating'.[3]

Box 8.6: Books Made More Exciting

Many schools deem traditional reading books no longer exciting enough to engage today's sensation-seeking child and instead use electronic reading schemes. My son's school trialled such a scheme (accessed via iPads or laptops) when he was 6 years old, allowing the child to log in using a unique code and access e-books online. Various books appear on the virtual 'bookshelf' and the child can pick what he wants to read and when. They read the book using arrow keys to turn the pages and they also look out for the little green bugs indicating that a question on the text requires an answer. Reward points for reading are collected and automatically stored; the child can log off and return at any point. The child's teacher can also monitor their reading and see how they are getting on.

Whilst my little boy loved the scheme and certainly pre-ferred it to the less stimulus-heavy traditional book (no buttons to press, no moving images, no sounds), I myself had misgivings about how such a scheme would impact on his boredom threshold and ability to concentrate and sustain attention on slower-moving stimuli. He was already enjoy-ing books in the traditional way and I didn't feel he needed this sort of scheme to engage him. Fortunately, many other parents shared my views and much to my son's disappoint-ment, the school returned to the old-fashioned book-reading scheme.

Other possible reasons why pupils and students are so bored at school include:

1 Mixed ability classes

The current trend for mixed ability classes could also lead to student boredom. According to a report in the *Daily Telegraph* in 2012, there has been a steady decline in streaming and setting in the UK over the past decade, with around 55 per cent of lessons being of mixed ability in 2010-11.[18] In the 1950s almost all lessons in the UK were 'streamed'.[19] The trend towards mixed ability classes is driven by findings that lower-ability pupils can be locked into 'a cycle of disadvantage'[20] whereby they are taught by less experienced and skilled teachers, who have low expectations of them. However, unless managed very well with differentiated work and teaching, mixed ability classes risk brighter children being bored by not being stretched and the less-bright becoming equally bored by being stretched too much.

A report in *Education Week*, the American education sector's newsletter, of 2012[13] pointed out that students who are forced to tackle work that is too hard for them have to use more working memory and are more likely to rate the work as 'boring' than simply too hard (perhaps as a protection mechanism against rating themselves as less able). As for the well-able student, a paper examining boredom amongst gifted students published in 2003 suggested that whilst a student need not be gifted to be bored, 'it helps'.[21] Gifted pupils, they suggest, grow bored with not only copying out material, memorising and regurgitating it (which all students may become bored with), but also with waiting for others to learn what they already know and with the repetition needed for the sake of less able students. Another researcher suggested that students get bored in mixed-ability classes because the teacher is forced to focus on those struggling students and go over the same topics until the weaker ones get it.[22] Both under- and over-challenge in the classroom is recognised as an important factor in student boredom.[10]

Ability streaming might well be the answer to this problem then; one recent study showed that gifted students' boredom due to being under-challenged decreased after they were moved to a streamed class for more able students.[10] Interestingly, Finland, where segregating children according to ability is illegal, has one of the highest pupil boredom rates according to Table 8.1 (page 141): 60 per cent compared to 54 per cent for the UK. Could this be connected to the boredom that may be experienced by more able pupils trapped in mixed ability classrooms?

2 Quality of teachers

Whilst most teachers are undoubtedly dedicated, passionate, enthusiastic and caring professionals, every schoolchild is aware that this is not the case for all the teaching staff that they come across. Good teachers use 'discovery, inquiry-based and hands-on methods'[21] to teach and vary their techniques and formats continuously. They make technology work by using it to enhance a lesson, rather than using it as the lesson itself. However, there is no doubt that some teachers are simply plain boring.

Ofsted acknowledged this in 2009 when it launched a crackdown on 'boring' teaching. [23] Part of the reason for less-engaging teachers might be burnout (see [10] for review) as exhausted and emotionally drained teaching staff must surely find it hard to make the effort to creatively engage with their students. According to a Monash University study of 612 Australian teachers in 2013, more than 1 in 4 new teachers suffer 'emotional exhaustion' due to lack of administrative support, onerous compliance measures (of which more later in Chapter 9) and much tougher emotional conditions than they expected to face.[24] If new teachers experience burnout so soon, there seems little hope for more experienced ones, so any 'boring' teaching is perhaps understandable.

3 Lack of meaningfulness

In Chapter 1, one of the causes of boredom was suggested as being lack of meaningfulness, and some educationalists feel that schooling often lacks such meaningfulness in the eyes of students. Pupils too often feel that what they are learning is useless and has no relevance to them and their lives – other than to pass exams.[7] Part of this problem might be to do with the culture of testing that plagues today's classrooms. In 2011, US President Obama claimed that 'too much testing makes education boring for kids'.[25] Too much testing and learning by rote leads to repetition and monotony – and less actual learning of new material that pupils find interesting and useful. Indeed, researchers have found that meaningful learning material can lead to a decrease in student boredom and that lack of meaningfulness predicted boredom even more than physical monotony did.[7] Indeed, Ofsted attributed too much preparation for tests as being the cause of the 'dull' and 'pedestrian' teaching in many schools in their crackdown on boring teaching of 2009.[23]

It is not only endless testing that leads to meaningless-ness but the lack of perceived or real usefulness of the lessons and subjects themselves. Schools in Finland (per-haps in response to their high rates of student boredom) have taken this issue seriously with their plan to abandon teaching kids handwriting in favour of typing from 2016.[26] Handwriting is clearly a skill whose usefulness is becom-ing extinct so it is likely that Finnish pupils will at least find more meaning in their keyboard lessons (even if they are unable to scrawl a note to the milkman in later life. But then again, almost certainly they won't have a milk-man to write a note to either!).

Roger C. Schank, the John Evans Professor Emeritus of Computer Science, Psychology and Education at Northwestern University, wrote a piece in the *Washington Post*[27] in 2012 about the uselessness of many academic subjects taught in schools; from Chemistry ('a complete waste of time. Do you really need to know the elements of the periodic table? The formula for salt? How to balance a chemical equation? Ridiculous'), to Biology ('Plant phyla? Amoebas? Cutting up frogs? It can't get any sillier'), to French ('No one says 'comment allez-vous?' in France. They say 'ça va?'). He advocates learning what interests you and what matters to you. It's an extreme view, but one shared more recently by Australia's chief scientist Professor Ian Chubb, who proclaimed in 2014 that most of the maths that children learn in school is irrelevant to the real world; this 'disconnect' makes what is taught meaningless to pupils.[28]

Box 8.7: Is Shakespeare too dull for today's kids?

According to Dr Mary Bousted, general secretary of the UK Association of Teachers and Lecturers, pupils nowadays get turned off by having to sit through entire Shakespeare plays and would be better off learning only the exciting and dramatic bits to start with, film-trailer style. For example, Dr Bousted, in an article in the *Times Educational Supplement* in the UK in 2013, suggested that a study of *Macbeth* should start in Act II after the murder of King Duncan, whilst students who are new to *Romeo and Juliet* should begin just before Tybalt's death, early in Act III. Her ideas have been widely criticised as pandering to 'computer game mentality', whereby it is all about drama and excitement and ignores the slower parts, which, traditionalists argue, are crucial to the appreciation of Shakespeare.[29]

University Students are Bored too

It is not just school pupils who, it might be argued, are in education from compulsion rather than choice, who happen to be bored. University students not only in the lecture theatre from choice, but who pay dearly for the privilege, are bored too. Research carried out for the *Independent* newspaper in the UK by OpinionPanel Research[30] in 2004 suggested that 27 per cent of university students fall asleep during lectures. Whether they do so because they are bored or tired is not clear, but the findings that 55 per cent eat during lectures, 63 per cent text and a whopping 72 per cent chat to friends at this time suggest they are simply not engaged during teaching sessions.

Findings like these led to my own research into student boredom at university. After all, I am a university lecturer and thus have a vested interest in engaging with my students. Together with a final-year undergraduate student, Andrew Robinson, I decided to investigate how much students were bored in lectures – and what they do when they are bored. The findings, published in *British Educational Research Journal* in 2009,[31] suggested that 59 per cent of the 211 students we surveyed were bored in at least half of their lectures, with 30 per cent bored in most or all of their lectures.

Andrew and I were also interested in what students do when bored. We found that the most common response was to daydream (75 per cent of students do this), followed by doodling (66 per cent). Both these boredom-reducing strategies are discussed elsewhere (Chapter 2). Fifty per cent chat to their friends (slightly lower than the findings reported above) and 45 per cent of students will text. We also found that 27 per cent leave a dull lecture as soon as they can, e.g. in the break – something that in school would be termed 'truanting'.

We also explored the factors contributing towards a boring lecture. Previous research by Bartsch & Cobern[1] found that students may be bored by poor or unstimulating teaching methods. Such methods are thought to include those that minimise student engagement, are less structured, less purposeful and involve less active learning. Fallis and Opotow[22] comment that 'for students, boring connotes a one-way, top-down, unengaged relationship with a teacher'. Work by Van der Velde, Feij and Taris[32] found that structured and purposeful use of time results in a lack of boredom. Students will be more likely to find tasks such as copying notes off overheads (un-stimulating, passive learning) more dull than active learning strategies. Collaborative learning, which inevitably takes place within a social context (for example, laboratory and group work) is thought to be more engaging[33] –especially for those students who score highly on the Boredom Proneness Scale (BPS). This led Shu-Sheng Liaw (2004) to suggest that for a learner to fully comprehend the complexity of a new subject it must be accessible to the learner in a more 'hands-on' nature (for example, through the employment of laboratory work and independent group learning).

We then explored a range of different teaching methods in terms of their contributions to the experience of boredom by students (see Table 8.2, below).

Table 8.2: Boring levels of various teaching methods	
Teaching method	Mean
Laboratory work	3.33
Computer sessions	3.17
Online lecture notes	3.14
Copying overheads in lectures	3.13
PowerPoint without handout	2.98
Workshops	2.97
Video presentations	2.74
Group work outside lectures	2.69
PowerPoint with handout	2.6
Seminars	2.57
Practical sessions	2.41
Group discussions in lectures	1.94

(Higher scores, i.e. nearer to 5 = higher boredom ratings)

Surprisingly, given the hands-on nature of these teaching methods, the highest boredom ratings were achieved for laboratory work and computer sessions; it would be expected from previous research that these methods would be the most engaging, not the least. However, these findings do concur with the view expressed by the Higher Education Academy's UK Centre for Materials Education, that 'students often find labs tedious and boring and do not take them seriously'.[34] One reason given is that many laboratory classes consist of 'controlled exercises' – simple exercises designed by the teacher with the aim of verifying something already known. Students, they say, can find these 'cookbook' classes 'dull and tedious' because of the predictability of the results and because they do not promote deep learning. Proper experimental designs (where the results are not known in advance) are thought to be more stimulating and more likely to promote deep learning, but these require more in the way of time and resources.

Computer sessions too have the potential to be stimulating or tedious; the findings of our study suggest that too many fall into the latter category. This could be due to the manner in which computer sessions are conducted (e.g. are the computer tasks relevant and interesting?), the resources available (e.g. is there a computer for each student?), the availability of support (are there enough teaching staff to help individual students?), etc. The fact that computers are a 'doing' activity is clearly not enough to eliminate boredom and this appears to be what one researcher[24] means when he says that 'doing in itself isn't enough'.

Online lecture notes and copying overheads in lectures come next in the boredom ratings, which this is less of a surprise. These teaching methods are the least engaging and involve very little learner engagement, as the student simply copies material down. This task can be achieved with little active processing or learning and thus can be expected to contribute to student boredom.

Our findings showed that high up on the list of 'boring' teaching methods is the use of PowerPoint. Over the past 15 years, this method has been widely adopted to replace traditional overhead projector transparencies and most universities and colleges have facilities for utilising such technology in all teaching rooms. A great deal of research exists to suggest that students do prefer PowerPoint-type presentations,[35] although evidence that such approaches actually improve student performance is less apparent; for example, one study demonstrated a decrease in student performance when the instructor switched from old-fashioned transparencies to PowerPoint.[36]

Of course, much depends on the complexity of using multimedia presentations; this can vary from simple text to using animation and sound effects that allow for greater stimulation. However, in order to reduce boredom, students must be engaged in their learning; as Kanevsky, Keighley and Roeper point out, 'learning is the opposite of boredom and learning is the antidote to boredom'.[37] In an article published in the *Guardian* in 2003,[38] mature student Tom Ward complains that whilst the increasing use of PowerPoint in higher education at that time was meant to enhance student learning, frequently it had the opposite effect, inducing 'boredom, frustration and disengagement'. The problem he found was that PowerPoint frequently fostered a teaching environment in which tutors did not connect with their students by making eye contact or engaging in exchanges. Instead, they just talked to the screen, read out material on the screen and often presented far too much material because it was so easy to do so; the presentations became a barrier between teacher and student and resulted in a learning environment 'so routine, so anodyne, so dull'. Ward complains bitterly of the 'disk dealers', whose efforts produce 'that dreadful mask of passive boredom' on students' faces. Indeed, our findings seem to concur with those of Ward: using PowerPoint presentations is clearly boredom-inducing. We found the least dull teaching methods to be seminars, practical sessions and group discussions. All these involve interaction and active learning rather than passive.

Part of the problem within higher education may lie within the traditional conception of the 'lecture', which implies a didactic transmission of material that students passively receive. Indeed, the notion of university lecturers actually needing any sort of training in how to teach is a relatively new one. As an article in the Education supplement of the *Guardian* points out, 'If you want to teach in a school you need a lengthy and intensive training, but to teach in a university you need a PhD and a handful of decent publications'.[39] Whilst most universities now provide training for teaching staff (like many of my colleagues, I have a Postgraduate Certificate in Teaching for Higher Education) and a wider range of teaching methods (and often use the term 'classes' rather than lectures), teaching staff are still called 'lecturers', so the traditional notion of teaching being a 'formal talk' (as defined in the Chambers Dictionary) is difficult to escape from.

Another issue perhaps equally difficult to get away from is that of students viewing the teaching they are presented with purely as a means to obtain the information necessary to pass exams or coursework. In other words, students themselves may actually resist attempts at what Ramsden[40] terms 'deep learning', i.e. where they approach their learning with the intention of understanding in favour of more superficial 'surface learning', in which there is an absence of the desire to understand. Students may bypass deep learning, even if this underpins the teaching and learning strategy of their institution, because their focus is on passing exams. In other words, although there may well be stated course objectives and outcomes as part of the teaching and learning policy, students may wish to find shortcuts and rules that will simply enable them to pass without the need to understand more than is necessary. That is, the surface learners are looking for the facts they think they will be tested on, not for the meaning of the material.

My university colleagues and I frequently come across this 'if it's not assessed, it has no value' attitude. Often we put on lectures and classes not directly assessed but designed to enable deeper engagement with material, but students invariably do not turn up. It is common to find less than 20 per cent attendance at teaching sessions that are not directly assessed.

Box 8.8: Truancy and poor grades: The effects of class-room boredom

Boredom in the classroom or lecture theatre is of grave concern. It has been linked with diminished academic achievement[15] and school dissatisfaction.[41] For example, pupils who rated themselves 'often bored' had generally lower scores on academic tests than those who were 'sometimes bored'.[42] Other research has found a negative relationship between boredom susceptibility and grade point average. Students who rated themselves 'often bored' had generally lower scores on academic tests than those who were 'sometimes bored'.

Student boredom has also been shown to be a contributory factor to truancy.[43] For example, boredom is one of the most frequently identified causes for students leaving school temporarily (e.g. skipping classes, feigning illness) or even permanently.[44] My own research with university students showed that the more time in lectures rated as boring, the more lecture time students missed.[31] Unsurprisingly, attending school regularly is likely to lead to better grades; pupils who do not miss classes have been shown to have higher performance scores.[45] My own research suggested that the more time

---

missed due to missing lectures, the more grade point average decreases.[21] As Fallis and Optotow (2003) point out in their study of high school students, 'class-cutting is a slippery slope: once begun, the academic damage is difficult to reverse'.[21]

The effects of student boredom are not limited to academic attainment, however. It also has pernicious impacts on their health. Bored students are more likely to smoke, drink alcohol, get depressed, use drugs and gamble too.[10]

A Revolution in the Classroom

To combat pupil and student boredom then, we need a revolution in the way we view teaching. Whilst we should stop over-stimulating kids, we cannot (or indeed *should* not) turn the clock back to the days of the chalk and talk. Instead we need to look for new solutions that do not depend on what Professor Michael Fullan and his colleague, Maria Langworthy, call 'pre-packaged, depersonalised learning experiences'.[16] They recommend new ways of learning, such as students tutoring each other (peer instruction) and teachers working with students to create individually tailored knowledge. Teachers thus become partners in the learning process, which encourages students to take responsibility for their own learning journey. This would also challenge the issues of constraint and lack of power or control that pupils currently have over their learning, which some researchers believe contributes to their levels of boredom.[11]

Other researchers emphasise the need to raise levels of meaningfulness for students and ensuring a good match between ability and challenge. Because this can be hard to do, developing students' ability to modify their own tasks and learning can give them the control to do this themselves.[46] Control of their own learning experience is thus key to students being motivated to learn and develop themselves.

Within higher education the traditional concept of the 'lecture' and 'lecturer' has almost certainly had its day. The 'sage on a stage' approach is considered by many as not only boring, but ineffectual too; undergraduate students in classes with traditional stand-and-deliver lectures are 1.5 times more likely to fail than students in classes employing more stimulating, so-called active learning methods.[47] The traditional lecture, relatively unchanged since the Middle Ages, is being rendered obsolete, partly because students' brains are being rewired by their access to digital media, portable electronics and games.[48] Students (and indeed school pupils) are also used to being able to access information at their own pace, when they want it, to pause or rewind or simply watch it again. Sitting still for up to two hours in a one-off passive opportunity no longer resonates with the rest of their lives. However, attempts to turn to what are considered 'active' methods, such as lab and computer classes, should be approached with caution, as my own findings suggest. Other techniques, such as using hand-held clickers, online interactive sessions, podcasts and peer instruction, can help transform passive into active learning.

Of course, the fact that pupils and students need such engagement is a product of society's over-stimulated making. If we did not over-stimulate our kids from birth, we might not now find ourselves in the uncomfortable position of looking for increasingly exciting ways to engage and entertain students. Indeed, as a university lecturer myself, my efforts to engage with jokes, witty anecdotes, funny YouTube clips and chat show-style audience interaction mean that I prefer to refer to myself as a 'Lecturetainer' – delivering performances rather than lectures. Unless we stem the tide of novelty and sensation-seeking expectation, I fear the need to entertain will overtake the need to educate. Could it only be a matter of time before teachers and 'Lecturetainers' will be taught fire-eating and juggling as part of their training?

Boredom in the Boardroom: Why Boredom in the Workplace is Rising

According to 2011 research by research and polling firm Gallup,[1] 71 per cent of American workers are either not engaged or are actively disengaged from their jobs, with highly educated and middle-aged workers the least likely to feel involved in, and enthusiastic about their work.

This chapter argues that the ever-burgeoning demands of meetings, paperwork, routinisation, information overload and bureaucracy within many job roles are creating a boom in the experience of workplace boredom – well beyond those mechanised jobs traditionally identified as highly boredom-inducing. Technological advances mean that we are ever more removed from the 'coalface' of our jobs, as we press more and more of the same type of (boring) buttons to achieve our tasks. The most boring jobs in the world will also be identified here (and yes, accountancy does feature).

The Prevalence of Workplace Boredom

My entire research interest in boredom began in 1999 when I embarked on my doctoral research at the University of Salford in the UK, into the experience of emotions in the workplace. Those were the days just before emotional intelligence became an everyday concept and the idea of emotions having any place at work was anathema. My research, which culminated in the publication of my first book, *Hiding What We Feel, Faking What We Don't* (Crimson Publishing), concentrated on examining emotion management at work and the concept of 'emotional labour' or the effort involved in having to control emotions because of workplace requirements. Part of this involved examining which emotions are suppressed and which expressed (and which faked) by ordinary office workers.

To my surprise, my research with over 300 office employees in the UK showed that the second most commonly suppressed workplace emotion was boredom (if you want to know what the most commonly suppressed emotion was, you will have to read my book!). It was this finding that we suppress boredom in a third of all interactions at work that sparked my new line of research into boredom, both at work and beyond.

Workplace boredom is a fairly under-researched area, probably for the same reasons that it is under-researched in education; it is largely a 'silent' emotion thought (wrongly) to be relatively benign. Early studies into workplace boredom focused on the idea that boredom is caused by low external stimulation such as that inherent in monotonous, repetitive work,[2] which led to a plethora of studies into blue-collar jobs requiring vigilance (involving the need for sustained attention with very little reward of variety or stimulation) or repetition. Thus, workplace boredom has been studied in the context of a limited range of tasks, such as mechanical assembly, vigilance tasks and continuous manual control. Professions studied include heavy truck drivers,[3] manual workers,[4] government clerks,[5] assembly autoworkers,[6] clerical employees,[7] long-distance truck drivers,[8] and repetitive press-operators.[9] Other jobs that involve the need for attention but offer stimulation as a reward for that attention in the form of variety, challenge, feedback, etc., were rarely the focus of boredom studies.

9.1: Bored at work statistics

- Nearly 45 per cent of hiring experts in a 1998 survey said firms lost top workers because they were bored with their jobs.[10]

- A third of Britons in a 2004 survey claimed to be bored at work for most of the day.[11]

- In the financial services industry, half were often or always bored at work.[11]

- Fifty-five per cent of all US employees were found to be 'not engaged' in their work in a survey reported in the *Washington Post* in 2005.[12]

- Twenty-eight per cent of graduates in 2004 claimed to be bored with their job in a survey by the Teacher Training Agency.[13]

More recently, however, research has begun to diversify into those jobs less likely to have the elements of routine and repetitiveness that so characterised the early research. White-collar boredom has been termed 'managerial malaise' or 'rust-out'. It is acknowledged now that 'boredom has a permanent seat in many workplaces, no matter the level of employee'.[14] It is because of this, and my 1999 finding that boredom is so commonly experienced in ordinary workplaces, that I began to research boredom in workplaces not traditionally associated with monotonous work. Over the past seven years I have looked at teachers, university lecturers, supermarket employees, lawyers, bankers and office staff – none of whom worked in the sort of vigilance-type task that traditional boredom research has tended to concentrate on. I have surveyed 310 people in total, roughly half of them male. Just over a fifth (21 per cent) reported being bored at work quite often or all the time (data not yet published).

Boredom at Work: Why It Matters

In fact, boredom at work matters because of what bored employees are apt to do (or *not* do) as a result of that ennui. Boredom has long been associated with a range of negative outcomes at work, such as anger,[15] accidents,[4, 3] absenteeism,[16, 17] errors,[18, 3, 2] stress, increased risk taking/thrill seeking,[18, 2, 20, 21] sleepiness, [22] stress-related health problems, e.g. heart attacks,[23] job dissatisfaction[24] and property damage.[3] Some of these consequences are clearly symptoms of the boredom experience; accidents, mistakes, sleepiness, etc. are all the result of being unable to sustain attention. Other consequences are a result of the ways in which individuals try to cope with their boredom; these coping strategies can be classified into two categories, as previously discussed in Chapter 2: (a) refocusing attention on the task and (b) seeking additional stimulation.

Previous research has identified a strong relationship between employees' workplace engagement and the overall performance of an organisation,[1] which is clearly an important long-term consequence. In addition, the less engaged employees are with their work and their organisation, the more likely they are to leave.[1] This could be because bored workers are simply not happy ones. For example, in a survey by Sirota Consulting LLC of more than 800,000 employees at 61 organisations worldwide,[25] those with 'too little work' gave an overall job satisfaction rating of just 49 out of

100, whereas employees with 'too much work' were far more satisfied – with a rating of 57.

A study on the link between counterproductive work behaviour (behaviour that harms an organisation) and boredom by researchers at Montclair State University and the University of South Florida, US, identifies six ways in which employees might harm their organisations due to their being bored: abusing others (usually verbal), 'production deviance' (purposely failing at tasks), sabotage, withdrawal (i.e. not doing their work properly), theft and horseplay.[26] Some of this is the result of resentment at being given such boring work, whilst some is about seeking extra stimulation to fill the void.

In my own research on the experience of boredom by 310 workers in the UK (similar to the smaller piece of research I have already reported on in Chapter 2), I divided the outcomes or consequences of boredom at work into three main categories:

Coping strategies: Here, I asked participants, '*What do you tend to do to try to combat any boredom you might feel at work?*' and offered a list of 12 possible coping strategies to select from, based on items generated in an earlier pilot study.[27] Some of these items could be classed as refocusing activities, such as taking a break (allowing fresh focus after the break), writing a shopping list (allowing distracting thoughts to be minimised after the list is written), thinking (if it is about the task) and drinking something (coffee, etc., a device often used to boost concentration). Other strategies are more stimulation-seeking, such as doodling, daydreaming, counting things, doing puzzles, chatting to colleagues, putting music on, eating or passing notes during meetings.

The most popular response to the question of what people do when they are bored is to 'think', with 55 per cent of respondents selecting this, followed by drinking something (50 per cent) Other common responses are chatting (45 per cent), taking a break (42 per cent) and eating something (40 per cent).

The full breakdown is shown in Figure 9.1, below, and is similar to that found in the smaller study discussed in Chapter 2. For an analysis of these coping strategies, see Chapter 2.

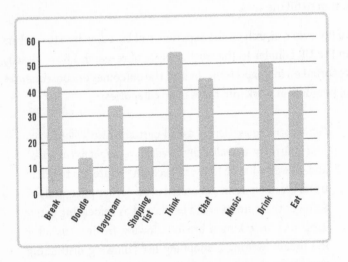

Figure 9.1: Percentage of respondents who engage in particular coping strategies when bored at work.

Outcomes: Longer-term consequences or outcomes of being bored at work were measured in a question asking, *'What are the consequences of being bored in your job?'* This was designed to tap into more general, longer-term consequences of being bored, such as causing mistakes or accidents at work, or leaving the job. Altogether, 11 items were listed.

The most common longer-term consequences of being bored in their job selected by respondents were that it causes them to 'lose concentration' (74 per cent of respondents selected this) and to 'make mistakes' (66 per cent). This is clearly due to the fact that attentional difficulties are a significant component of the experience of boredom; we find it hard to maintain attention on a dull task or have to exert considerable efforts to do so.

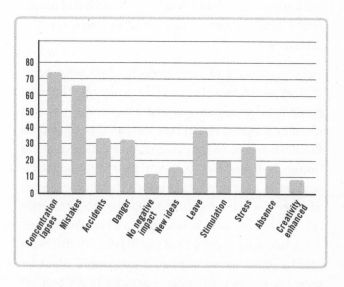

Figure 9.2: Consequences of being bored at work

Thirty-nine per cent of respondents felt that their boredom at work might lead them to consider leaving their job, whilst around a third were of the view that their workplace boredom caused them stress, that being bored could lead to an accident and boredom in their job could be 'potentially dangerous'. This concurs with many previous findings that boredom leads to lower performance, decreased concentration and increased difficulty to maintain attention, all of which are likely to increase the chance of errors and accidents.[28] Many of the world's worst disasters have been blamed, at least partly, on bored employees making errors; for example, the 1979 Three Mile Island incident, near Middletown, USA, the 1984 release of methyl isocyanate (MIC) gas in Bhopal, India, and the 1986 nuclear plant disaster at Chernobyl in the Ukraine all involved people tasked with dull assignments, who committed judgemental blunders, resulting in tragedy.[29]

Eighteen per cent of participants felt that being bored at work might lead them to take a day off. This relationship between boredom and absenteeism was first found by boredom researchers Steven Kass and Stephen Vodanovich with their colleague Anne Callender at the University of West Florida, USA, in their 2001 study of 292 workers of a manufacturing plant[30] and they wondered whether the link between the two was job satisfaction (which has been well documented to be related to boredom). However, 12 per cent of participants felt that being bored at work had no negative consequences, whilst for some there were positive consequences; 16 per cent felt being bored helped them come up with new ideas and 9 per cent believed that it helped them become more creative at work (see also Chapter 11 for more on this).

Causes of Workplace Boredom

There are two main categories that are thought to cause individuals to experience boredom in the workplace: those to do with the task or work environment itself and those to do with the individual who is doing that work.

Task/environmental effects: This category is concerned with the nature of the job itself. Previous research suggests that tasks which are high in skill variety, task significance (i.e. they have meaning for the worker), autonomy (where workers feel in control of how they carry out the task) and feedback (whereby workers know whether they are doing a good job or not) are thought to produce less boredom.[31] One previous study found that 55 per cent of boredom-related incidents were due to quantitative underload (i.e. not having enough to do), [32] whilst a 2004 study carried out by the Teacher Training Agency in the UK, in which 28 per cent of employees claimed to be bored with their jobs, found that the most common reasons given by respondents to explain why their jobs were boring were to do with the nature of the job: lack of challenge, not using skills/knowledge and routine in their jobs were the top causes for being bored.[13]

In my study I found that the most common aspect of the work environment that is likely to contribute to workplace boredom is repetitive work (62 per cent), followed by routine (53 per cent). This concurs with previous studies that have found repetitiveness to be a significant cause of workplace boredom; indeed, it is why so many of the early studies of workplace boredom were concerned with repetitive tasks, such as those involving mechanical assembly, inspection, monitoring and continuous manual control.[2]

A third of my respondents claimed that not having enough work to do caused boredom (less than in previous research), whilst over a quarter cited (a) not having enough *interesting* work to do, (b) undemanding work, (c) not needing to think much and (d) having little control over what tasks they do or how they do them are aspects of the work environment likely to induce boredom for them (see Table 9.1, below). This concurs with the previous findings mentioned above.

Some of these causes of boredom, then, are directly as a result of organisational practices rather than elements of the task itself. For example, restrictions on talking or constraint on what workers can do to vary the amount of stimulation they receive are rules imposed by the organisation for various reasons (usually to do with what they consider acceptable practice). Talking can help relieve the monotony but is often seen by managers as counter-productive, either for the image of an organisation if customer-facing (shop assistants standing around chatting is *not* a good image), or in terms of lowering productivity (office workers gossiping are perceived to be not doing their job).

It is interesting that more people complain that they are more bored by work not being demanding enough than by it being too demanding. Previous research has shown that both under-challenge (including qualitative underload, which is not having enough challenging work to do, and quantitative underload, which is simply not having enough to do) and over-challenge (or qualitative overload) is boring,[33] but my research suggests under-challenge is a much bigger problem, possibly because of so many employees being over-skilled (which 21 per cent of my respondents felt they were) or over-qualified for their job; I will discuss this later on in the chapter.

Fourteen per cent of participants complain that other people are the source of their boredom. Whilst other people can be a means of alleviating boredom, clearly they can also be a source of tedium too – *if* they are boring people. What makes someone boring is discussed at length in Chapter 10, but Cynthia Fisher, a pioneer in workplace boredom, seemed to predict this finding when she pointed out in 1987 that 'uninteresting, unfriendly or uncommunicative co-workers' was a source of boredom for many.[32]

Table 9.1: Aspects of the work environment that contribute to workplace boredom

Aspects of the work environment contributing to workplace boredom	% of employees citing this as a source of their workplace boredom
Repetition	62
Routine	53
Not enough work to do	33
Not enough interesting work to do	29
Not having control over the type of work (e.g. when to do tasks/ how to do them)	29
The work is not demanding enough	27
There is no need to think at work	26

Being overskilled	21
Restrictions on talking	17
Too much paperwork	16
Other people are boring	14
The work is too demanding	9

'Person' effects: The other category that causes workplace boredom is to do with the individual who is bored. The tendency to be easily bored has been viewed as a personality characteristic that differs from person to person and this tendency has been termed 'Boredom Proneness'. This is discussed in greater detail in Chapter 5 but in relation to job boredom, it has been found that those high in BPS have more **extrinsic** work value whereas those low on BPS have higher **internal** work value;[33] this suggests that boredom-prone individuals might be best suited to jobs that provide external, tangible rewards since they will be less motivated by any internal feelings of satisfaction associated with, for example, doing a job well. Other studies have found a direct relationship between Boredom Proneness and job satisfaction; for example, both restaurant workers and teachers in a 1997 study who were more boredom-prone also reported lower job satisfaction.[34] Other 'person' factors (termed 'individual differences' by psychologists) found in relation to job boredom include:

Extroversion: Extroverts perform better on boring tasks than introverts when the task is enriched by other stimuli, such as noise or music. As discussed in Chapter 5 (see page 85), this is almost certainly because extroverts need extra stimulation in order to prevent them becoming bored.[33]

Experts: Experts who have mastered a task and no longer need to think very hard about it are also at risk of boredom.[33] Studies suggest that experts feel more bored, suffer more attentional lapses and have more accidents – a surprising finding as you might expect them to make fewer errors, not more.

In my own research that I have been describing, I also conducted analysis to investigate which of the aspects of the work environment (see Table 9.1 above) contributed most significantly (in the statistical sense) to the experience of boredom – and whether these mattered more than the personality trait of Boredom Proneness, which I also measured. Using a statistical technique called 'multiple regression', I found that Boredom Proneness indeed contributes most to the experience of boredom, followed by repetition and routine. In other words, however dull certain aspects of work might be, being boredom-prone is the most important factor that will influence how bored an employee will be.

The Role of Distraction

Whilst the role of distraction in the experience of boredom is not something I examined in the study discussed above, it would seem to be an important consideration since there is no doubt that we encounter an ever-increasing number of external distractions in the workplace now. Phones, email, texts and social media all bleep to draw our attention towards them but there is also the increasing use of noisy open-plan offices, home-working (with all the distractions the home environment offers) and, of course, the old-fashioned (but still highly prevalent) face-to-face interruptions from colleagues or clients. These interruptions distract attention from focus on the current task, and the attempts we make to return our attention can contribute towards the feeling of boredom.

Such distractions fall into three categories: those that are temporary and, once attended to, allow the worker to continue with their task (e.g. dealing with a colleague's enquiry), those that are longer-lasting in that even after they are attended to, thoughts about the distracting event continue to preoccupy and intrude (e.g. taking a phone call about your school-age son that leaves you worried), and finally, those that do not require attending to but still pull attention away from the task (e.g. the noise of a building site just outside your window). It is expected that the middle category would have the most detrimental effect on boredom as it involves both external and internal distractors.

Internal distractions take the form of non-task-related thoughts which can intrude, such as mind wandering, daydreaming, anxieties, thoughts about other events and what is termed 'current concerns'.[35] Current concerns could be about what to buy for lunch or what to do with your elderly and ailing mother, and it is estimated that 65 per cent of our daydreams are related to current concerns.[35] Concerns most likely to intrude into our thoughts are those that are highly valued (i.e. issues that are important to us), or require immediate action, and it is likely strong current concerns can be so distracting that workers will label a task as 'boring' as it seems unable to capture our attention. Of course, it works the other way around too; workers who are already bored are more likely to be distracted by current concerns. They might even deliberately seek to engage with these internal thoughts as a way of gaining relief from the boring task.

Our thoughts do tend to shift very frequently from topic to topic (about every 5–30 seconds on average [36]), with such shifts happening less often when we are working on a more complex and varied task. Adding meaning to the task, e.g. in the form of financial reward, can also decrease the frequency of these internal interruptions,[35] which suggests if we pay people more, they might be able to sustain attention on boring jobs. Of course the very opposite tends to happen in that the lowest paid work often involves simple, repetitive and non-complex tasks.

The effect of distractions on the experience of workplace boredom depends then on both the type of distractor and the type of task. A simple task requiring little attentional processes might have its boredom for the worker alleviated by distractions such as chatting or daydreaming. Another study by Cynthia Fisher showed just that; external interruptions (someone speaking) helped prevent boredom on a simple, repetitive manual assembly task that required low levels of sustained attention[35] (see also box 9.2, below). More complex tasks require greater sustained attention and thus might be more distractible by even low 'cost' interruptions and thus in this case, distractions would serve to make us feel more bored.

Box 9.2: How distractions can help bored drone pilots

Operating a drone can be 'mind-numbingly boring', with seasoned fighter pilots typically spending most of their 12-hour shift just watching and waiting. Like many automated vigilance tasks today, this involves a highly skilled human 'effectively baby-sitting the automation'. The problem is how to keep workers alert when there is so much tedious downtime. Researcher Missy Cummings, a systems engineer at MIT, said, 'We're automating the world more and more, and a side effect of this increased automation is that people are going to be bored monitoring those systems.' She found that workers stay more alert when external distractions such as a book or computer game are available. Organisations that don't allow workers access to such distractions, she says, are setting them up to fail. Keeping workers alert with external distractors might help because it prevents them getting involved in what might be more attention-grabbing internal distractors.[37]

The Most Boring Job in the World?

You might sometimes think that you have the most boring job in the world, but spare a thought for Helen Southall, who works as a 'grass seed analyst' in Lincolnshire, UK. Helen is paid to watch grass grow; she spends her working days in fields and lawns, individually counting out hundreds of grass seeds – and going through each blade manually to measure growth. She claims to love her job and doesn't find it at all tedious.[38]

© Carters News Agency Limited

If Helen does ever get bored of watching grass grow then she might be interested in swapping with Dr Thomas Curwen – he is paid to watch paint dry. The research scientist from Twyford, Berkshire in the UK works for Dulux Paints, where he spends his working day watching the changing colour of paint as it dries – often through a microscope (but on walls too). And, guess what? He claims to love his job too.[39]

Which all goes to show that there is no such thing as a boring job – what is boring for one person could be wildly exciting for the next. One web-based organisation, however, has come up with a more objective way of calculating what the most boring jobs around are. Salary Explorer, a salary comparison and career resources website,[40] collects data from thousands of workers who rate their job for levels of boredom. The lower the rating from 1–5 (i.e. the closer to 1), the more boring that job is rated to be. They found that the most boring jobs (at the time of writing) were in cleaning and housekeeping, with the least boring being in fundraising and non-profit work. The data presented below are correct at the time of writing (October 2015) but are ever-changing as more people rate their jobs (and you could rate yours too by going onto the website: www.salaryexplorer.com/rate-your-job.php).

Type of Work	Boredom rating (1–5 where 1 = most boring)
Cleaning and Housekeeping	2.82
Courier/Delivery/Transport/Drivers	2.86
Customer Service and Call Centre	2.87
Banking	2.90
Administration/Reception/Secretarial	2.88

Real Estate	2.99
Accounting and Finance	2.98
Insurance	3.05
Pharmaceutical and Biotechnology	3
Law Enforcement/Security/Fire	3.06
Factory and Manufacturing	3.06
Construction/Building/Installation	3.05
Facilities/Maintenance/Repair	3.10
Engineering	3.08
Government and Defence	3.19
Sales: Retail and Wholesale	3.12
Legal	3.07
Human Resources	3.15
Information Technology	3.13
Gardening/Farming/Fishing	3.22
Health and Medical	3.21
Architecture	3.23
Marketing	3.24
Food/Hospitality/Tourism/Catering	3.23
Teaching/Education	3.27
Advertising/Graphic Design/Event Management	3.3
Executive and Management	3.32
Public Relations	3.36

Fashion and Apparel	3.36
Counselling	3.43
Care Giving and Childcare	3.44
Petcare	3.43
Photography/Media/Broadcasting/Arts/ Entertainment	3.56
Recreation and Sports	3.54
Fitness/Hair/Beauty	3.51
Fundraising and Non-Profit	3.59

Box 9.3: The accountancy firms that are 'proud to be boring'

Accountancy has long suffered a reputation of being boring, but there are some firms who are using this perception to their advantage. Lithgow Nelson in Surrey, UK (http://tomlynham. wordpress.com/2013/11/26/proud-to-be-boring-5)adoptedthe strapline 'proud to be boring' when they realised that people see 'boring' as being obsessed with accuracy, compliance and attention to detail – something that Lithgow Nelson are happy to admit they are.

And they are not the only ones to realise that being perceived as 'boring' can have its advantages. On their website MGO in Sacramento, USA (http://www.mgocpa.com/go/mgo/ benefits-of-boring) describe themselves as 'proud to be boring accountants'. They boast of having not only 'boring partners', but also a staff numbering over 230, all of whom are 'proud to be boring'.

The Boom of Workplace Boredom

In 2007, I wrote an article for *The Psychologist*,[41] – the journal of the British Psychology Society – entitled 'The Boredom Boom', in which I argued that workplace boredom had dramatically increased over the past few decades due to changing work practices. Ignoring for the moment variations in individual propensity to boredom (boredom proneness), workplace boredom is, as we have shown, a function of task and environmental effects. For example, work tasks that are varied, have high significance (and meaningfulness) for the worker, are performed under the control of the worker and elicit feedback about performance to the worker (which can add meaningfulness) are thought to be less boring. As far as the working environment is concerned, boredom can be mediated by the presence of 'interesting' co-workers, or by the introduction of boredom-busting organisational practices such as less controlling environments, in which people are free to organise their own work schedule and take breaks when they want.

In the absence of any valid comparative data, of course, it is difficult to declare with any accuracy that workplace boredom has grown over time. What *is* clear is that the nature of work has changed dramatically and many of these new work practices are thought to be boredom-inducing. For example, workplaces today are increasingly automated, with faceless technology being the interface through which many tasks are completed. Jobs that in the past involved skill use, decision-making and contact with people can now be achieved with the press of a few (boring) buttons. Back in 1969, when automation was in its infancy, researchers examined the effects of introducing a new automated process in a tin plate mill; they showed that whereas under the old manual system it was physical labour that caused fatigue, with automation it was boredom that caused fatigue.[42] I recently visited a famous chocolate factory in the UK, where myself and the other visitors marvelled at the multi-armed packaging robots that could each now do the work of 20 men. The sole human survivor of this automated invasion, a middle-aged gentleman, was sitting at a computer, his glazed eyes gazing somewhat mournfully at the screen monitoring the robots. I could only imagine that he would rather have been shifting the cartons himself.

Similarly, imagine the highly trained pilot forced to spend most of the flight sitting back, whilst autopilot takes over. A recent study in 2014, reported in the journal *Human Factors*, suggests that whilst automation in the cockpit is designed to free pilots from paying attention to the mundane 'vigilance'-type flight tasks (such as watching displays and monitoring equipment) and allow them to concentrate on the bigger picture, this does risk leaving them bored and frustrated.[43] The problem is that their minds may then wander off-track to non-flight related matters as they search for the stimulation they are lacking. They can't even reduce the boredom anymore by inviting children into the cockpit to show them what all the buttons do – such practices are becoming increasingly rare due to post-9/11 security.

Box 9.4: Bored pilots struggle to stay alert

In 2009, an aircraft missed its destination by 241 kilometres (150 miles) because the two pilots weren't 'paying attention' to either their instruments or air traffic controllers (which subsequently cost them their licences). The problem is that once a plane is airborne, there isn't much to do, other than stare at instrument gauges (that rarely change much), which can lead to pilots being easily distracted. Many airlines prohibit pilots from taking anything aboard that is too distracting, such as reading material or laptops, but they cannot stop them chatting or daydreaming to while away the hours.

The pilots of a Colgan Air flight were 'idly chatting' even as their plane descended below 3,048 metres (10,000 feet) near Buffalo, New York, USA, in February 2009, as a National Transportation Safety Board investigation found. That plane crashed, killing the two pilots and 48 others onboard. Meanwhile, a transcript of cockpit conversations from another incident showed that two Comair pilots were chatting about their families and schedules just before their jet crashed whilst attempting to take off on the wrong runway in Lexington, Kentucky, USA, in 2006.[44]

Mounting paperwork is an all-too common feature of the modern workplace that produces ripe conditions for a boredom boom. According to the British Chamber of Commerce, the UK Government introduced almost 900 new regulations affecting workplaces between 1997 and 2004 (British Chamber of Commerce, 2004[45]). A quick search on the internet using the term 'mounting paperwork' reveals concerns about the toll that burgeoning paperwork is taking on their working life being expressed by a range of different professional bodies across the globe – for example, farmers' unions in Northern Ireland talk of the 'bewildering avalanche of paperwork',[46] family doctors in the UK lament the fact that 'mounting paperwork "takes valuable time away from patients"',[47] sheltered housing providers in the UK complain of the mounting paperwork which they believe is draining a 'disproportionate' amount of resources',[48] whilst UK nurses similarly complain of 'drowning in a sea of paperwork', with over 17 per cent of their time now spent on it.[49]

Box 9.5: Teaching and form filling

The teaching profession is just one example of where monotonous and dull paperwork, form filling and bureaucracy have taken over from the job of actually teaching children. One trainee UK teacher, who quit his course due to 'death by paperwork', wrote in the *Guardian* that had he pursued his dream of becoming a teacher, he would have spent his life being a 'dull bureaucrat'.[50] He was not alone; research suggests that 4 out of every 10 new teachers abandon the profession after three years in the job.[51] My own research into teacher boredom suggested that 50 per cent claimed excessive paperwork was the main cause of their boredom.[27] The sort of 'paper shuffling' that UK teachers today are expected to do before they even get in the classroom includes APPs (Assessing Pupil Progress), extensive weekly or daily plans, documentation, administration surrounding assessments and report writing. This sea of paperwork is not restricted to UK teaching: a columnist in the *Washington Post* lamented the rising paperwork associated with the 'mania for more student data, more meetings to discuss the data and more high-level monitoring of the data' in US schools.[52] The reason for this obsession with data (and its associated paperwork) is, he says, down to the national school reform movement over the past decade that has emphasised the role of standardised tests to measure student achievement. An article in the Panama City *News Herald* in 2012[53] lists some of the paperwork requirements incumbent on teachers as they are expected to meet the requirements of:

- The Federal Government, including those associated with the No Child Left Behind Act, the Individuals with Disabilities Education Act, Section 504 of the Vocational Rehabilitation Act of 1973, and many other requirements related to issues such as keeping track of free or reduced lunch eligibility.

- State Department of Education (FDOE), which includes compliance (written documentation) with the Florida Comprehensive Assessment Test (FCAT) testing program requirements; capturing and reporting accurate student daily attendance records, accurate preparation and maintenance of individual student 'special education' related records and student Individualised Education Plans (IEPs) developments.

- The local School Board, including CPD (Continual Professional Development) requirements; development of written weekly lesson plans, written progress documentation for each individual assigned student; submission of daily classroom attendance via computer data entry; preparation every few weeks of progress reports for each pupil; preparation each term of report cards for every student and maintenance of the 'parental portal' – an electronic system that keeps parents updated about their child's progress.

Constant meetings also contribute to what one author called 'Death by Meeting'.[54] Eighty-two per cent of working adults report spending almost one-third of their working week in either formal or informal meetings (Steelcase Workplace Index Survey, December 2000[55]). It is estimated that wasted time in meetings costs the UK £8 billion a year in lost productivity; this is calculated on the basis that if the average £30,000-a-year manager spends one hour a week in meetings where they don't pay attention, the total cost to British industry is £7.8 bn a year[56] (the cost is even higher when travel costs, refreshment and room hire, etc. are taken into account). The problem is that we seem to be having more meetings than ever; as more work becomes teamwork-based, the need to meet increases. Meetings also seem to increase visibility – if we have a meeting that is minuted and recorded, then we reassure others that we must be working really hard (rather than quietly and invisibly getting on with actually doing the work). In these increasingly insecure times, anything we can do to increase our visibility is often seized upon.

Box 9.6: The bored MP caught playing Candy Crush in a meeting

Conservative Amber Valley Member of Parliament Nigel Mills was caught playing the popular computer game on his iPad for over two hours during a parliamentary committee meeting on pension reforms in December 2014. His actions were roundly condemned and he offered various apologies, but some people were sympathetic. Conservative MP Sir Edward Leigh excused his colleague's attempts at alleviating his boredom during long, drawn-out meetings, saying in a BBC report, 'I survived nine years as chairman of the Public Accounts Committee and I just about managed not to go to sleep and not to play computer games but my god, it was boring!'[57]

If these meetings weren't so turgid, the increase might not contribute to increased workplace boredom quite so much. Part of the reason why today's meetings are so dull is their over-reliance on PowerPoint slides; a meeting is not seen as a proper meeting without a slide presentation. This over-reliance on visuals can result in the same problems discussed in the context of the lecture theatre in Chapter 8 – lack of eye contact, distraction by animations, too much text, etc. (see also page 159).

New working practices, such as those in call centres, also severely restrict job autonomy and worker control, leading to an upsurge in conditions traditionally identified as boring. According to contact centre industry analyst ContactBabel, there were 5,675 call centres in the UK by 2013, employing nearly 4 per cent of the workforce.[58] This is up from the estimated 2.3 per cent in 2002.[59] And with the rise in call centres comes a rise in bored employees. According to CallCenterOps.Com[60] boredom is a major factor in staff turnover in call centres, with the following cited as main boredom-boosters: the repetitive nature of the work, excessive control by managers, supervisor or team leaders, limited career progression opportunities and limited job variation. A study by Call Centre College and Lucent Technologies[61] revealed that 28 per cent of staff leaving call centres cited boredom as the main reason. Call centres were also cited amongst the most boring industries in the self-ratings of job-holders (see also page 181).

The burgeoning 24/7 work culture also contributes to the boredom boom, as lonely night workers miss out on the more sociable camaraderie and interaction that their day-worker colleagues enjoy. Another problem is the misfit between skill and workplace demands; there are now many more graduates than there used to be: so many have had to accept jobs for which they are over-qualified and over-skilled. Inability to utilise our abilities in favour of tasks that do not use up our cognitive capacity leads to lack of fulfilment and that feeling of understimulation that we recognise as boredom. This could explain why half of new graduates say that they 'often feel bored at work'.[62]

The global rise of the need for 'self-actualisation' or self-fulfilment means that we want more mental stimulation and autonomy in our working lives. We expect jobs to be more than just sources of income; we expect them to be stimulating and fulfilling. There is more on this growing need for meaningfulness in Chapter 4 (see page 79). Yet this need for fulfilment is often at odds with the relentless industrial pressure to drive down costs, which seems to involve controlling aspects of employee work with ever-greater precision. Jobs are becoming more efficient, uniform and predictable, reducing work to a formula so resisted by the employee, who is driven by the desire for self-fulfilment.

Boredom-Busters – How to Halt the Boom

Clearly, there are no quick-fire easy solutions to the problem of boredom at work. As is so often said, the world of work is changing and the clock cannot be turned back to the arguably more exciting (yet more dangerous) days when workers really were at the coalface. But, strategies that acknowledge the psychology of boredom should be put into place. These must respect the known causes of workplace boredom, as well as understand the human need for optimal levels of stimulation. Boredom-busters need to be realistic since total business process re-engineering to combat boredom is unlikely to be a feasible option. Suggestions, then, include:

- The impact of automated workplaces needs to be considered by researchers and practitioners. Ergonomics experts are adept at adapting workplace designs to meet human functioning and sometimes they recommend decreasing reliance on automation and computer control in order to increase the skill needed by the operator. Other systems can create a virtual 'coalface' (or whatever) so that although the operator is merely pressing buttons, they can actually 'see' the results of their efforts.
- The de-robotisation of call centre employees so that they do not have to read scripts or work in highly controlled environments is recommended. Of course, this is unlikely to change

simply because of the boredom created for employees. Labour is cheap and turnover rates at call centres an expendable cost, so the only way that practices will change is almost certainly with union or employee right input.

- The over-use of meetings in many organisations needs to be re-examined. Meetings should either be run more efficiently (i.e. tightly chaired, highly focused and, above all, brief), and/ or replaced, where possible, with other procedures such as email discussions or video conference calls. The culture of one-hour meetings should be challenged – schedule 30 minutes instead.

- It is difficult to get over the problem of over-legislation and bureaucracy. Initiatives such as trying to give more administrative work to support staff (as tried by Surrey Police Force[63]), public awareness campaigns to relieve GPs of unnecessary paperwork[64] and use of new technologies such as PDAs (Personal Digital Assistants) to take school registrations without the administration[65] go some way towards solving the problem. Research should also be carried out to help identify the best way for individuals to cope with these increasingly necessary, but boring tasks. For example, interspersing such tasks with more interesting work, breaking down form filling into smaller chunks, playing music in the background – these are all individual strategies that companies should allow to go some way towards coping.

- Working conditions of all job roles should be re-examined so as to allow as far as possible utilisation of job rotation schemes and less controlling environments in which individuals are free to organise their own work schedule and take breaks when they want (see below).

- One set of researchers suggest that managers can reduce boredom by 'qualitatively' improving the work of employees[26] – for example, by allowing staff to work on multiple stages of a project and not just one; thus crafting hundreds of car doors every day is considered more boring than creating five full cars each day and feeling the satisfaction of seeing a final completed product. People also experience more personal responsibility (and thus more meaningfulness) from seeing a full car than a full door. The car analogy might be a crude one but serves its purpose here.

- Organisational control and constraint practices should be examined – for example, those that limit talking, breaks, etc. as these may reduce the amount of stimulation and variety that can alleviate the boredom of dull work tasks. These also contribute to psychological reactance, which is where workers may crave those activities that are forbidden to them (such as talking).[66] Being distracted by such cravings for engaging in forbidden activities may thus make it harder to attend to the task and workers may therefore rate it as more boring. Thus, only allowing breaks at prescribed times might make workers focus on that break more (as they crave it even more because they can't have it) and consequently find their work more boring. Excessive control is often in place to ensure that employees work hard, but this can be counter-productive due to 'over-justification'; workers figure that they need to be controlled in order to work hard so they decide that the work must not be interesting enough to do for its own sake.[66] Thus, they rate it more boring.

- A slightly more controversial idea is to be selective about whom to employ for boring or routine work. Whilst choosing 'boring' people for 'boring' tasks is one way of putting it, screening out the most boredom-prone might be sensible.

Box 9.7: The upside of workplace boredom

It is worth mentioning that monotonous work is not always perceived as negative. Some people might regard tedious work that does not demand much attention as a good opportunity to daydream, contemplate and reflect. In my study, a significant number of respondents felt it helped them become more creative (see also page 171). Researchers in 2006 even proposed that 'mindless' work that is low in cognitive demands might be a good way to increase creativity and problem-solving at work;[28] they suggested intermingling challenging with mindless tasks to achieve optimal performance at work (see also Chapter 11 for more on this).

Humour: The Antidote to Workplace Boredom?

Henry Ford, one of the earliest protagonists of mass working practices, famously claimed that 'When we are at work, we ought to be at work. When we are at play, we ought to be at play. There is no use trying to mix the two'.[67] Indeed, he is documented for having fired a worker on his factory floor for smiling – having already committed an earlier offence of 'laughing with the other fellow'.

Things may not be quite that bad today, but humour, fun and work are still generally thought of as mutually exclusive activities – and never more so, perhaps, than in these rather sombre days of austerity in the workplace. Play and fun at work are seen as anathema to the concept of the wage exchange (the idea of doing a day's work for a day's pay – and not inter-mingling that work with non-work pleasure activities). Indeed, having fun at work also blurs the distinction between work and leisure and whilst employers may not mind work impinging on leisure time, generally they do not want it the other way around. This was demonstrated starkly when I was carrying out the boredom research outlined above. Attempting to recruit organisations to allow me access to survey their employees about their experience of workplace boredom, I hit against a few brick walls from employers who were not only adamant that their employees were never bored, but also frowned upon the idea of them taking time out from their work to under- take any boredom-reducing strategies. One employer actually told me in an email, '*With the current economic climate as it is, it is impera- tive that all our staff are as pro-active as possible in generating work, etc. Some of the questions, therefore, I do not feel are appropriate. If any one of our staff were doing any one of these things in work time, I would be seriously worried. Hopefully not one of our staff would be doing this*'. The list of activities that the employer was concerned that their staff should never, ever do at work included:

- Taking a break
- Doing puzzles
- Doodling
- Chatting to colleagues
- Daydreaming
- Putting music on in the background
- Drinking something (e.g. coffee)
- Thinking.

These activities are, in the main, stimulation-enhancing and could help the employee reduce his/her experience of boredom at work, but to the employer they were simply leisure activities that had no place in work time. Yet, if we are increasingly bored at work, the antidote is surely laughter, frivolity, fun and play. Play is, after all, the 'very opposite of ennui and indifference'.[68] If we can bring such things back into our lives, even in these difficult times, then might we not be less bored, or at least more able to tolerate boredom?

9.8: What is so funny?

We all enjoy a good laugh, but what makes something funny? Although this largely depends on an individual's sense of humour and the context, most humorous incidents tend to fall within certain categories:

Incongruity: This is where we find something amusing because of its unexpected nature, its ambiguity, its lack of logic or its inappropriateness. As receiver of the humour, we are led down a certain path, only to be abruptly switched to another path by the punchline. However, the point is that the shift actually turns out to make sense; what at first appeared incongruous turns out to be reconciled once we understand the punchline.

Superiority: This is when we find something funny because of someone else's mistake or failings. Hearing of something rather bizarre or embarrassing that someone else has done allows us to feel superior and consequently we can find it funny (though we mightn't laugh if we ourselves had made the mistake).

Relief: Here, the premise is that a build-up of stress and tension can put us into a frame of mind whereby we find something funny as a form of relief. This is why 'dark' or 'black' humour such as that used by medics or emergency workers can be effective.

Engaging in humour and fun at work has been found to be a good antidote to workplace boredom.[69] In an article entitled 'Work, Play and Boredom' in 2011, the authors assert that 'play promises to relieve the monotony and boredom of work.[17] They go even further in suggesting that play is not the antithesis of work, as some believe but 'an important ally in the fight against tedium'. And if having fun, having a laugh and being playful keeps boredom at bay, then job satisfaction, productivity and the bottom-line dollar will all increase too. Thus it 'pays to play,' as researchers in 1998 so succinctly put it.[70]

Managed Fun

There are many ways to bring back fun into the workplace. Fun team-building exercises and games, puzzles, office parties, dress-down days, office banter, notice-board jokes, revues . . . the list of possibilities is endless. These might blur the boundaries between work and leisure somewhat, but that separation is no longer as distinct as it was anyway, with more and more of us working remotely, using email and computer-mediated technology well into our supposed non-work time.

Many companies, especially in the United States, have caught onto the fact that fun workplaces are more productive. Indeed, many go so far as to employ people or give existing employees special roles, such as 'Fun Officers' or 'Happiness Engineers',[18] whose role it is to organise fun events in the workplace. This 'fungineering'[71] has been criticised by some as forced or managed fun, but as an antidote to workplace boredom, it would certainly seem effective. Examples of fun workplaces include:

- Southwest Airlines: they are well known for their emphasis on fun and employees are encouraged to dress up, play practical jokes and generally enjoy themselves. The company was the top-rated to work for on Glassdoor.com, a website that compiles anonymous employer reviews.[72]

- Quad/Graphics (a large printing company) celebrates fun by holding an annual Management Revue – a song and dance programme, where employees can 'share laughs and even look downright silly together'.[73]

- Virginia Credit Union's call centre holds wacky contests (such as broom races), develops skits and generally 'extracts joy from the job'.[74]

- Ben & Jerry's, the ice-cream people, have a 'joy committee' offering grants to improve workplace happiness.[75] Their motto is: 'If it's not fun, we don't want to do it'.

- Kodak have a huge 'humour room' for employees to take a 'fun break' in.[76] It is stocked with Monty Python films and *Candid Camera* shows, amusing books and other props, such as juggling equipment and fancy dress, to help employees have fun.

- At Sun Microsystems, one of the world's leading makers of server computers based in Santa Clara, California, USA, spectacular April Fools' Day pranks are encouraged. For example, on 1 April 1986, Eric Schmidt, Sun's product development chief and now chief executive of Google, discovered that a Volkswagen Beetle had replaced all the furniture in his workspace. Two years later, Scott McNealy, then chief executive of Sun Microsystems, walked into his office and found it transformed into a par-four golf hole.[77]

- British Airways employed a 'corporate jester' in 1994; one of the things the jester, Paul Birch, did to promote creativity was to encourage managers to chase one another with water guns.[78]

- Appriver, an email security firm based in Gulf Breeze, Florida, USA, created a specially devised film featuring a stuffed monkey to amuse staff because, as their director of marketing comments, 'It's important that our people have fun at work.'[79]

- Google are probably the best-known example of fungineering at work. The internet giant's Californian headquarters includes a volleyball pitch, a rock-climbing wall and a games room.[79] But it's not just the headquarters that features managed fun; Google offices all over the world are like adventure playgrounds, with everything from a slide in Zurich to an indoor bike lane in the Netherlands. And it's one of the few places where goats mow – and fertilise – the lawn.

Bloomberg/Getty Images

- ThinkGeek is an online retailer based in The Fairfax, VA, USA, selling all kinds of cool stuff, including SpyCam pens. Playing with toys is part of the job, whether reviewing a gadget to sell or inventing one from scratch. Staff also have games and other recreational things to help them let loose. One room is chock-full of videogames, arcade-style games, a football table and guitars. 'I like ThinkGeek because I can wear my *Ghostbusters'* uniform to work and get high fives,' said product buyer Chris Mindel.[80]

- Innocent Smoothies have a Services to Fruit scheme ('The most amazing person of the month gets a top hat or tiara to wear'), Friday beers ('We like to wind down properly before the weekend. Sometimes there are crisps involved too'), free smoothies and a jokes/photos blog (taken from their website).

Box 9.9: Funny business

Comedian John Cleese, best-known for his roles in *Monty Python's Flying Circus*, *A Fish Called Wanda* and *Fawlty Towers*, is (according to his agent) the world's largest producer of business training films through his company, Video Arts, largely through the skilful use of humour.[81]

I'm Not Boring You, Am I?

If there is one social impairment most of us fear, it is that of being boring. We can probably tolerate all manner of negative personal descriptors, from accusations of being obnoxious to opinionated, but call us boring and that is one insult too much. The intense fear of boring another person leads many of us to anxiously monitor our conversational partners for any possible hint of ennui. Spotting a surreptitious glance at the clock or a half-suppressed yawn is often all it takes for most of us to enquire plaintively, 'I'm not boring you, am I?' (usually accompanied by a self-deprecating chuckle). Such queries are undoubtedly met by firm denials and hastily ushered explanations for being caught clock-watching, but for many of us, the seed of doubt is sown and the fear of being boring continues to haunt us.

And yet, regrettably, not everyone seems to be quite so concerned about being boring. We all know someone who, quite frankly, bores us rigid. In my own research, over 300 people were asked what bored them at work. Fourteen per cent of respondents claimed that the source of their workplace boredom was another person (see Chapter 9). We all know someone for whom even the most lengthy gaze at our wristwatch or blatant edging towards the door fails to interrupt the flow of tedium that gushes unrelentingly from their lips. Whenever I am unfortunate to encounter such an individual, I am reminded of the scene from the classic movie *Airplane!* where an excruciatingly dull passenger so bores his fellow passengers with the painstakingly uneventful (but very lengthy) story of his life that one by one, they are driven to suicide.

What is it that makes such a person so boring? Researchers have identified a range of traits that make up a 'boring' person's spoken repertoire, from their conversational manner to their verbal range, that are likely to render their audience numb with boredom. This chapter, then, is for all of us who break out into a cold sweat at the mere thought of anyone considering us even remotely boring.

Before we look at what makes a person boring, for all those who have ever entertained that prickle of fear that they might be somewhat dull, here is a quiz to help you find out just how tedious you might be.

Quiz: How Tedious Am I?

How much do you agree with the following statements?

1. I tend to speak more slowly than most people.

1	2	3	4
Strongly disagree	Disagree	Agree	Strongly Agree

2. I tend to take a lot of pauses when I am speaking.

1	2	3	4
Strongly disagree	Disagree	Agree	Strongly Agree

3. When I tell a story or anecdote it tends to take me a long time.

1	2	3	4
Strongly disagree	Disagree	Agree	Strongly Agree

4. I think it is important when retelling a story or anecdote to include every detail.

1	2	3	4
Strongly disagree	Disagree	Agree	Strongly Agree

5. Using jargon or acronyms impresses people as it shows my insider knowledge.

1	2	3	4
Strongly disagree	Disagree	Agree	Strongly Agree

6. I tend to bring conversations round to things about myself.

1	2	3	4
Strongly disagree	Disagree	Agree	Strongly Agree

7. I think it is funny and smart to quote from my favourite movies or TV shows.

1	2	3	4
Strongly disagree	Disagree	Agree	Strongly Agree

8. A lot of interesting things have happened to me in my past that I like to share with people.

1	2	3	4
Strongly disagree	Disagree	Agree	Strongly Agree

9. Often I find myself going off the point when telling a story or anecdote.

1	2	3	4
Strongly disagree	Disagree	Agree	Strongly Agree

10. I prefer it when I can speak more and listen less.

1	2	3	4
Strongly disagree	Disagree	Agree	Strongly Agree

11. I am emotionally very calm when I speak.

1	2	3	4
Strongly disagree	Disagree	Agree	Strongly Agree

12. I am not the sort of person who is always laughing, smiling or joking.

1	2	3	4
Strongly disagree	Disagree	Agree	Strongly Agree

13. Being quite critical, I do tend to point out what is wrong in the world.

1	2	3	4
Strongly disagree	Disagree	Agree	Strongly Agree

14. I keep my voice stable as much as possible rather than trying to vary the pitch and tone.

1	2	3	4
Strongly disagree	Disagree	Agree	Strongly Agree

15. When talking, I tend not to look people in the eye much.

1	2	3	4
Strongly disagree	Disagree	Agree	Strongly Agree

16. I prefer to keep my emotions to myself.

1	2	3	4
Strongly disagree	Disagree	Agree	Strongly Agree

17. I like to tell jokes which people tend to groan at – but I know they like them, really.

1	2	3	4
Strongly disagree	Disagree	Agree	Strongly Agree

18. Life is a serious business – I don't have much time for frivolity.

1	2	3	4
Strongly disagree	Disagree	Agree	Strongly Agree

19. I am very interested in a small number of topics and tend to talk about these a lot.

1	2	3	4
Strongly disagree	Disagree	Agree	Strongly Agree

20. I have a few good anecdotes that I tend to tell a lot.

1	2	3	4
Strongly disagree	Disagree	Agree	Strongly Agree

21. People like it when you praise them a lot in conversation.

1	2	3	4
Strongly disagree	Disagree	Agree	Strongly Agree

22. I tend to use certain words a lot, such as 'really?'

1	2	3	4
Strongly disagree	Disagree	Agree	Strongly Agree

23. I prefer to let people speak without bothering them with questions.

1	2	3	4
Strongly disagree	Disagree	Agree	Strongly Agree

24. If people are talking about something uninteresting I will immediately try to change the subject.

1	2	3	4
Strongly disagree	Disagree	Agree	Strongly Agree

25. I don't have many hobbies or interests.

1	2	3	4
Strongly disagree	Disagree	Agree	Strongly Agree

Scores range from 25–100. The higher your score, the more of the following 'boring habits' you are likely to employ in your interactions.

Thirty Habits of Boring People

What makes a person boring? Is there such thing as a 'boring' person, or can someone who really bores one person fascinate and enthral the next? Clearly, it is possible that whilst there might be a trait of 'boringness', being boring can also be situational. That is, what one person finds boring, another might find thrilling. If a professor of historical French literature engaged me in a long, detailed conversation about his or her area of expertise, I might well find them boring, but a fellow expert would no doubt be hanging onto every word.

That said, there are a number of traits that an individual may possess that can significantly add to their Boring Quotient. Behavioural researcher Dr Mihaly Csikszentmihalyi points out that, 'We're all boring at one time or another, although some people are so chronically boring they're held back socially and in their careers – but sadly, they don't know why.'[1] There is surprisingly little empirical research into what makes someone boring, but fortunately, a group of researchers at Wake Forest University in the 1980s [2] identified a range of conversational characteristics that they have found other people to consistently rate as boring.

When considering what makes people boring, it is helpful to go back to the concept of what boredom is and why we feel bored (see Chapter 1, pages 14–17). According to the Wake Forest researchers, people feel bored when they need to 'exert concerted effort to maintain their attention'.[2] It is more than being uninterested in what someone is saying; if we are simply not interested in what the other person is talking about, we can, in theory, simply not pay any attention and ignore them. The problem is that it is not socially acceptable to walk away from someone in the midst of a conversation, so instead we find ourselves struggling to maintain a semblance of interest in what they are saying. We are socially obliged to try to pay attention to them. Boring people not only speak about things that don't interest us but they do so in a way that requires effort on our part to sustain attention to what they are saying. In other words, it is not simply that what they say is uninteresting to us, but that the way they say it makes it hard for us to follow and understand them. This is why a really dynamic and engaging speaker can make the dullest topic fascinating, yet a tedious speaker can kill dead a subject that ought to be really engaging.

M. R. Leary and colleagues at Wake Forest University analysed the characteristics of really boring people and found they typically fall within a number of categories.[2] These include:

Category of Explanation Boring-ness	
Egocentrism	Focusing too much on themselves which in turn is less engaging for others.
Banality	Talking about trivial matters so that listeners struggle to find material to engage their attention.
Emotion	Inappropriate display of emotion whilst talking which makes it harder for the listener to maintain attention.
Passivity	Not engaging enough with the world around them so they have little to add that grabs the attention.
Seriousness	Being humourless or too serious; again this makes it harder for the listener to maintain interest.
Distraction	Their conversational style makes it hard to follow and involves too much cognitive effort to follow; it is too distracting.

Think about someone who really bores you. What is it specifically about them that you find such a turn-off? I asked 105 of my students at the University of Central Lancashire to do just that. Using the Wake Forest categories as a basis, I created a list of characteristics that boring people have; some of these were gleaned directly from previous research and others from focus groups that I myself conducted. The students were asked to think about someone who bores them and to select the five characteristics from this list that they believe makes someone really boring. The results are ranked in the table below.

	Boring Characteristic	% who rated this one of the top five boring qualities
1.	Telling long, rambling stories that never seem to get to the point	52
2.	Speaking very, very s-l-o-w-l-y	49
3.	Not varying their tone of voice	45
4.	Not allowing the other person to input	34
5.	Telling the same stories repeatedly	34
6.	Talking about themselves all the time	30
7.	Complaining all the time	30
8.	Showing little enthusiasm	28
9.	Including lots of irrelevant detail when explaining something	22
10.	Taking everything very seriously	20
11.	Taking long pauses when talking	18
12.	Using key words or phrases, like, repeatedly, you know?	18
13.	Telling jokes that just aren't funny	17
14.	Having little of interest in their life to talk about	13
15.	Using jargon and acronyms that their audience don't understand	13

16.	Being obsessed with one topic	12
17.	Avoiding eye contact	10
18.	Not showing any emotion	10
19.	Not smiling	10
20.	Getting side-tracked easily	8
21.	Using as little facial expression as possible	8
22.	Asking a lot of simple questions	7
23.	Changing the topic suddenly	7
24.	Not asking any questions at all	6
25.	Talking about trivial matters a great deal	6
26.	Repeating perfunctory responses (e.g. 'really'?)	5
27.	Constantly quoting from movies/TV shows	4
28.	Always talking about the past	4
29.	Being ingratiating	2
30.	Not checking to see if you are interested	2

It is worth going through each category (starting with the most boring) to see what can be learnt to ensure that we never risk being labelled 'boring'.

1. Telling long, rambling stories that never seem to get to the point

What makes a good story? According to a group of Californian researchers, a good story should have three main elements: an appropriate pace that matches the audience's ability to follow it; details that hold the audience's attention; and finally, it should create an impression by 'either piquing the audience's curiosity and making them want to learn more, or conveying a deeper meaning than your normal, everyday run-of-the-mill sequence of causally-related events'.[3]

Inability to tell a good story was labelled as boring by over half my respondents. Boring people never quite master the art of story-telling. We see them approaching us and so we head for the hills, lest we become embroiled in some complex rendition of an event that may or may not have happened (we never really know as they never seem to get to the point).

Specific techniques employed by Boring People to transform engaging anecdotes into rambling tales include:

- Making sure the story goes nowhere. This means that when the end is finally reached, it is reached abruptly, with no obvious or logical conclusion.

- Ensuring the tale is as irrelevant as possible, so that it has little connection with any previous topic of conversation, nor with any other topical occurrence. Casual small talk about the weather, for example, is regarded by the Boring Person as a good enough cue to launch into a totally unrelated story about how they once visited a shop to buy a bread knife.

- Padding the story out with plenty of inconsequential detail. Boring People firmly believe that their listener needs to know everything even vaguely related to their story, including what they were wearing, why they were wearing it, where they bought said clothing from, how much it cost, how they once saw someone else wearing the exact same top (but in a different colour), how they hate button-down polo shirts, etc., etc. A further rambling anecdote about something incidental to their main thesis adds an extra boring factor – and, in fact, this can lead to a mind-addling 'Russian Doll' effect, whereby each tale opens up another inconsequential tale until they (and their audience) have totally lost sight of the original yarn.

• Making sure to include reference in their stories to lots of people whom their audience has never heard of. These characters tend to be introduced into their narrative with a lengthy explanation as to how the Boring Person knows them. Adding a long anecdote about something 'hilarious' (the hilarity is often so subtle as to be missed by most of their listeners) that each of these extraneous characters once did (or that their mother or sister or auntie's best friend did) only adds to the depth of boredom they are inadvertently creating.

2. *Speaking very, very s-l-o-w-l-y*

This is the second most boring habit according to my research, with nearly half the respondents selecting this. People who speak with exaggerated slowness during a normal conversation are often boring. This is because their audience is waiting for them to get to the punchline, but becomes frustrated with the delay. Research has shown that people who speak too slowly are perceived as being overly pedantic,[4] as if they are more concerned with selecting and enunciating each word and syllable than with the point they are trying to make. Listening to a slow speaker can be extremely irritating and also quite distracting; we find ourselves so mesmerised (initially, at least) by the abnormal pace that we lose track of the content – so subsequently become bored as we are no longer able to follow the thread of what they are talking about.

3. Not varying their tone of voice

> *'People who speak in a monotone are boring'*

Participant in my boredom research

The third most commonly selected characteristic of a boring person was chosen by 45 per cent of respondents. Varying the tone in your voice injects energy and clarity into your message, so people become more boring simply by keeping their tone the same all the time. By tone, I mean pitch (squeaky or growly), volume (loud or quiet), pace (fast or slow) and using emphasis to stress a point. A varied tone rises and falls and emphasises key words and phrases.

A monotone voice has little variety, conveys no emotion (see **18**), it stays at the same pitch and there is a lack of stress variation; this makes it harder for people to listen and understand so makes them more likely to be bored. Using a monotone voice also suggests to your listener that you really don't care whether they are interested in what you are saying because you can't be bothered to make your conversation more engaging for them.

4. Not allowing the other person to input

> *'Boring people go on and on, and don't seem to care that your eyes are glazing over. If you try to interject, they just talk over you and eventually you just give up and shrivel away.'*

Participant in my boredom research

One third of research respondents cited the failure to allow another party to engage in the conversation as one of their top-five qualities that makes a person boring. To be really boring, it is essential to keep up a conversation without anyone else's input. Technically, of course, this is a monologue, but Boring People blithely assume their audience will be delighted to sit back and let them take over. They tend to disregard any subtle (or even quite blatant) signs from their conversational partner (see *30*) that suggest that s/he might want to contribute.

5. Telling the same stories repeatedly

Some people seem to have a 'party piece', which they will trot out at every conceivable occasion. Clearly, this will be boring for those who have heard it all before. This is illustrated nicely by the comments of psychologist John Bargh, reported in Malcolm Gladwell's classic book, *Blink*.[5] The bane of many psychology researchers is the repetitive nature of running experiments repeatedly on many participants. Bargh relates one study which involved the same instructions being given continuously to participants and laments, 'I had to listen to the same conversation over and over again. It was boring, *boring!*'

Apart from being a problem for psychology researchers, hearing the same tales repeatedly is a particular problem for couples in long-term relationships, who have heard it all many (many) times before. In fact, according to one report, more and more women are leaving their husbands out of boredom.[6] Endless recycling of the same stories could be a contributing factor.

6. Talking about themselves all the time

We all love talking about ourselves but most of us resist the urge to do so too much. The problem is that Boring People don't seem to know what 'too much' is. Nearly a third of respondents in my research said that this was one of the top five qualities that make someone boring. Boring People manage to bring every topic of conversation back to themselves and talk almost exclusively about either themselves, or topics that interest them. When someone else relates an anecdote, they immediately explain how this reminds them of something that happened to them. Boring People tend to be 'story-toppers' – i.e. by topping any tale that anyone else tells, with what they consider to be a far better story of their own.

Actually, to be fair to Boring People, research has shown that our brains like it when we talk about ourselves. In a study conducted by Harvard University researchers, a series of experiments was designed to assess how much people liked talking about themselves and why. In the first study, they scanned people's brains whilst those people either talked about themselves or judged the personalities or opinions of others. In another experiment, researchers tested whether people preferred to answer questions about themselves, other people or neutral facts. Yet another study explored whether people wanted to share their answers with others or keep them to themselves.[7]

In all the studies, the researchers, led by Diana I. Tamir and Jason P. Mitchell at Harvard's psychology department, found similar findings: humans get a boost in the reward centres of their brain when they talk about themselves. We get more of a boost when others are listening to us (or when we think they are) than when they are not. All of which explains the appeal of talking about ourselves. It could be that Boring People have a greater need for this brain boost than less boring people, which might be why they don't seem able to stop.

Box 10.1: How to deal with boring people

'When I have a conversation with someone boring, I amuse myself by deciding not to use a certain letter in my words – say "e" – and see how I manage'

Steve Pearlman, retired teacher, Manchester (in Facebook comment with the author)

---

7. Complaining a lot

Nearly a third of respondents in the survey claimed that people complaining a lot are amongst their top five boring 'hates'. People who are very negative about everything can be boring because of the lack of enthusiasm and interest this conveys. Negativity can be very energy-sapping and makes people feel lethargic; this means it is harder for them to maintain the cognitive effort to attend to what the complainer is saying.

The predictability of always complaining also adds to the Boring Quotient. Those who react in predictable, pro-typical ways are seen as more boring than more spontaneous individuals.

Being forced to listen to people who complain a lot also has other effects on us, which could help to explain why we find such people so boring. According to Trevor Blake, entrepreneur and author of the business self-help guide, *Three Simple Steps: A Map to Success in Business and Life*, research has shown that prolonged exposure to negativity and complaining diminishes the brain's capacity for problem solving. Or, to put it more simply (though less scientifically), listening to other people complain 'turns your brain to mush'.[8] It is probably reasonable to assume that 'mushy' brains that are unable to engage creative problem solving are bored brains.

8. Showing little enthusiasm

In February 2013, internationally renowned movie star Bruce Willis was forced to apologise for delivering a 'boring' interview on British television. His crime, apparently, was 'appearing listless and disinterested' whilst being interviewed about his new film (*A Good Day To Die Hard*) and for struggling to work up 'much enthusiasm' (he later admitted, 'I was a little boring' but blamed it on jet-lag).[9]

Enthusiasm is engaging. I always say that a person can get away with quite a lot (e.g. having little of substance to say) as long as they are enthusiastic. Boring People may have fascinating things to say but if they are delivered in an unenthusiastic manner, they will simply bore their audience (even if they are Bruce Willis). Lack of enthusiasm suggests you are bored. According to researchers in The Netherlands[10] there are a number of distinct ways, in addition to the above, that Boring People display their boredom and lack of enthusiasm. For example, speaking quietly without varying voice pitch at all (see 3) conveys a lack of interest, whilst 'drooping' uses body language to create an overall lethargic, 'droopy' impression. Slumped posture is a sign of low arousal so conveys the impression that the person is disinterested, unenthusiastic and bored.[10] Keeping hand gestures to a minimum is another way that lack of enthusiasm is conveyed as this suggests a lack of energy and zeal; people who use a lot of hand gestures when they speak can convey a dynamism that is incompatible with boredom.

9. Including lots of irrelevant detail

It's all in the detail, they say, and indeed there is an art to numbing an audience's minds with detail.

Example: Suppose someone at work asks when a report will be ready.

Regular (Non-Boring) Response: 'I hope to get it finished by Thursday evening, Friday tops'.

Response of a Boring Person: 'Well, I was hoping to have it finished for Thursday evening – Thursday night is my Bingo night with Kelly and Chloe – you know, from accounts? Kelly had a big win two weeks ago, you know! She promised to treat us all to curry tonight to celebrate. Anyway, I am not sure I will have it finished by Thursday because of the problems I'm having with my car – I had to take it in yesterday after it was making a funny whirring noise about a minute after switching the ignition on. I took it to the garage and Mike, that's the mechanic, said he'd have to take it on a little run to be able to hear the noise and try to diagnose it properly. So, I went with him – we ended up driving on the ring road and well, you know how busy that gets, so by the time we got back it was half 11. Anyway, I had to leave it with Mike – he thinks it's a gasket problem – and get the bus in, so I lost half a morning's work, which really delayed me . . .' (etc., etc.).

The problem with all this detail is that it both distracts from the main story (thus making it hard to follow) and also changes pace so quickly that the listener isn't given any time to engage with the content. Researchers have shown that in reading fiction, relevant detail, imaginative metaphors and attentive descriptions of people and their actions afford the reader the opportunity to enter fully into other people's thoughts and feelings – which often engages different parts and networks of the brain.[11] When these opportunities are not offered (by the inclusion of lots of irrelevant, trivial and extraneous information), readers are less likely to engage different brain processes (other than the language-processing areas) and are thus more likely to be bored. Whilst this research was carried out, using brain scans, with written text, it is likely to be just as applicable with the spoken word too.

10. Taking everything very seriously (and 19. Not smiling)

> '*I know someone who you can never have a laugh with. He is a very serious person and resists any attempt to banter with them. If you make a joke about something he will respond by pointing out why your comment is just not funny. My heart sinks when I see him approach*'

Participant in my boredom research

Telling unfunny jokes is bad enough (see **13**), but not finding the humour, fun or light-heartedness in anything is perhaps worse. Humour has an important role as an antidote to boredom, so individuals unable or unwilling to use this tool fail to make their world a less boring place. See Chapter 9 for more on the role of humour.

11. Taking long pauses

Boring People often take inordinately long pauses before answering any and every question. They might also pause for too long between words and clauses, but at the same time may refuse to allow their audience to jump into the pause, perhaps by silencing them with a hand firmly held aloft or a stern glare. Such techniques are guaranteed not only to bore their audience, as they wait with growing impatience for them to finally get their point across (and lose their attention whilst waiting), but also to irritate them by refusing to allow them to 'close the gap'.

12. Using key words or phrases, like, repeatedly, you know?

Some people pepper their speech with the same banal and redundant words. Common words include:

- Like (as in, 'he, like, said, he was happy, like')
- Basically (as in, 'basically, what happened was that she basically ran away')
- Know what I mean?/You know?
- Totally (as in 'he was so totally into me')
- Whatever!
- It's not rocket science
- Absolutely!

If you repeatedly use the same phrase or word, the repetition will bore people. This is because our brains learn to ignore the extraneous phrases and thus our attention turns away whilst you are saying them – it is then hard to drag our attention back to you. The net effect is that you are perceived as boring.

13. Telling jokes that just aren't funny

Part of the reason why other people bore us is to do with the need to maintain attention on themselves when we'd rather not. When someone tells us a 'joke', there is a social expectation that we show the appropriate response, which, at the very least, normally ought to involve some display of pleasure. When Boring People tell boring jokes, we find the need to maintain attention and obey the expected display rule difficult and thus experience boredom.

So, what is it that makes a joke boring?

- It could be the way it is told. A good joke can be killed simply in the telling; using emphasis in the wrong place, forgetting the punchline, delivering it with bad timing, etc. Precision is vital: to reach precision, the joker must choose the words in order to provide a vivid, in-focus image. To properly arrange the words in the sentence is also crucial to get precision. Boring People tend not to do that.

- If the joke is old, no one will find it funny. According to psychologist Edward de Bono,[12] one of the foremost experts in the fields of creativity, who coined the term 'lateral thinking', the mind is a pattern-matching machine, and works by recognising stories and behaviour and putting them into familiar patterns. When a familiar connection is disrupted and an alternative unexpected new link is made in the brain via a different route than anticipated, then humour is experienced as the new connection is made. Jokes are thus only funny the first time they are told: once told, the pattern is established so there can be no new connections, there will be no humour. Unfortunately, no one has told Boring People this.

- For the same reason, telling the same jokes over and over again is just not funny.

- 'You had to have been there' – a humorous event that was only funny in the context but when retold later is often just not funny.

- The joke is too long; Isaac Asimov, in his *Treasury of Humor*,[13] points out that attempting to tell a long joke 'bears its corresponding risks'. The joke, he says, must have 'intrinsic interest' but should also have 'mild humour' throughout. If it is only interesting, the audience may take the story too seriously and the punchline, when it comes, can fall into what Asimov so aptly calls 'a well of dreadful silence'. Boring People often fail to insert the necessary subsidiary humour to keep the story buoyant and funny.

14. Having little of interest in their life to talk about

> 'Boring people lead boring lives so don't have much to say that is
> of interest to most other people.'

Participant in my boredom research

Naturally, if a person has no hobbies, doesn't go out much or do much that is different in their day-to-day lives, they will have less engaging material to draw on. Whilst some people have the gift of making even a trip to the dentist sound enthralling, most of us need better material to bring out the best in us. So, if you don't have any interesting experiences with which to engage your audience, go out and get some!

15. Using jargon and acronyms that their audience don't understand

Boring People seem to think that by using lots of acronyms and jargon, they will sound clever. They don't – the overall effect is that the listener is unable to follow the thread of the conversation and thus loses interest quickly. Listeners may also feel that the speaker is trying to impress them with their in-depth inside knowledge, but rather than be impressed, they are likely simply to tune out. Other related habits of Boring People include over-use of clichés, 'management speak', using pompous language and use of two words where one will do.

Boring Example: I approached the customer-facing interface with caution as befitting an Ambient Replenishment Controller such as myself.

Non-Boring Translation: I was a bit wary about going to the Customer Service desk as I am only a shelf-stacker.

Boring Example: With all due respect, I am basically trying to address the issue, which is a 24/7 concern. What we need is some blue sky thinking so we can think outside the box. It's not rocket science, but I am between a rock and a hard place. You'll have to bear with me at this time as the goalposts keep moving, which makes it hard to ensure we are all singing from the same hymn sheet.

Non-Boring Translation: I am trying to sort this out, but I need a new, more creative solution. I'm in a difficult position, but I want to make sure we are in agreement with this.

Boring Example: As ASL, I need to engage an ASOP to carry out a new corporate BBS.

Non-Boring Translation: As an Assistant Section Leader I need to ask an Assistant System Operator to create a new Bulletin Board System.

Jon Warshawsky, co-author of *Why Business People Speak Like Idiots: A Bullfighter's Guide*, has kindly identified the five most overused business-jargon terms, so if you want to avoid being boring at work, these are the ones to avoid:

- Empower
- Value (as in 'value-add', 'deliver value' or 'value proposition')
- Thought leadership
- Mindshare
- Customer-focused.

16. *Being obsessed with one topic*

'I have this acquaintance who is obsessed with her dog. Every attempt to draw her away from her pet fails – she steers every topic of conversation back to her precious pooch. We have to view updated photos of the dog at every meeting and hear about every tiny detail of his life since we last met. Yawn.'

Participant in my boredom research

Scientists have shown that when we hear a story or tale, we want to relate it back to our own experiences. When someone talks to us, we busy ourselves with looking to our own experiences to see how it fits within our existing schema – we try to relate to the material. When someone talks about a very narrow topic area that we cannot relate to, we struggle and quickly lose interest.

17. *Avoiding eye contact*

Did you ever play the 'staring' game as a child? This is where you and a friend sit and stare at each other without laughing – the first to look away is the loser. It is hard to do so because it violates the social norms of appropriate eye contact between two people. Normally, the listener pretty much gazes at the speaker, but the speaker doesn't constantly gaze back; usually they glance away every so often whilst they talk.

But what happens if the speaker violates the normal rules and avoids eye contact with the listener far more than is usual? If the speaker is glancing away too much, it becomes harder to understand them because eyes are very expressive; when this medium of communication is removed, it is more difficult for us to pay attention (and thus adds to the likelihood of our becoming bored). When someone is not looking at us, it is also easier for us, the listener, to look away and become distracted by other things that our gaze takes in. This all adds to our boredom as we rapidly lose interest in the speaker and become more engaged in our immediate surroundings.

Eye contact also makes listeners feel more included. Dr Roel Vertegaal, an expert on eye communication, conducted a study which showed that the amount of eye contact a person received during a group conversation was proportional to how much s/he participated.[14] Researchers at the Universities of Wolverhampton and Stirling in the UK have also shown that eye contact forces us to pay attention more: they recorded clips of someone gazing directly into the camera for varying amounts of time whilst talking and found that viewers remembered more of what the speaker said if s/he looked directly into the camera at least a third of the time.[15]

18. Not showing any emotion (or conversely getting over-excited by trivia)

It is particularly irritating when you announce some thrilling piece of news to someone, only for their reaction to be a flat 'oh, right'. Lack of emotional affect makes for a very dull, tedious interaction, but it is more than that which is boring: it is the lack of appropriate or expected emotion that turns people off.

Speaking without any attempt to convey emotion (either by facial expression or tone of voice) makes it harder for listeners to attend to your message. Listeners might become distracted by your lack of emotion, or simply give up putting the cognitive effort into trying to understand a message that is missing its vital emotional nuances.

Conversely, some Boring People show too much emotion; they get over-enthusiastic about the most trivial things. An extra piece of cucumber in their sandwich, a new fragrance a colleague is wearing, or bumping into an old friend unexpectedly can send them into a frenzy of thrilled excitement. This delight in trivia can appear boring since most people won't share the sentiments and thus cannot relate to the emotions being expressed.

20. Getting easily side-tracked

We all know people who are simply unable to tell a tale from A to B. Instead, they meander leisurely all around the proverbial houses, getting side-tracked by every new and random path of consciousness that streams through their minds. Each train of thought sparks new avenues so the more they talk, the further away they get from the original point. This haphazard jumping from one topic to another leaves the listener struggling to follow the incessant stream of chatter. And the harder it is to follow the conversation, the more likely we are to disengage and become bored.

Example:

(Non-Boring Person): 'Oh, Cassie, I have that book you wanted! Here it is.'

(Boring Person): 'Oh, Cassie, I have that book you wanted – it's funny because just after you told me that you wanted it, I bumped into James – he is the one who told me about the book in the first place – he was actually on his way to hospital when I saw him cos his mum was taken in last night – lovely lady she is, and doing so well for 83, you wouldn't know it to look at her – reminds me of my gran, she does, as they both love knitting – actually, knitting is very fashionable these days, isn't it? I once went with my gran to a local knitting group called The Nutty Knitters – I only went the once, though, it really wasn't my thing . . .'

(See also 1 and 9.)

21. Using as little facial expression as possible

Facial expression and other non-verbal media account for over 50 per cent of our message. This means that more than half of what we are trying to communicate comes from the way we arrange our face, and less than half from the words we use. This is why phone conversations may be less engaging than those that are face-to-face.

Boring People reduce the ability of people to be able to understand them by minimising their facial expression; this forces their audience to maintain more cognitive effort to understand their message, which is hard for them and contributes to the emotional state that they will recognise as 'boredom'.

Expressionless faces also convey the impression that they are bored,[10] which adds to the overall tedium. (See also 18.)

22. Asking a lot of simple questions

Simple questions reflect politeness; more complex questions reflect genuine curiosity. People who tend to ask a lot of simple questions may do so in order to cover the fact that they are not really listening, may not want to reveal much about themselves or make any other more engaging contributions to the conversation.

Examples:

Simple question: So, then what?

Complex question: So, did you manage to get to the show in time?

Simple question: What happened?

Complex question: What was his reaction when you did that?

Simple question: Was it good?

Complex question: What did you do when you arrived?

23. Suddenly changing the topic

Conversations normally have a natural flow but Boring People often make abrupt changes of topic without warning – for example, by inserting complete non-sequiturs in random places. In the midst of a discussion about last night's football game, they might say, for instance: 'People who have varicose veins often have piles too'. Or, during a conversation about the merits of online supermarket shopping, ask, 'Would you like to see a picture of my gran?'

24. Not asking any questions at all

Asking lots of simple questions is probably better than not asking any questions at all. Of course, some people are shy and uncomfortable in social situations, and as such may be inhibited about asking questions. Sadly, however, someone who sits there passively can be perceived as dull. If their conversational partner says something that invites an enquiry (e.g. 'So, then he dropped his bombshell') but the expected question fails to materialise, then the impression is given that the listener is simply not interested. This apparent lack of curiosity would seem to reflect an uncurious, dull individual, who fails to engage with the outside world: that is, a Boring Person.

25. Talking about trivial matters a great deal

Of course, what is trivial to one person is essential information to the next. It's all in the context. If you are engaged in a deep discussion about serious health issues, the Middle East Crisis or the latest terrorist deterrents, and someone tries to interject (repeatedly) with their concerns about the blemish that their hamster has got, then their conversational topic might be perceived as boring.

26. Repeating perfunctory responses

Wow! Really? Gosh! Cool! These are the sort of repetitive responses that don't really add anything to the conversational flow and can end up just being irritating background noise. It is boring because of its repetitive nature; as we discovered in earlier parts of this book, one of the main causes of boredom is repetition as this obscures our need and search for novel stimuli. The perfunctory responses are also passive in that they don't invite much, if any, input or participation from the other person. Utterances that are passive are less engaging as they don't require much attention.

Boring People might be reassured to learn that they are not alone and even celebrities are not immune from this trait; apparently the singer Britney Spears was labelled 'boring Britney' for repeatedly using the word 'amazing' in her role as judge on *The X Factor* talent show in the US.[16]

27. Constantly quoting from movies

Boring People think they are being cool, hip and 'on trend' by constantly throwing out quotations from their favourite movies or TV programmes. Occasional, relevant quotes can be very amusing, but repeated regurgitation of their favourite *Star Trek* moment is not. Again, it is the repetition here that is key to creating boredom: either the repetition of the same line or the same concept (of quoting from movies).

Examples:

- Every time someone says 'surely', they respond with 'and don't call me Shirley!' (*Airplane!*, 1980).
- When they want to be philosophical: 'Life is like a box of chocolates, you never know what you're gonna get'. (*Forrest Gump*, 1994). This is great once, not so great the tenth time they say it.
- Every time they leave the office to get their sandwich: 'I'll be back' (*The Terminator*, 1984).
- Whenever someone else leaves the building: 'May the Force be with you' (*Star Wars*, 1977).
- Whenever they intend trying to persuade someone to do something: 'I'm gonna make him an offer he can't refuse' (*The Godfather*, 1972).

The Boring Quotient is increased when poor attempts at accents are made in employing these quotes. Isaac Asimov, an expert in humour, points out rather astutely that 'the number of people who think they can handle some particular accent is far greater than the number of people who actually can.'[7] Boring People seem to demonstrate his point rather well.

28. Always talking about the past

'My husband's best days seem to have been in his teens and he talks about those times constantly. He brings up events from 25 years ago as if they are still relevant. They are not, it's boring.'

Participant in my boredom research

Boring People use most of their conversational currency by talking about the past. This is dull because such tales lack relevance to the current situation. Constantly talking, for example, about a holiday you took 23 years ago, a person you knew in school, a sports event you attended as a teenager, that time when you got your kitchen refitted in 1979, etc., is banal and boring because listeners will struggle to relate your insights to their own lives today. There is also the danger that if you tend to live in the past, you will end up repeating these old 'classic' anecdotes (see 5), which adds significantly to your boredom factor.

29: Being ingratiating

'Much has been written on the misuse and overuse of praise. The bottom line: it's boring.'

This was written on the parenting site, Positive Parenting Connection (http://positiveparentingconnection.net/praise-is-boring), but applies equally to other social arenas. Praising someone too much is monotonous and boring.

People who try too hard to please can thus appear boring. They constantly pepper their conversation with repeated sycophantic comments, such as 'Wow, that's so cool!', 'You are amazing!' or 'That's hilarious!' At first, this can seem flattering to the speaker, but when done repeatedly, we habituate (or get used to the stimuli), tune it out and it just becomes boring.

30. Not bothering to monitor their audience for signs of disinterest

Boring People are peculiarly immune to the effects that they have on their audience. They will ignore the most obvious cues that they are being boring and refuse to acknowledge even the possibility that they are less than engaging. Perhaps it is selective blindness, or lack of social cue reading, but the following list of signs that you are boring someone might help.

How to tell if you are boring someone:

- They look at their watch more than once
- They say things like, 'Well, enough about you . . .'
- They avoid eye contact with you whilst you are speaking
- You are monopolising the conversation
- They start doing something else whilst you are talking
- They keep trying to change the subject
- They fidget a lot
- They tap their feet or a pen
- Their eyes seem to glaze over
- They don't ask questions, but just nod politely.

How Dare You Bore Me!

Boring People are not just perceived as boring: their very tedium leads to a whole range of associated personality traits. The Wake Forest researchers,[2] who identified the categories of boring behaviour referred to earlier, carried out another study in which they asked people to listen to taped conversations that were rated as either boring or non-boring. They were then asked to rate the boring and interesting speakers on a range of scales. Results revealed that the 'boring' people, when compared with 'interesting' people, were perceived as less:

- Friendly
- Likeable
- Competent
- Enthusiastic

- Reliable
- Strong
- Secure
- Interested in others
- Popular
- Capable of being leaders.

The researchers in this study offer an intriguing explanation for these findings. There is a social norm, they say, that prohibits the 'wholesale boredom of others'. In other words, whilst no one is expected to be consistently entertaining and fascinating, there is huge social pressure and expectation not to be downright boring. Boring people violate this accepted social norm and this is why they evoke such negative reactions from those whom they have bored.

It should be noted, however, that the same study also found that the participants rated boring people as being more intelligent than interesting people, so there are at least some benefits to being perceived as boring!

Is Boring-ness Part of a Social Deficit Syndrome?

Boring People have difficulty holding the attention of others. This is because they may disclose too little about themselves, or too much, or be socially anxious or inhibited. According to earlier research in the 1970s,[13] they may also possess poor role-taking abilities, be unable to work out what other people find interesting, be overly self-focused or have general social skill problems. All this can lead to loneliness, lowered self-esteem and even depression. Social skills training to help those who seem to be boring, or who perceive themselves as boring, might be a very beneficial way forward and indeed such training should perhaps be made available in schools.

Some people who appear to be boring may actually have a learning difficulty that prevents them from reading social cues, such as Asperger's syndrome or they could be on the Autistic Spectrum Disorder, as discussed more in Chapter 7.

But Hang On, Is Boring Always Bad?

US President Barack Obama was famously pronounced boring by his college roommate – 'You're becoming a bore,' he complained.[17] The reason for this accusation, Obama explains in his memoir, *Dreams From My Father*, was that he was 'concentrating on his studies, running three miles a day, fasting on Sundays. And no more getting high.' All in all, his was becoming a somewhat predictable, disciplined life.

Clearly, being boring is not always bad. Those who might be considered boring tend to be hardworking, conscientious, stable and health-conscious (and make good state leaders). A growing body of research shows that being 'boring' might even predict a longer life. In fact, scoring low for conscientiousness is as detrimental to longevity as cardiovascular disease, according to Brent Roberts, a professor of psychology at the University of Illinois, Urbana-Champaign.[18] 'Boring' people tend to be responsible and disciplined. They eat healthily, exercise regularly, see their doctor more often and refrain from smoking and excessive drinking. They're more likely to succeed at work, enjoy stable marriages, have larger families and engage with their community. So why does 'boring' get such bad press?

There is actually anecdotal evidence that such qualities are beginning to be increasingly appreciated. Indeed, a number of people and organisations are beginning actively to promote being 'boring' and are coming out as 'boring and proud'. Being a 'geek' or 'nerd' (an intellectual perceived as boring) is now fashionable, as illustrated by an astonishing array of clothes currently available that proudly proclaim its wearer to be boring:

cap from Sports Direct

Is boring really becoming the new interesting? Has the time come for boring people everywhere? Certainly, accountancy firms, traditionally thought of as 'boring', are beginning to reclaim the negative label as a positive one, as seen in Chapter 9. But it is not just accountancy firms that are happy to be labelled as boring anymore.

Proud to Be an 'Anorak'?

> '*In British slang an "anorak" is a person who has a very strong interest, perhaps obsessive, in niche subjects. This interest may be unacknowledged or not understood by the general public. The term is sometimes used synonymously with geek or nerd.*'

> Wikipedia

The description 'anorak' has traditionally been a term of mild abuse directed almost exclusively at 'boring' men. According to a description by a reader of the *Guardian*, 'such men are usually obsessively interested in an obscure subject and/or activity – the archetypal one being trainspotting. Such activities often require the participant to spend hours out of doors, not doing much and occasionally writing something in a little book. Hence, such people often wear anoraks because they are (a) cheap (b) practical (c) have lots of pockets for flasks, notebooks, pencils, other pencils etc.'[19] And yet, I feel the tide is turning for anoraks. It appears to be more acceptable now to admit to being boring, and possibly this is even something to be proud of (even if you are not an accountant). The Dull Men's Club (http://www.dullmensclub.com) is an international web-based group made up of men (and some women), who are proud to be 'anoraks'. Their website celebrates all that is boring with 'dull-lights' (rather than highlights) being discussions of park benches, airport carousels and roundabouts. Their motto is 'It's OK to be dull'. The Club began as a real group in New York City, with 17 members (the number of chairs available in the meeting room), but their Facebook page now boasts 3,386 likes at the time of writing – that's a lot of people proud to be boring!

One man who knows all about being labelled boring is Peter Willis, whose unusual hobby has earned him the title of the Most Boring Man in Britain. This unenviable (perhaps) title was bestowed on him by the mass circulation newspaper, the *Daily Mirror*, and has since been reported in various media outlets across the world. The hobby that earned him this title is taking photos of letterboxes the length and breadth of Great Britain. The *Daily Mirror* explained, '*If there was a competition to have the dullest ever ambition then Peter Willis might just have pipped everyone to the post. The former postie dreams of taking a photo of all of Britain's 115,000 postboxes.*'[20]

Certainly, this might well be the sort of narrow interest that could rightfully earn the label of 'anorak', but is Willis really the most boring man in Britain? And if so, how, I wondered, did he feel about this? In an effort to find out, I tracked Peter Willis down to his home in Worcester; his initial reluctance to talk to me clearly reflected an unhappiness with the title and indeed, the media officer of the Letter Box Study Group, Robert Cole, who reluctantly passed my details onto him, warned me that my request, '*could cause at least mild offence*'. Robert went on to explain, somewhat defensively, '*others may think Peter is boring. Others may think our hobby is boring. Neither is true.*' Clearly the Letter Box Study Group do not view the labelling of their hobby as 'boring' as a positive descriptor.

Peter did agree to talk to me and this led to a series of (not at all boring) email discussions about his hobby and the subsequent 'honour' bestowed on him by the world's media. Willis, 68, explained:

> I think the title given to me of 'most boring man in Britain' is unfair. Other people might find my hobby boring, but then I find horse racing or angling boring. Postboxes are more interesting than you might think. I do know about boring – I have had many boring jobs in my time; in one job when I was young, my day was so slow and uninteresting that I was constantly watching my watch, umpteen times each hour. The highlight of my working

> *day was making a cup of tea. That type of inactivity, both within*
> *the brain, and not being able to use one's thinking processes*
> *much or at all, is what I sum up as boredom. So I know what it is*
> *to be doing boring things and in my view, boring things are char-*
> *acterised by inactivity. Yet my hobby is a very active occupation*
> *and definitely not boring. There are lots of post boxes, some*
> *never seen before, in different places, some good, some really ter-*
> *rible. The boxes are also different anyway, with many styles, but*
> *they are also in different states of repair and condition. I have*
> *a database and I have acquired a list from Royal Mail of those*
> *115,000 boxes, so one can carry out some research beforehand,*
> *using the splendid digital mapping from Ordnance Survey. Like*
> *stamps, some types of boxes are more scarce than others, so all*
> *in all, this hobby is to me anything but being boring.*

In talking to Peter, it does become quickly apparent that he may
well have been unfairly labelled as 'boring', at least according to
the list of '30 qualities of boring people' outlined earlier in this
chapter. For example, in our conversations it became clear that
Peter has a wide range of interests (including theatre, as well as
other, more quirky ones, such as drain covers, milestones, inn
signs and war memorials), and is clearly sociable and well able to
talk about a range of topics in an engaging and humorous way. But
his story does raise the interesting issue of why we tend to label a
hobby as 'boring' and whether having a 'boring' hobby means that
you are a 'boring' person, as the *Daily Mirror* assumed.

Boring Hobbies = Boring People?

'Boring' hobbies tend to be those that demand obsessive attention
to details too technical, obscure or narrow in range to interest
very many people. This leads to the hobbyist having excessive
knowledge about something that only a small minority of people

share even a passing interest in. Often the subject of their interest tends to be something rather mundane and everyday, such as letter boxes, park benches, etc.

I thought it would be interesting to ask people what hobbies they consider boring so I decided to ask my students (always a captive audience for an academic's research), but I didn't want to give them a list of hobbies – I wanted to see what hobbies they would pluck from thin air themselves. Fifty-eight students took the time to answer and the most commonly mentioned boring hobby was stamp or coin collecting (mentioned by 43 per cent of respondents), followed by train/plane or bus spotting (19 per cent) and fishing (16 per cent). Others included bird watching, knitting, politics, collecting objects such as stones or shells, 'taking pictures of pylons', 'making things out of matches' and 'metal detecting in areas where there is nothing to find'.

Many of these 'boring' hobbies are characterised by their being predominantly solitary activities (or those where other people's input is not required), or, as one respondent put it, 'Collecting things that have no use – there is no point to them – and having long periods of waiting in between adding something to the collection'.

It is highly likely that enthusiasts of any of these hobbies will object to either them or their hobbies being described as 'boring' (as Peter Willis and Robert Cole did) simply because if it grabs their interest and engages them, it cannot be boring to them. So maybe it is time to stand up for trainspotters, stamp collectors and yes, those who photograph letter boxes and reclaim the 'boring' label'. After all, what is boring to one person might be fascinating to the next. Indeed, this is the theory behind the annual Boring Conference, which is held in the UK as a celebration of 'the mundane, the ordinary, the obvious and the overlooked';[21] subjects which, according to the Boring Conference website, are 'often considered trivial and pointless, but when examined more closely reveal themselves to be deeply fascinating'. Previous topics discussed at the conference, which has been running for four years now, include sneezing, toast, IBM tills, the sounds made by vending machines, the Shipping Forecast, barcodes, yellow lines and the features of the Yamaha PSR-175 Portatone keyboard. Boring topics? The events are a sell-out each year, with over 500 people happy to pay £20 each to attend. Perhaps there is more to these 'boring' topics after all.

The point about 'boring' hobbies, and perhaps even people labelled as 'boring', is that they do focus on the mundane rather than the grandiose. Perhaps in our fast-paced world, where nothing seems to sustain our attention for long unless it is 'exciting', there is something charming about taking the time to appreciate the beauty and joy of simple, everyday life. In fact, as a mental health practitioner one piece of advice I always give to depressed clients is to look for the pleasure in simple, ordinary things. Maybe if more of us stopped to appreciate the small stuff, fewer of us would get depressed in the first place.

I put this theory to 'Boring Tweeter', a man who has been using Twitter to send 'boring' messages to all those who follow him (some 173K at the time of going to print). Boring Tweeter @ Boringtweets is someone committed to penning boring tweets as an antidote to what he refers to as 'the grandiose tweets' that many tweeters write. 'The mundane is interesting,' he told me (in a private tweet), 'because it is something that each and every one of us experiences every day'. He might tweet when bored, but strongly believes there is a 'big difference with being bored and actually being boring'. Examples of his 'boring' tweets include:

@Boringtweets My bath was too hot earlier on, so I added some cold water and then it was just right.

@Boringtweets If I get tired of standing up and there's a chair nearby, then I sit down.

@Boringtweets I thought it was about 5pm and when I looked at the clock it was actually 5.04pm. I wasn't far out. I'm pleased with that.

Each of these tweets was retweeted around 200 times by some of his hundreds and thousands of followers – far more than many celebrities, with their thrilling lives, achieve. Of course for most of the followers it is probably the deliberate dullness of the tweets that is so entertaining; in a world populated by people trying to be seen as leading exciting lives, perhaps 'exciting' is simply becoming boring and the mundane is quietly celebrated.

So if you feel like being part of this boring revolution, here are some special interest groups you might wish to consider joining:

British Brick Society (http://britishbricksoc.co.uk)

The Pylon Appreciation Society (http://www.pylons.org)

Round-A-Bouts of Great Britain (http://www.round-aboutsofbritain.com)

The Traffic Cone Preservation Society (http://www.trafficcone.com)

The Letter Box Study Group (http://www.lbsg.org)

The American Pencil Collector's Society (http://www.pencilpages.com/misc/apcs.htm)

The Benefits of Boredom

This book has shown how most of us see boredom as the enemy, as something to fear and avoid:

- As workers, we worry that being bored means we are unfulfilled and unimportant – maybe it is time to look for another job?
- As employers, we fear that if our staff are bored, they will be less productive, may leave or even start using company resources unwisely.
- As mothers (or fathers), we possibly fear boredom the most. We are terrified to allow our kids to be bored because this reflects our own shortcomings as parents. We want them to be fulfilled, busy, creative and, above all, occupied, so when that whine of 'I'm bored!' singsongs through the house, our hearts sink and our very beings quiver with failure.
- As teachers or university lecturers, we fear the consequences of allowing our students to get 'bored'. We are indoctrinated with the belief that we must provide constant entertainment and stimulation in order for them to be able to learn. As educators, failure on our part to do this can only result in lost custom as our students (at university) choose other institutions or we risk poor ratings (in school).
- As a society, we seem especially concerned about allowing teenagers to get bored. We fear the havoc caused by their attempts at boredom-busting: the drugs, the stolen cars, the vandalism, etc.

Yet, there are many sections of society to whom boredom is not a dirty word. They like boredom because to them it represents income:

- The entertainment industry relies on our need to be entertained as a boredom-avoidance strategy. They want to fill our leisure time with boredom-busting (and costly) experiences, such as cinema and TV.
- The retail industry too relies on our need for new stuff to beat the boredom. Without our increasing boredom, there would be no need for new versions of iPods, Nintendo Wiis, etc. As an example, I remember when the new and exciting Tamagotchi virtual pet arrived when I was a teenager. This was an exciting toy, the zeitgeist of the day, and we played feverishly with them. Nowadays, the Tamagotchi is still around, but each year, a new and 'improved' version is brought out, presumably to cater for jaded tastes and pique new interest. We get bored with the old model so quickly, so to keep it fresh, a new one has to reappear with increasing frequency. This applies to all manner of white goods designed to entertain us. Mobile phones are another great example – how quickly we tire of these new-fangled devices and start yearning for more!
- Online gambling and shopping providers benefit hugely from our never-ending search for stimulation. We waste hours and hours on the internet, googling, fingers dancing over the keys, as we wait impatiently for pages to beam onto our screens to keep us occupied.

But why should only other parties benefit from our boredom? Why shouldn't we too learn to benefit from this great emotion that nature has bestowed within our repertoire? This chapter will show you how to harness the power of boredom – and it will also teach you never to fear that boredom again.

The Functions of Boredom

All emotions have a purpose; that is why we have them. For example, anger is invaluable for communicating to others our displeasure and also in motivating us to do something about perceived injustices. Sadness allows us to show others that we need looking after or help in some way. Disappointment tells us that we have been let down, whilst jealousy can make us ambitious as we strive to achieve what others have.

Boredom is a complex emotion that is (probably) not innate or primary (see Chapter 1, pages 6–8, for more on this). As a complex emotion, it is thought to have a complex range of functions or purposes. Researchers, psychologists and philosophers have long pondered the purpose of boredom, so here is as exhaustive a list as I can find of its proposed uses:

1. *Communication to others*

Displaying boredom on our faces sends a powerful message. Believe me, as a university lecturer, I know full well how that expression of boredom can send the heart of the recipient plummeting (*not* that I see it myself very often, of course!). We dread to see boredom written on the faces of those with whom we converse, whether they be our colleagues, friends, clients, or, indeed, students. Of all the emotions that we might not wish to see, boredom is probably top of the list (though anger is rarely welcome either).

When we realise that we have bored our audience, we know something has gone wrong with our message: we have delivered it wrongly, it has been misunderstood, it is inappropriate or in some way just not hitting the mark. We know all this from simply one surly expression of boredom. And this, then, is its invaluable function – to communicate the clear message that we are bored

– and, more specifically, that you are boring us. This allows us to plead with you to do something to change the situation so that we are no longer bored. Indeed, many recipients of this message will quickly adapt their approach, perhaps missing a few pages out, changing tack, asking questions or even calling it a day. Success! The emotion has served its communicative purpose.

Communicating our boredom is important even if the target of our communication isn't the one who is responsible for our boredom. In other words, the communicative purpose is not just to get someone to stop boring us. Imagine you are at an opera, a classical concert, a pop concert ... whatever bores you rigid; or in a meeting at work with new suppliers, or in a lecture at university on environmental issues. Conveying your boredom in these cases may be about communicating your beliefs, values and interests rather than as a means of getting the boredom to cease. A good example of this is when I took my young daughter to see a Gilbert and Sullivan operetta (*The Mikado* – jolly good it was too). She immediately honed in on the only other child in the audience, observed her for a while and then commented (rather disdainfully) on how bored she looked. 'That girl obviously doesn't appreciate Gilbert and Sullivan,' she fumed. From the expression on her face, the other girl had communicated not simply her boredom, but a whole set of information about herself, her attitudes and her interests too.

This, of course, is why we are often so careful to mask our boredom, lest others make judgements about us. We may well fake enthusiasm and interest in a range of dull activities in order to create an 'appropriate' image of ourselves. It certainly wouldn't do for our boss and colleagues to see that we are bored during a rather dull presentation on the Statistical Variants within Structural Equation Modelling; to communicate boredom might give away the secret that we do not find Structural Equation Modelling as exciting as they do.

2. *Adaptive mechanism against societal noise or information overload*[1]

According to this approach, boredom is a protective emotion that allows us to 'switch off' from some of the information and noise that we are constantly bombarded with. Imagine if we never got bored with anything! See what happens to Aidan in Box 11.1, below:

Box 11.1: Imagine never getting bored

Aidan woke up at 7 a.m. when his clock radio alarm went off. He bolted upright, fascinated to hear the traffic report beaming through the radio: 'This is an amazing invention! To think that thousands of people all over the city can hear this at the same time.'

It is some time before Aidan is able to get out of bed; he is too preoccupied with stroking the soft sheets, enjoying the décor of his bedroom (in which he has lived for 18 months now) and listening to the music now emanating from the radio. Eventually, he goes into the bathroom and steps into the shower – wow! Aidan is thrilled with the speed of the water jets, the scent of his shower gel, the feeling of warmth and wetness at the same time. He gets out and manages to get dressed ('What lovely clothes! So clever the way zips work! And Velcro, what an invention!').

At breakfast, Aidan avidly reads the cereal box from cover to cover ('Cool, this can help my heart!') and watches the kettle boil several times ('Fascinating!') before getting ready to leave the house. Before he leaves, he gets distracted by items on breakfast TV and by junk mail on the hall mat. It takes him four hours to leave for work that day.

> Stepping (eventually) out of the house, he marvels at the dew covering the grass, even bending right down to get a closer look. Twisting and turning, he examines it from every angle, fascinated by the way the sun glints through the wet droplets.

The case of Aidan demonstrates nicely what occurs when we simply don't get bored with stimuli. Everything continues to be exciting and interesting – and consequently, distracting (incidentally, Aidan's experiences might sound familiar to those who have the condition of Autistic Spectrum Disorder. The relationship between boredom and conditions like this is discussed earlier, see also pages 134–9). This is how the world is to toddlers for whom everything really is new and exciting – if I told you the tale of Aidan, a 3-year-old boy in Box 11.1, above, you would probably chuckle with recognition. Certainly, parents of small children know only too well how fascinating everyday detail is to them and how it can take an age just to walk down the road.

As adults, however, we live in a world in which we are constantly bombarded with so much information that we would not be able to cope without 'habituating' to much of it and switching off. Thus, we habituate or get used to the radio, junk mail, messages on the back of cereal boxes, etc. – all in order to free our minds from having to think about them. Getting bored with things allows this to happen and frees up our brains to concentrate on those aspects of life that demand more careful consideration. Hurrah, then, for boredom!

3. A 'shield against self-confrontation'[1]

On a deeper level, boredom can take a self-protective purpose. By claiming that we are 'bored' we can avoid confronting all kinds of less desirable parts of ourselves. For example, imagine that you are still in that lecture on Structural Equation Modelling, as mentioned on page 245. Everyone else around you is nodding sagely but the truth is you just don't understand it. Rather than admit this to yourself (or to others), it is far less damaging for your self-esteem to simply claim to find the whole thing 'boring'. It's not that you are stupid, oh no – it's just that the topic bores you.

This same logic can apply in any one of a range of settings – the opera is 'boring' (rather than admit to myself I find it unintelligible), that quality broadsheet newspaper is 'boring' (better that I should call it boring than admit that I don't always follow what it is saying), learning Spanish is 'boring' (better for my self-esteem than to acknowledge that I find it too hard to learn at my age), and so on and on. The label of boredom allows us to dismiss that which threatens our self-esteem. Teenagers may well do this too when they dismiss school as 'boring'.

4. To demonstrate a lack of 'presence' – that you don't want to be here

Oh, how teenagers are adept at using this function of boredom! Drag them on a family holiday, or a day trip to see Auntie Agnes's new tea cosy and there you see it – a teenager whose bored expression is clearly demonstrating a lack of 'presence'. They are there in body only, and don't they want you to know it! Their real self is very much elsewhere, and there is no better way to communicate this to Mum and Dad than with that surly and well-practised expression of boredom.

The point of this function is that we can go along (reluctantly) with the plans of others, but use this powerful expression to illustrate that we would rather be elsewhere – indeed, our minds *are* elsewhere. In other words, you can drag a teenager to Auntie Agnes, but you can't make them drink her tea.

Box 11.2: The President's kids who could not hide their boredom

© Jacquelyn Martin/AP/Press Association Images

Barack Obama may be the President of the United States, but to his teenage girls, Sasha and Malia, he is just Dad – and just as boring as any other parent. During a Thanksgiving tradition in which the President 'pardons' a turkey and saves it from becoming Thanksgiving dinner, the girls were seen to be 'shuffling awkwardly and rolling their eyes' – making no attempt to appear anything other than 'bored stiff' during their dad's attempts at humour. Indeed, they appeared 'rigid and disinterested' according to one media report, clearly indicating they were bored.[2]

5. Functions as an excuse or justification[3] – for example, for non-involvement or need for respite

'I am bored of this dull task – I need a break.' This can be a useful tool in many ways. It can communicate to others your boredom as a way of establishing your superiority: 'I am far too important and intelligent to be satisfied with this kind of activity'. Expressing boredom allows us to save face by distancing ourselves from the sort of people who would normally engage in the type of activity from which we wish to gain respite: 'I need someone to type up my letters – I find typing so boring'.

Boredom is also a fairly acceptable excuse for non-involvement in something within society; most people know what it is to feel bored so expressing boredom can sometimes provide a credible rationale for our behaviour. 'I find going to these social functions such a bore!' is acceptable, whereas 'I don't like going to these events because I never know what to say to anyone' indicates a flaw in our personality that the expression of boredom can conveniently cover up.

6. Evolutionary value

Boredom is thought to have an important evolutionary value in two regards: firstly, in terms of habituating to repeated stimuli (see 2) – if we did not habituate, or get used to information and stimulants, we would never be able to process everything and still function. This is put nicely by one researcher, who comments that 'it is adaptive to grow bored with stimuli that, after many repeated exposures, have never been associated with any type of positive reinforcement.'[3] In other words, as long as a stimulus proves itself not to be either dangerous or rewarding, it is appropriate that we should lose interest in it and turn our attention to other things that may either offer greater reward or need monitoring for danger.

The second evolutionary benefit is thought to be in our reaction to boredom: when bored, we seek out novel and new stimuli and it is this that is thought to be of evolutionary benefit. Would early man have invented fire, or the wheel, if he had not had time on his hands in which to develop new ideas? Similarly, today it is often boredom that causes us to seek out new things, develop new ideas and come up with new inventions (see 7) – all of which benefit man as a species.

7. Stimulates the 'production of fantasies, awakening creativeness'[4]

Boredom is a paradoxical phenomenon in that it can both stifle and stimulate creativity. In my own research, I found that some people claimed that being bored makes them so lethargic that they can't be bothered to do anything; indeed a quarter of my participants said that being bored makes them want to sleep (see also Chapter 2, page 40). Yet, a significant minority (20 per cent) claimed that being bored actually makes them more creative (see Chapter 2, page 43) – with 16 per cent claiming that being bored out of their minds helps them come up with new ideas at work (see Chapter 9, page 194)! So, how can this be? How can boredom stifle and stimulate creativity at the same time? This may depend on the type of boredom you experience – see Chapter 1, page 18 – but also on whether you daydream when bored.

Box 11.3: 'Time' to be bored: Creative achievements in prison

There are probably few more boring environments than the confines of prison. The boredom of prison life has been discussed earlier in this book (see pages 55–6), but there are also upsides to all that downtime. Would any of the following classic works have been achieved without this enforced downtime?

- Martin Luther King wrote 'Letter from a Birmingham Jail' whilst jailed for organising a non-violent protest against racial segregation in Alabama.

- O. Henry (pen name for William Sydney Porter), who is famous for, amongst other achievements, coining the phrase 'Banana Republic', wrote his famous short stories whilst in prison for embezzlement.

- *Don Quixote* by Miguel de Cervantes is considered to be the first modern European novel and its hero the original knight in shining armour. Cervantes penned part of his *magnum opus* whilst serving time for his debt troubles in seventeenth-century Spain.

- Oscar Wilde penned *De Profundis* (published posthumously) whilst imprisoned for two years for his 'indecency with men'.

- Nelson Mandela wrote *Conversations with Myself*, which includes letters and diary entries that he penned during his 27 years in prison.

Mind you, Adolf Hitler wrote *Mein Kampf* in jail too . . .

The idea that boredom can lead to a search for 'variety' was taken up in 2011 by Genevieve Bell,[5] who suggested that boredom might well boost creativity. When bored, individuals find it difficult to focus their attention on the task, and thought processes shift to other areas that can provide more stimulation. When the bored individual cannot physically escape the task to undertake a more engaging one, this attention shift is often from an external focus on the task to a more internal focus on inner thoughts, feelings and experiences. This inner focus allows a way of gaining the stimulation that is being craved and that is missing from the dull task. This internal focus could involve a search for new ways to carry out the task in order to make it more engaging[6] or might involve thinking about unrelated problems or ideas whose consideration is more appealing than the task at hand. It is this attention shifting that is termed 'daydreaming' and is thus a common by-product of boredom.[7] Indeed, previous research has shown that individuals use daydreaming to regulate boredom-induced tension,[8] thus suggesting that daydreaming is used as a coping strategy for dealing with the unpleasant state of boredom.[9]

In concordance with the above, Singer in 1975[10] described daydreaming as shifting attention from the external situation or problem to the internal representation of situations, memories, pictures, unresolved things, scenarios or future goals. Schank (1982)[11] proposed that daydreaming is a part of dynamic memory. Dynamic memory is the ability to re-evaluate information and possible solutions with the re-examining of a problem or unresolved scenario. The act of daydreaming can thus provide individuals with the opportunity to re-examine a problem or situation that is preoccupying their mind as many times as they wish, in varied ways, and each time incorporating new information and possible solutions. The benefit of daydreaming, then, is that seemingly illogical ideas can be explored in ways that may not be practically feasible and through this exploration a new or more suitable solution to problems or unresolved situations may be found. This, then, can lead to creative problem-solving[9] and thus suggests a link between daydreaming and creativity. More recently, this theme was taken up in an article in *Newsweek* (2009), which described daydreaming as a 'propitious mental state for creativity, insight and problem solving',[12] in which 'truly novel solutions and ideas emerge' due to the daydreaming brain being able to bring together unrelated facts and thoughts.

I recently tested these ideas out in an intriguing study[13] designed with one of my undergraduate students, Rebekkah Cadman. We wanted to see if boring tasks really do make people more creative. We got people really bored by asking them to copy out phone numbers from a phone book – the most boring and meaningless task we could think of. Because we were aware of the link of daydreaming with creativity, we also had a second condition in which we asked participants to read out phone numbers rather than copy them; this was because the writing task might hinder the daydreaming by interfering with the propensity for attention to wander. This was suggested by previous research; for example, doodling when bored improved cognitive performance for students and it is thought this was due to it interfering with daydreaming.[14]

© Lasse Kristensen/Shutterstock

We then gave the 170 participants various tasks of creativity; for example, we asked them to come up with as many uses for plastic cups as they could (a divergent creativity task inevitably affording many answers) and asked them to solve word problems called 'remote associations'; these consist of three stimulus words, and the task is to generate the fourth word that combined with each of the stimulus words. For example, the answer to the three stimulus words 'MEASURE', 'WORM' and 'VIDEO' would be 'TAPE' (tape measure, tape worm and video tape). This is a convergent task of creative potential, where there is one right answer rather than infinite numbers of possible answers.

The results suggested that participants came up with significantly more answers to a creative task following a boring task than without such a boring task. The number of answers (and correct ones in the case of the convergent test) also differed significantly between the reading and writing conditions such that more answers were produced in the reading condition. This adds evidence to the belief that boredom can lead to an increase in creativity across a range of creative tasks. Dull tasks involving reading rather than writing can, in some circumstances, lead to even greater increases in creativity than similarly dull writing tasks. This is thought to be due to the greater possibility for daydreaming afforded by reading compared with writing tasks.

1. Motivating force/catalyst for action

Related to the above is the idea that boredom possesses motivational properties. This is perhaps the strongest defence of an otherwise apparently negative emotion. The philosopher Nietzsche commented that creative individuals 'require a lot of boredom if their work is to succeed',[15] whilst boredom researcher Gaylin declared, 'Boredom is an alerting phenomenon that all is not well and something must be done'.[16] In this way, boredom serves as a 'catalyst for action'[4]; it causes us to seek challenges, be creative, look for new directions, etc. Boredom gets us going again and in this sense can, somewhat paradoxically, be an energising force. By avoiding boredom, or escaping it, we can change our lives for the better (more on how to do this later in the chapter).

2. A contributor to self-reflection

Some argue that it is only through boredom that individuals tend to engage in introspection and self-reflection. When we are busy, occupied and fulfilled, we rarely stop to ponder on our abilities, attitudes and qualities; it is only when we have the luxury of being bored that we have time for such introspection. Of course, this is assuming such self-reflection is a good thing and leads us to become better people, with better ideas, qualities, attitudes, etc (see the case study in Box 11.4, below).

Box 11.4: Bored and introspective

Jamie was bored. He sat at his computer at work staring at the report that needed to be completed. It really ought to be about ten pages long and so far he had completed two pages – and that was over two days and with numerous coffee breaks, etc. As his mind wandered, he started to think about other matters intruding into his mind: what would he have for lunch? Should he buy the new DVD he was thinking of? Did Angela in the cubicle opposite like him? Then he started thinking about his job, his work, his role in the office . . . He began to wonder what he was doing, wasting time sitting writing a report that should take a day, maximum, to complete. Why was it taking so long? Why did he find this job so unappealing? Was he really cut out for this sort of work?

Jamie began to think about those aspects of the job that he enjoyed and found stimulating, and the ones that totally numbed him with boredom. He began to think about why some tasks bored him, and whether the interesting bits of the job outweighed the boring bits. He started to wonder if he should be looking at a career move – perhaps another job would stimulate him more so that he wasn't bored like this? Or maybe he should gain some new skills – perhaps this report was too taxing and that was why it was boring him.

Such a view is backed up by researchers, who have discovered those people who are more prone to boredom are more likely to engage in self-reflection.[17] This is thought to be particularly true regarding self-reflection that relates to self-evaluation and self-criticism. Indeed, one study of students found that the vast majority of those surveyed felt that boredom could be beneficial – and that the most positive aspect of the emotion was that it provided opportunities for thought and reflection.[18]

3. Encourages pro-social behaviour

According to a study entitled 'Bored George Helps Others: A Pragmatic Meaning-Regulation Hypothesis on Boredom and Prosocial Behaviour',[19] boredom can inspire people to seek out ways of being altruistic and empathetic and to engage in pro-social tasks, particularly more difficult ones such as donating to charity, volunteering or even giving blood. According to Wijnand van Tilburg, co-author of the paper from the University of Limerick, when we are bored, we lack meaningfulness and thus have a yearning for meaningful activities. Pro-social behaviours can give us the meaningfulness that we seek. Through a series of seven studies, the researchers found that boredom increases pro-social motivation that impacts on positive behaviours lasting far beyond the length of time of the boring activity itself.

How to Harness the Power of Boredom

Hopefully, by now you are convinced of the benefits of boredom, but how can you turn this boredom into a positive, motivating, creative force? There are two kinds of boredom that can be harnessed: existential boredom (when life itself is boring) or task-specific boredom (when what we are doing right now is boring). Here is how you can harness the power of both kinds of boredom:

Existential boredom:

1. Look around you as if you are in a new place. What can you see? Gaze at the world with fresh eyes. This is what children do when they find animal shapes in clouds – they are just looking at clouds, but seeing something fantastic within them. We can do this too by looking at the world around us as if viewing it for the first time. Marvel at the details; look for things that are exciting and innovative (see also the section on mindfulness in Chapter 7). Never mind not sweating the small stuff – delight in the small stuff and find something interesting everywhere you go. How can you be bored?
2. Become curious. Find interest in all that is around you by emulating young children. Toddlers rarely get bored because they are curious about everything – how does this work? What happens if I do this? Can this be taken apart? What is this made from? Such curiosity prevents boredom from kicking in by making the dullest things more interesting. Researchers have shown that being curious not only helps us remember the things we are curious about, but also helps us recall the things we are not curious about. It is thought that curiosity puts our brains into a state that is helpful for memory and learning – which helps maintain our interest in things that might otherwise have seemed boring.[20] Curiosity also brings its own benefits. According to Todd Kashdan, author of *Curious? Discover the Missing Ingredient to a Fulfilling Life*, learning, growing and exploring makes us happier.
3. Talk to people, find out about their lives and what they do. Other people lead surprisingly interesting lives – if only we can be bothered to enquire about them.

4. Learn something; take up a new hobby. It is hard to be bored when you are busy. Find something that grabs you, engages you – something that meets your need for the stimulation lacking in your life. It might be something that involves risk-taking to satisfy your need for extra stimulation; extreme sports are often taken up by those searching to introduce a relatively safe element of risk into their lives (see also pages 53–4).

5. Turn the TV off. That goes for the internet, Facebook and Wii too. These offer two-dimensional stimulation when our brains need three or four dimensions to be stimulated in order to feel satisfied. We cannot meet our need for neural stimulation by virtually visiting the seaside; we need to smell the sea, feel the sand beneath our toes, hear the seagulls and taste the salty air. Living life through virtual, 2D formats will lead to an increase in boredom, so get out and about to immerse yourself fully in life!

6. Take a digital Sabbath – this is a new trend to turn off all electronic media and get 'unplugged' for one day each week. Embrace life free from distractions and from viewing the world through a screen. You can take this a step further with a digital detox holiday; leave your phone and devices at home and enjoy some time when you are able to be at one with yourself and your surroundings.

Box 11.5: Digital detox

Digital detoxing is a growing trend. Increasing numbers of organisations and individuals are beginning to see the value of a digital sabbatical and the trend is predicted to grow even bigger over the next few years. Randi Zuckerberg, sister of Facebook founder Mark, recently advocated a digital-free Sunday, claiming she had reached the point 'when rather than owning a computer, a phone and a tablet, the devices were owning me'.[21] She told the *Daily Mail* in 2013 that she had stopped living in the moment and a weekly digital detox helped redress the balance.

Car manufacturer Daimler recently introduced an out-of-office auto-delete option, whereby all emails that arrive in staff inboxes whilst they are on vacation are automatically deleted,[22] thus encouraging employees, at a time when more than 4 in 10 Americans reported checking work email while on vacation,[23] to take a 'disconnected' break. Other companies, such as Intel in the UK and Cellular, Deloitte and Touche in the US, have been encouraging email-free Fridays for years.[24]

With 61 per cent of US travellers saying they use social media whilst on vacation[25] and 84 per cent of respondents in an international poll claiming they couldn't go for one day without their smartphones,[26] more and more travellers are looking to disconnect whilst vacationing. Seventy-seven per cent of travellers believe that time spent without gadgets would actually liberate them.[23] The *Japan Times* reported in December 2014 that whilst many tourists go to great lengths to always be digitally accessible, a growing number of gadget-weary travellers in Japan are ditching their phones and tablets for 'digital detox holidays'.[27] Because stressed-out executives find it so difficult to log off, digital detox retreats (also known as 'black hole breaks'), such as Camp Grounded in northern California and the Westin Dublin Hotel in Ireland, are springing up across the globe.[23]

7. Change your job. If you are suffering from chronic boredom at work, listen to what your boredom is telling you. In these austere times we are all grateful for a job and the joy of having a fulfilling occupation may not be the top priority. But there is no harm in trying to make changes. What is it about your job

that is boring? Can the tasks themselves be changed or must a new job be sought? What do you need to do, e.g. further training, to enable a career change?

8. Boredom is the neediness for something 'exciting' to happen. It's the craving for drama, the desire for experiencing physical sensations. To reduce the boredom in your life, you need to acknowledge and satisfy those needs in a safe way. Starting a riot would be one way to bring drama into your life, but here we are talking about safe, socially desirable actions. Research shows that engaging in 'pro-social' behaviour (behaviour that helps other people) can satisfy the craving for stimulation that comes through boredom. So, give blood, volunteer in a residential home, visit the sick, start a campaign, save the world . . . any of these 'do-good' actions can do the trick.

9. Boredom is the inability to accept life for what it is, as it is, in this very moment. Bored people are constantly looking over their shoulder for something more interesting to come along. They channel hop in the hope of something better, not just in front of the TV, but in life itself – they change romantic partners, clothes, cars, phones and friends constantly so as to be sure that they are not missing out on something more exciting out there. Advertisers rely on this need for novelty and the fear of missing out by constantly reminding us of all we are missing. We can stop the cycle by refusing to play. Learn to be content with what you have and resist the urge to keep checking the other side to see if the grass is greener (it probably isn't).

10. Get back to nature. According to Dr Teresa Belton of the School of Education and Lifelong Learning, University of East Anglia, 'Nature is the antidote to boredom'.[28] This is because, she says, natural environments provide stimulation that does not require focused attention, in contrast to most of the stimulation in our day-to-day lives that often requires

sustained effort. In the natural environment it is easier to let our thoughts go with the flow, to allow ourselves to become distracted by birds, animals, leaves or flowers, and to enjoy gentle, slow-moving sensation without the need to work at it. If you want to try this, be warned: at first it can seem a bit of a culture-shock compared to the fast-moving stimuli we are used to, but once we allow the slower world of nature to 'turn us on', we can adapt and learn to appreciate a less stimulus-heavy environment. Once we learn to need less stimulation, we are on the way to lowering our boredom threshold.

Task-specific Boredom

1. Treat boredom, such as when waiting in a queue, as luxury time. We live such busy lives that the joy of being able to take a breath sometimes should be pounced on with delight. Use the queuing time in the supermarket or the traffic jam time in the car to do something useful: think (over half of respondents in my research think when they are bored), write a shopping list, text a friend, solve the Middle East Crisis . . . anything that makes creative use of the time will eliminate the boredom.

2. Get back into the 'flow'. Founder and co-director of the Quality of Life Research Center (QLRC) Mihaly Csikszentmihalyi[29] is well known for the notion of 'flow' in creativity. He describes flow as 'being completely involved in an activity for its own sake . . . time flies . . . Your whole being is involved, and you're using your skills to the utmost.' In his book, *Beyond Boredom and Anxiety: Experiencing Flow in Work and Play*, Csikszentmihalyi examines motivation based on a study of a half-dozen groups of people involved in pursuits such as rock climbing, composing, dancing and playing chess. He chose these groups in an effort to understand more fully what motivates people to stop

watching television shows and instead engage in activities that are extremely challenging or offer few external rewards (like writing a poem, or pondering a chess move). They all managed to get into the 'flow' and this is what motivated them, he found. Find your own flow by truly engaging with the task in hand. Aim to do it as well as you can, as creatively, as skilfully – and enjoy the challenge of achieving that.

3. Refocus your attention by finding interest in the task at hand. Tasks are more likely to be boring if they are repetitive or routine. Try to make them less so by finding a different way to do the task, by breaking the task down into smaller parts or by focusing on the end result. Bored people feel their actions are meaningless and so they are motivated to engage in meaningful behaviour (see Box 11.6, below), so search for something meaningful in what you are doing.

Box 6: The antidote to boredom is not fun but meaningfulness?

One Story Ministries is the non-profit publishing arm of Pear Orchard Presbyterian Church (PCA) in Ridgeland, MS, USA. John C. Kwasny, Ph.D is its director and he wrote a blog about how to challenge the boredom that Christian children might experience during Sunday school. Whilst his comments might be aimed at religious teachings, they could apply equally well to any kind of teaching environment. Kwasny laments the teachers who aim to make their Sunday class the most 'exciting' in the area – teachers who want their charges 'to have more FUN here than they have doing anything else, anywhere else'.[30] This is an impossible ambition, given the wealth of other, more exciting options constantly available out there for kids today, he feels.

Whilst he doesn't advocate dull, unengaging teaching, Kwasny argues the antidote to boredom is not fun, but meaningfulness. The teachers described earlier in this book who use drumming to teach maths or who want to dumb down Shakespeare to make it more engaging (see pages xx) are probably missing the point if Kwasny's view is correct (and I am inclined to feel that he certainly has a point): 'When teachers are excited about what they are teaching, it is contagious for our children. It's not about telling more jokes, or doing a tap dance, or trying to be silly.'[30] It is about injecting meaningfulness into the material and getting kids excited about that.

4. Change the scenery: a change is as good as a rest, or so they say. Going for a quick walk, a comfort break or having a water cooler moment can help break the monotony and refocus attention back to the task in hand.

5. Reward yourself for doing the boring stuff. Every half an hour on the dull task earns a reward. Rewards could be a break, something edible, a chat, sending a text … even allocating time to do a more rewarding task. This is the operation of the 'Premack Principle',[31] which states that we can motivate ourselves to do the less desirable tasks with the promise of doing more desirable ones as a reward.

6. Eliminate distractions. When bored, we are constantly seeking stimulation so even the slightest distraction can seem appealing when competing with a dull task. Thus, the ironing can be a desirable alternative when faced with a pile of reports to write at home. This principle can be used to your advantage by scheduling the really boring jobs alongside the slightly less boring ones; the appeal of the slightly less boring ones will jump instantly!

7. Do something more stimulating at the same time. Sometimes

we can provide the missing extra stimulation we crave by adding another dimension to our physical sensations whilst we labour on the boring task. Playing music, for example, can meet this need, as can having the TV on in the background – when your teenager maintains the TV helps them concentrate on their homework, they could be right! Chewing gum provides the extra dimension for some people – it is all about finding the extra stimulation that works for you and fits in with the environment (having the TV blaring is not always a practical solution in a work environment!).

Concluding Comments

Having read this book, you might be left feeling a little confused. After all, on the one hand I have presented a fairly thorough argument for the dark side of boredom; all the doom and gloom associated with being bored at work, leisure and in the classroom. And yet on the other hand, I am advocating that boredom is good for us and we need more of it. So, which is boredom – a necessary evil or a force for good?

In fact it is both of these things. Too much boredom is harmful, but then so is too little. Boredom is the most paradoxical of emotions; in order to reduce the harmful effects of boredom in our lives, we need to increase our boredom. If we want to stop being so bored, we need to be a little bit *more* bored.

This book has argued throughout that the obsession society seems to have today with eliminating the merest hint of boredom in our lives means we are becoming so accustomed to filling every moment with stimulation that we are developing a lower threshold for boredom, which in turn means we bore more easily. And the more bored we get, the more we try to fill that boredom with our 'junk food devices'; just as junk food provides easily accessible but empty calories, so our devices provide easily accessible but empty stimulation. Filling up on junk food means we are unable to eat the healthy stuff that provides the vitamins and nutrients we need to develop; trying to cure our boredom with a junk diet of passive electronic stimulation means we are unable to access the more active stimulation that leads to healthier development. And so boredom begets boredom.

The cure, then, is to allow downtime back into our lives. We must stop over-stimulating ourselves and our children so we become less reliant on a fast-paced, constantly changing stream of novel stimuli to keep the ennui at bay. We need to reduce our cravings for this unhealthy diet and start to enjoy the boost that downtime can give us. In other words, we need to embrace, not fear, boredom.

I dream of a society where people stare into space, gaze out of train windows, turn off their electronic devices, stop feeding their kids with stimulating junk, shun the TV and computer and simply live life in 3D again; a society where, in our downtime, we engage with our minds and souls, or even with each other. I dream of seeing real downtime incorporated into our working day, where we can cut the virtual apron strings tying us down to dependency on passive stimulation and free ourselves to soar within our own creativity and imagination.

Bored is good. Downtime has its Upside.

Notes

Introduction

1. Frostrup, Mariella, 'Luxury Travel: Simple Pleasures', *The Times*, 25 January 2014 (http://www.thetimes.co.uk/tto/public/article 3985064.ece).

Chapter One: The Quest for Engagement: What is Boredom?

1. Eastwood, J. D., Cavaliere, C., Fahlman, S. A. and Eastwood, A. E., 'A Desire for Desires: Boredom and Its Relation to Alexithymia', *Personality and Individual Differences*, 42 (2007), 1035–45.

2. 'Britons Bored for More Than Two Years of Their Lives', *Daily Telegraph*, 20 July 2009 (http://www.telegraph.co.uk/news/uk news/5868721/Britons-bored-for-more-than-two-years-of-their-lives.html).

3. Anthony, Andrew, 'One Big Yawn: Boredom is Not Just a State of Mind', *Observer*, 17 July 2011 (http://www.theguardian.com/books/2011/jul/17/boredom-peter-toohey-andrew-anthony).

4. http://www.telegraph.co.uk/science-news/8160622/Computer-identifies-the-most-boring-day-in-history.html

5. http://www.thestudentroom.co.uk/showthread.php?t=2522948&page=2

6. Mann, S., 'Counting Window Panes: An Investigation into Boredom-reducing Strategies Used by Teachers and the Causes and Consequences of Their Workplace Boredom', presentation at the Annual Conference of the Division of Occupational Psychology of the British Psychological Society, Glasgow, January 2006.

7. Wallbott, H. G., 'Bodily Expressions of Emotion', *European Journal of Psychology*, *28* (1998), 879–96.

8. Gosline, Anna, 'Bored?' *Scientific American*, 27 December 2007.

9. Fisher, C., 'Boredom at Work: A Neglected Concept', *Human Relations 46* (1993), 395–417.

10. Maslow, A., *Motivation and Personality* (New York: Harper & Row, 1954).

11. James, W., 'What Is an Emotion?' *Mind*, *9* (1884), 188–205.

12. Dutton, D. C. and Aron, A. P., 'Some Evidence for Heightened Sexual Attraction Under Conditions of High Anxiety, *Journal of Personality and Social Psychology*, *30* (1974), 10–17.

13. Schachter, S. and Singer, J., 'Cognitive, Social, and Physiological Determinants of Emotional State', *Psychological Review*, *69* (1962), 379–99.

14. London and Monell, 1974, in Damrad-Frye, Robin and Laird, James D., 'The Experience of Boredom. The Role of the Self-Perception of Attention', *Journal of Personality and Social Psychology*, volume 57: 2 (1989), 315–20.

15. Damrad-Frye and Laird, 'The Experience of Boredom: The Role of the Self-perception of Attention,' volume 57: 2 (1989), 315–20.

16. Pekrun, Reinhard, Goetz, Thomas, Daniels, Lia M., Stupnisky, Robert H. and Perry, Raymond P., 'Boredom in Achievement Settings: Exploring Control–value Antecedents and Performance Outcomes of a Neglected Emotion', *Journal of Educational Psychology*, volume 102: 3 (August 2010), 531–49.

17. Hebb, D. O., *A Textbook of Psychology* (London: W. B. Saunders Company, 1996).

18. Mikulas, W. and Vodanovich, S., 'The Essence of Boredom', *The Psychological Record, 43* (1993), 3–12.

19. Pilkington, Ed, 'Bush's Great Ambition: Wealthy Boredom', *Guardian*, 3 September 2007.

20. Csíkszentmihályi, Mihály, *Flow: The Psychology of Optimal Experience* (New York: Harper & Row, 1990).

21. Moran, Joe, 'The Ideas Corner: A Chronic Malady', *New Statesman*, 4 September 2006.

22. Vodanovich, S. J., 'Psychometric Measures of Boredom: A Review of the Literature', *Journal of Psychology*, volume 137: 6 (2003), 569–95.

23. Goetz, Thomas, Frenzel, Anne C., Hall, Nathan C., Nett, Ulrike E., Pekrun, Reinhard and Lipnevich, Anastasiya A., 'Types of Boredom: An Experience Sampling Approach', *Motivation and Emotion,* volume 38: 3 (2014), 401–19.

24. 'Boredom: An Emotional Experience Distinct from Apathy, Anhedonia, or Depression', *Journal of Social and Clinical Psychology*, volume 30: 6 (2011), 647–66.

25. German, D. and Latkin, C. A., 'Boredom, Depressive Symptoms, and HIV Risk Behaviors Among Urban Injection Drug Users', *AIDS Behavior*, volume 16: 8 (November 2012), 2244–50.

26. Barbalet, J. M., 'Boredom and Social Meaning', *British Journal of Psychology*, volume 50: 4 (1999), 631–46.

27. Van Tilburg, W. A. P. and Igou, E. R., 'On Boredom: Lack of Challenge and Meaning as Distinct Boredom Experiences', *Motivation and Emotion, 36* (2012), 181–94.

28. Van Tilburg, Wijnand A. P., Igou, Eric R. and Sedikides, Constantine, 'In Search of Meaningfulness: Nostalgia as an Antidote to Boredom', *Emotion,* volume 13: 3 (June 2013), 450–61.

Chapter Two: What Do We Do When We Are Bored (Or, Why Boredom is Propping Up the Confectionery Industry)

1. Mann, S, 'A Mars a Day Keeps the Boredom Away?', BPS Division of Occupational Psychology Annual Conference, Chester, January 2012.

2. Abramson, E. E. and Stinson, S. G., 'Boredom and Eating in Obese and Non-obese Individuals', *Addictive Behaviours*, volume 2: 4 (1977), 181–5.

3. 'Comfort and "Boredom"-eating Rife', Monday 23 August 2004 (http://news.bbc.co.uk/1/hi/health/3590086.stm).

4. Koball, A. M., Meers, M. R., Storfer-Isser, A., Domoff, S. E. and Musher-Eizenman, D. R., 'Eating When Bored: Revision of the Emotional Eating Scale With a Focus on Boredom', *Health Psychology 31* (2011), 521–24.

5. Abramson and Stinson, 'Boredom and Eating in Obese and Non-obese Individuals', *Addictive Behaviors*, volume 2: 4 (1977), 181–85.

6. Janko, M. Lozar Prolegomena, 'Boredom with Husserl and Beyond', *Prolegomena*, volume 13: 1 (2014), 107–121.

7. Toohey P., *Boredom – A Lively History* (New Haven: Yale University Press, 2012).

8. Harmon, Katherine, 'Addicted to Fat: Overeating May Alter the Brain as Much as Hard Drugs', *Scientific American*, 28 March 2010 (http://www.scientificamerican.com/article/addicted-to-fat-eating).

9. Sullivan, S., Cloninger, C.R., Przybeck, T. R. and Klein, S., 'Personality Characteristics in Obesity and Relationship with Successful Weight Loss', *International Journal of Obesity 31* (2007), 669–74.

10. Lovett, Richard, 'Coffee: The Demon Drink?' *New Scientist*, *2518*, 24 September 2005.

11. Kelly, Jon, 'Coffee Addiction: Do People Consume Too Much Caffeine?' *BBC News Magazine*, 23 May 2013 (http://www.bbc.co.uk/news/magazine-22530625).

12. Loke, Wing Hong, 'Effects of Caffeine on Mood and Memory', *Physiology & Behavior*, volume 44: 3 (1988), 367–72.

13. Einöther, Suzanne J. L., 'Caffeine as an Attention Enhancer: Reviewing Existing Assumptions', *Psychopharmacoloy*, volume 225: 2 (January 2013), 251–74.

14. Spiegel, Alix, 'Bored? Try Doodling to Keep the Brain on Task', 12 March 2009 (http://www.npr.org/templates/story/story.php?storyId=101727048).

15. Francis, Mandy, 'What Your Doodles Really Say About You', *Daily Mail*, 12 September 2011 (http://www.dailymail.co.uk/femail/article-2036328/What-doodles-really-say-Arrows-ambition-flowers-family.html).

16. Andrade, Jackie, 'What Does Doodling Do?' *Applied Cognitive Psychology*, volume 24: 1 (January 2010), 100–06.

17. http://www.musicworksforyou.com/news-and-charts/news/202-is-music-a-legal-drug-that-improves-performance

18. Ünal, Ayça Berfu, Steg, Linda and Epstude, Kai, 'The Influence of Music on Mental Effort and Driving Performance', *Accident Analysis and Prevention*, volume 48 (September 2012), 271–8.

19. Naish, John, 'It's NOT a Sign of Boredom. It DOESN'T Boost Oxygen in the Brain. So Why DO We Yawn?' *Daily Mail*, 11 December 2011 (http://www.dailymail.co.uk/news/article-2072877/Its-NOT-sign-boredom-It-DOESNT-boost-oxygen-brain-So-DO-yawn-html).

20. http://www.dailytech.com/Study+Workers+Spend+60+or+More+of+Day+Web+Surfing+for+Personal+Reasons/article29856.htm

21. Websense, Inc. Web@Work (2006) (http:www.securitymanagement.com/archive/library/websense_technofile0906.pdf).

22. Jaschik, Scott, 'Texting in Class', insidehighered.com, 21 October 2013(https://www.insidehighered.com/news/2013/10/21/study-documents-how-much-students-text-during-class).

23. 'Americans and Their Cell Phones', Pew Research Center, 15 August 2011 (http://www.pewinternet.org/2011/08/15/americans-and-their-cell-phones).

24. Hunt, Daniel, Atkin, David and Krishnan, Archana, 'The Influence of Computer-Mediated Communication Apprehension on Motives for Facebook Use', *Journal of Broadcasting & Electronic Media*, volume 56:2 (2012), 187–202.

25. Gross, Doug, 'Have Smartphones Killed Boredom (And Is That Good)?' CNN, 26 September 2012 (http://edition.cnn.com/2012/09/25/tech/mobile/oms-smartphones-boredom).

26. Zillmannb, Dolf, 'Using Television to Alleviate Boredom and Stress: Selective Exposure as a Function of Induced Excitational States', *Journal of Broadcasting*, volume 28: 1 (1984), 1–20.

27. http://sleepfoundation.org/sleep-topics/drowsy-driving

28. Massey, Ray, 'Two Million Exhausted Drivers a Year Falling Asleep at the Wheel', 12 September 2007 (http://www.dailymail.co.uk/news/article-481469/Two-million-exhausted-drivers-year-falling-asleep-wheel.html).

29. Gordon, Bryony, 'In Hot Water? Have a Bath and Relax', *Daily Telegraph*, 14 October 2002 (http://www.telegraph.co.uk/health/alternativemedicine/4711987/In-hot-water-Have-a-bath-and-relax.html).

30. Mann, S., 'Counting Window Panes: An Investigation into Boredom-reducing Strategies Used by Teachers and the Causes and Consequences of Their Workplace Boredom', presentation at the Annual Conference of the Division of Occupational Psychology of the British Psychological Society, Glasgow, January 2006.

31. 'Teachers Reveal Exam Hall Games', BBC News Channel, 24 May 2004 (http://news.bbc.co.uk/1/hi/education/3742915.stm).

32. Harvey, Joan, Heslop, Simon and Thorpe, Neil, 'The Categorisation of Drivers in Relation to Boredom', *Transportation Planning and Technology*, volume 34:1 (June 2011), 51–69.

33. De Lacey, Martha, 'Trying to Impress a Man? Steer Clear of the Sales. Men Get Bored Shopping After Just 26 MINUTES... Women After 2 Hours', *Daily Mail*, 5 July 2013 (http:www.dailymail.co.uk/femail/article-2356781/Men-bored-just-26-MINUTES-shopping--women-2-hours.html).

34. Grosser, Travis J., Lopez-Kidwell, Virginie, (Joe) Labianca, Giuseppe and Ellwardt, Lea, 'Hearing It Through the Grapevine: Positive and Negative Workplace Gossip', *Organizational Dynamics 41* (2012), 52–61.

35. Call Centre Helper.com (http://www.callcentrehelper.com/how-to-curb-call-centre-gossip-29989.htm).

36. Webb, Jonathan, 'Do People Choose Pain Over Boredom?' BBC News, 4 July 2014 (http://www.bbc.co.uk/news/science-environment-28130690).

Chapter Three: Drugs, Truancy and Riots: What Boredom Does to Us

1. Pelisek, Christine, 'Inside the "Boredom" Killing That Has Shocked Oklahoma', the dailybeast.com, 23 August 2013 (http://www.thedailybeast.com/articles/2013/08/23/inside-the-boredom-killing-that-has-shocked-oklahoma.html).

2. Clemons, Steve, 'We Were Bored... So We Decided to Kill Somebody', the atlantic.com, 20 August 2013 (http://www.theatlantic.com/national/archive/2013/08/we-were-bored-so-we-decided-to-kill-somebody/278858).

3. 'Disbelief in Some Quarters After NRA Calls For Armed Guards at Every School, Blames Movies', U.S. News, 21 December 2012 (http://www.nbcnews.com/health/mental-health/boredom-blamed-murders-true-killing-impulse-f6C10963043).

4. Connors, Bob, 'Teens Killed Because They Were Bored: Judge', nbcconnecticut.com, 2 December 2010 (http://www.nbccon necticut.com/news/local/Teens-Killed-Because-They-Were-Bored-Judge-111189404.html).

5. Roberts, Georgett, Cusma, Kathryn and Fredericks, Bob, '"Bored" Teen Charged with Murder After Blaze Kills Cop', *New York Post*, 11 April 2014 (http://nypost.com/2014/04/011/bored-teen-charged-with-murder-in-blaze-that-killed-cop).

6. 'GCSO: Suspects Killed Young Father Because They Were "Bored"', Wyff4.com, 22 May 2014 (http://www.wyff4.com/news/gcso-suspects-killed-young-father-because-they-were-bored/26103478).

7. Wardell, Anne, 'Boredom Didn't Make Injury Employer's Fault', lawchat.com.au, 27 August 2012 (http://www.lawchat.com.au/index.php/boredom-didnt-make-injury-employers-fault).

8. Rogers, Simon, Sedghi, Ami and Evans, Lisa, 'UK Riots: Every Verified Incident – Interactive Map', *Guardian*, 11 August 2011.

9. Johns, Lindsay, 'The London Riots One Year On: What Still Needs to Change If We Are to Avoid a Repeat of Last Year', dailymail.co.uk, 6 August 2012 (http://www.dailymail.co.uk/debate/article-2184359/London-riots-year-What-needs-change--.html).

10. Ross, Tim, 'Rioting Teenagers "Were Bored in Long Summer Holiday"', *Daily Telegraph*, 29 August 2011 (http://www.telegraph.co.uk/news/uknews/8728524/Rioting-teenagers-were-bored-in-long-summer-holiday.html).

11. 'Arson Investigators Say Boredom Spurred Most Suspects in Region's Wildfires', Fox News, 16 November 2001 (http://www.foxnews.com/story/2001/11/16/arson-investigators-say-boredom-spurred-most-suspects-in-region-wildfires).

12. 'Big Increase in Arson Attacks', BBC News, 20 August 2008 (http://news.bbc.co.uk/1/hi/england/7572398.stm).

13. Thalji, Jamal and Stanley, Kameel, 'Police Say Boredom Sparked

Teens' St. Petersburg Arson Spree', *Tampa Bay Times*, 2 February 2009.

14. 'Boredom to Blame for Attacks on Bus', Get Reading.co.uk, 22 June 2011 (http://www.getreading.co.uk/news/local-news/boredom-blame-attacks-bus-4212830).

15. Sullivan, Gail, '"Bored" Man Sentenced to 21 Months for Aiming Laser Pointer at Police Helicopter', *Washington Post*, 5 August 2014 (http://www.washingtonpost.com/news/morning-mix/wp/2014/08/05/bored-man-sentenced-to-21-months-for-aiming-laser-pointer-at-police-helicopter).

16. Mercer, K. B. and Eastwood, J. D., 'Is Boredom Associated with Problem Gambling Behaviour: It Depends What You Mean By "Boredom"', *International Gambling Studies*, volume 10: 1 (2010), 91–104.

17. Smith, R. W. and Preston, F. W., 'Vocabularies of Motives for Gambling Behaviour', *Sociological Perspectives*, 27 (1984), 325–48.

18. McNeilly, D. P. and Burke, W. J., 'Late Life Gambling: The Attitudes and Behaviours of Older Adults', *Journal of Gambling Studies*, 16 (2000), 393–415.

19. Boffey, Daniel, 'Boredom Led to My Gambling, Says Rooney', *Mail on Sunday*, 22 July 2006 (http://www.dailymail.co.uk/news/article-397114/Boredom-led-gambling-says-Rooney.html).

20. Bargdill, Richard, 'The Study of Life Boredom', *Journal of Phenomenological Psychology*, volume 31: 2 (2000), 188–219.

21. 'Boredom "Fuels Teen Alcohol Use"', BBC News, 4 August 2009 (http://news.bbc.co.uk/1/hi/health/8181289.stm).

22. St Clair, Jane, 'Boredom and Substance Abuse: A Dangerous Combination' (http://www.crchealth.com/addiction/drug-addiction-rehab/drug-addiction-rehab-2/home-2/drug_addiction/boredom-substance-abuse-a-dangerous-combination).

23. Jones, Cass, 'Paul Gascoigne: Boredom Drove Me Back to Drink',

   Guardian, 21 March 2013 (http://www.theguardian.com/football/2013/mar/21/paul-gascoigne-alcohol-addiction).

24. http://www.dailymail.co.uk/news/article-2583426/Drug-addict-dialled-999-begging-police-sent-prison-BORED-living-Church-Stretton.html

25. Patoine, Brenda, 'Desperately Seeking Sensation: Fear, Reward, and the Human Need for Novelty Neuroscience Begins to Shine Light on the Neural Basis of Sensation-Seeking', dana.org, 13 October 2009 (http://www.dana.org/News/Details.aspx?id=43484).

26. Ericson, John, 'Extreme Sports Cause 40,000 Head And Neck Injuries Each Year: How Can Organizers And Parents Improve Safety?' *Medical Daily*, 16 March 2014 (http://www.medicaldaily.com/extreme-sports-cause-40000-head-and-neck-injuries-each-year-how-can-organizers-and-parents-improve).

27. 'Hardwired for Thrills – Extreme Sports: Faster, Riskier, More Outrageous', Canadian Broadcasting Corporation Online Archives, 25 February 1998 (http://www.cbc.ca/archives/entry/extreme-sports-hardwired-for-thrills).

28. 'Living on the Edge: Extreme Sports and their Role in Society', Summit Post Org, 2006 (http://www.summitpost.org/living-on-the-edge-extreme-sports-and-their-role-in-society/214107).

29. 'OJ Turns to Baseball Out of Boredom', 1 PageSix.com, 5 April 2010 (http://pagesix.com/2010/04/15/oj-turns-to-baseball-out-of-boredom).

30. 'Report Says Castle Huntly Prisoners Bored Due to "Poor Quality of Recreation"', *Daily Record*, 5 September 2012 (http://www.dailyrecord.co.uk/news/scottish-news/prison-inspector-worried-that-prisoners-are-bored-1304711).

31. Ben's Prison Blog – Lifer on the Loose (http://prisonerben.blogspot.co.uk/2010/04/riot-and-reform.html).

32. Morris, Steven, 'Family of Murdered Prisoner Express Shock at

Actions of "Bored" Inmates', guardian.com, 20 September 2013 (http://www.theguardian.com/uk-news/2013/sep/20/subhan-anwar-murder-prison-inmates).

33. 'Drugs as Antidote to Prison Boredom', *Herald*, 24 August 1995 (http://www.heraldscotland.com/sport/spl/aberdeen/drugs-as-antidote-prison-boredom-1.665151).

34. Johnson, Andrew, 'Boredom, Drugs and Violence... The Reality of Cell Life in Pentonville Prison', *Islington Tribune*, 26 August 2011 (http://www.islingtontribune.com/news/2011/aug/boredom-drugs-and-violence-reality-cell-life-pentonville-prison).

35. 'Police Surround HMP Ashwell After Riot By Prisoners', Press Association 11 April 2009 (http://www.theguardian.com/uk/2009/apr/11/hmp-ashwell-prison-riot-lockdown).

36. Taylor, David, 'Young Scot Locked Up For His Part in the World's Biggest Hacking Scandal Blames Life on Shetland For Driving Him to Cybercrime', *Daily Record*, 19 October 2013 (http://www.dailyrecord.co.uk/news/scottish-news/shetland-computer-hacker-blames-boredom-2468090).

37. '"Bored" Computer Hacker Given Suspended Sentence in District Court', News.com.au 14 January 2011 (http://www.news.com.au/national/bored-computer-hacker-given-suspended-sentence-in-district-court/story-e6frkp9-1225987235707).

38. Copeland, Alexa, 'Computer Equipment Seized From Home of Darlington 16-Year-Old Following Hacking Attempt', *Northern Echo*, 4 October 2012 (http://www.thenorthernecho.co.uk/news/9964294.Teenage_computer_hacker_in_police_raid).

39. Campbell, Q., & Kennedy, D. M., Chapter 12: The Psychology of Computer Criminals, in Bosworth, et al. (eds.), *Computer Security Handbook* (New York: John Wiley & Sons, Inc., 2009).

40. Dittrich, D. and Himma, K.E., 'Hackers, Crackers and Computer Criminals', in H. Bidgoli (ed.), *Handbook of Information Security*, volume 2 (New York: John Wiley & Sons, Inc., 2006).

41. Hoare, Rose, 'Is Workplace Boredom "the new stress?"', CNN, 2 May 2012 (http://edition.cnn.com/2012/05/02/business/work place-boredom-stress).

42. Mann, S., 'Counting Window Panes: An Investigation into Boredom-reducing Strategies Used By Teachers and the Causes and Consequences of Their Workplace Boredom', presentation at the Annual Conference of the Division of Occupational Psychology of the British Psychological Society, Glasgow, January 2006.

43. Mann, S. and Robinson, A., 'Boredom in the Lecture Theatre: An Investigation into the Contributors and Outcomes of Boredom Amongst University Students', *British Educational Research Journal*, volume 35: 2 (2009), 243–58.

44. Mann, S., 'Boredom at the Checkout: Causes, Coping Strategies and Outcomes of Workplace Boredom in a Supermarket Setting', *Journal of Business and Retail Management Research*, volume 6: 2 (April 2012), 1–14.

45. Merrifield, C. and Danckert, J., 'Characterizing the Psycho-physiological Signature of Boredom', *Experimental Brain Research*, volume 232: 2 (February 2014), 481–91.

46. Shelley, A., Fahlman, Kimberley B., Mercer, Peter Gaskovski, Eastwood, Adrienne E. and Eastwood, John D., 'Does a Lack of Life Meaning Cause Boredom? Results from Psychometric, Longitudinal, and Experimental Analyses', *Journal of Social and Clinical Psychology*, volume 28: 3 (2009), 307–40.

47. German, D. and Latkin, C. A., 'Boredom, Depressive Symptoms, and HIV Risk Behaviors Among Urban Injection Drug Users', *AIDS Behavior*, volume 16: 8 (November 2012), 2244–50.

48. Britton, Annie and Shipley, Martin J., 'Bored to Death?', *International Journal of Epidemiology*, volume 39: 2 (2010), 370–71.

49. Harrington, Suzanne, 'It's Official: We Get Bored After Two Years of Marriage', *Irish Examiner*, 14 January 2013 (http://

www.irishexaminer.com/lifestyle/features/humaninterest/its-official-we-get-bored-after-two-years-of-marriage-219463.html).

50. 'Middle-aged Women Missing Passion (and Sex) Seek Affairs, Not Divorce', Phys Org News, August 2014 (http://phys.org/news/2014-08-middle-aged-women-passion-sex-affairs.html).

51. Harasymchuk, Cheryl and Fehr, Beverley, 'A Script Analysis of Relational Boredom: Causes, Feelings, and Coping Strategies', *Journal of Social and Clinical Psychology*, volume 29: 9 (2010), 988–1019.

52. Chaturvedi, Vinita, 'Are You Getting Bored in Your Marriage?' Times News Network, *The Times of India*, 2 November 2014 (http://timesofindia.indiatimes.com/life-style/relationships/man-woman/Are-you-getting-bored-in-your-marriage/articleshow/37702436.coms).

Chapter Four: How Modern Society Fosters Boredom: The Causes of Boredom

1. Voysey, Sheridan, 'Terry Waite – Break My Body, Bend My Mind, But My Soul Is Not Yours to Possess', hope1032.com.au, 24 April 2013 (http://www.hope1032.com.au/stories/open-house/terry-waite-you-can-break-my-body,-bend-my-mind,-but-my-soul-is-not-yours-to-possess).

2. Svendsen, 2005 in Martin, Marion, Sadlo, Gaynor and Stew, Graham, 'The Phenomenon of Boredom', *Qualitative Research in Psychology 3* (2006), 194.

3. Eccles, Louise, 'Stop Taking Food Snaps, Plead Chefs: French Restaurant Bans Cameras After Head Cook Complained About Diners Taking Pictures of Their Meals', *Daily Mail*, 17 February 2014 (http://www.dailymail.co.uk/news/article-2560940/Stop-taking-food-snaps-plead-chefs-French-restaurant-bans-cameras-head-cook-complained-diners-taking-pictures-meals.html).

4. Bunzeck, Nico and Düzel, Emrah, 'Absolute Coding of Stimulus Novelty in the Human Substantia Nigra/VTA', *Neuron*, volume 51: 3 (3 August 2006), 369–79.

5. Whitney, Lance, 'Facebook "Boring": 1 in 3 Users Are Tuning It Out', CNET, 5 June 2012 (http://www.cnet.com/news/facebook-boring-1-in-3-users-are-tuning-it-out).

6. Mimms, Christopher, 'How the Internet Became Boring', *MIT Technology Review*, 5 June 2012 (http://www.technologyreview.com/view/428087/how-the-internet-became-boring).

7. Thompson, Damian, '"Electronic cocaine": A New Look at Addiction to Computers', *Telegraph*, 21 June 2012 (http://blogs.telegraph.co.uk/news/damianthompson/100166830/electronic-cocaine-a-new-look-at-addiction-to-computers).

8. Saunders, Doug, 'Work? Leisure? It's All a Blur These Days', *The Globe and Mail*, 30 August 2014 (http://www.theglobeandmail.com/globe-debate/work-leisure-its-all-a-blur-these-days/article20259972).

9. Aguiar, Mark and Hurst, Erik, 'Measuring Trends in Leisure: The Allocation of Time over Five Decades', bostonfed.org, January 2006 (https://www.bostonfed.org/economic/wp/wp2006/wp0602.pdf).

10. Khaleeli, Homa, 'How to Get More Free Time in Your Day', *Guardian*, 7 June 2013 (http://www.theguardian.com/money/shortcuts/2013/jun/07/how-get-more-free-time).

11. '7 Charts That Show How Americans Spend Their Free Time', Vox Media, 2015 (http://www.vox.com/2014/4/11/5553006/how-americans-spend-their-time-in-6-charts).

12. Haller, Max, Hadler, Markus and Kaup, Gerd, 'Leisure Time in Modern Societies: A New Source of Boredom and Stress?' *Social Indicators Research*, volume 111: 2 (April 2013), 403–34.

13. Wang W.C., Wu, C. C., Wu, C. Y. and Huan, T. C., 'Exploring the Relationships Between Free-time Management and Boredom in Leisure', *Psychol Reports.*, volume 110: 2 (April 2012), 416–26.

14. Meeker, Mary, 'Internet Trends 2015 – Code Conference', KPCB, 27 May 2015 (http://www.kpcb.com/internet-trends).

15. van Tilburg, Wijnand A. P., Igou, Eric R. and Sedikides, Constantine, 'In Search of Meaningfulness: Nostalgia as an Antidote to Boredom', *Emotion*, volume 13: 3 (2013), 450–61.

16. 'Overview of the Time Use of Canadians', General Social Survey, 2010 (Ottawa: Statistics Canada, 2011), catalogue no. 89-647-X.

17. Levine, Bruce E., 'Does TV Help Make Americans Passive and Accepting of Authority?' Alternet, 26 October 2012 (http://www.alternet.org/culture/does-tv-help-make-americans-passive-and-accepting-authority?page=0%2C2).

18. Graham, Ian, 'Television Viewing: Countries Compared', *NationMaster*, 31 March 2005 (http://www.nationmaster.com/country-info/stats/Media/Television-viewing).

19. Springen, Karen, 'Hooking Up at the Big House', *Newsweek*, 6 January 1992 (http://www.newsweek.com/hooking-big-house-198794).

20. Konnikova, Maria, 'How Facebook Makes Us Unhappy', *New Yorker*, 10 September 2013 (http://www.newyorker.com/tech/elements/how-facebook-makes-us-unhappy).

21. Damrad-Frye, R. and Laird, J. D., 'The Experience of Boredom: The Role of the Self-perception of Attention', *Journal of Personality and Social Psychology*, volume 57: 2 (1989), 315–20.

22. Focus Manifesto (http://focusmanifesto.com/the-age-of-distraction).

23. Van Tilburg, W. A. P. and Igou, E. R. 'On Boredom: Lack of Challenge and Meaning as Distinct Boredom Experiences', *Motivation & Emotion, 36* (2012), 181–94.

24. Stephens, Sam, 'How I Quit My High-Paying Job to Pursue My Dream', *Huffington Post*, 3 December 2014 (http://www.huffingtonpost.com/sam-stephens/how-left-my-finance-job-for-dream_b_4602096.html).

25. 'Facebook and Twitter: We May Love Them, But They Make Us Feel Inadequate and Ugly', *Herald*, 25 July 2014 (http://www.heraldscotland.com/news/home-news/facebook-and-twitter-we-may-love-them-but-they-make-us-feel-inadequate-and-ugly.1406270293).

26. 'Britons Can't Switch Off From Work When On Holiday', *Daily Telegraph*, 21 October 2013 (http://www.telegraph.co.uk/finance/jobs/10393412/Britons-cant-switch-off-from-work-when-on-holiday.html).

27. Doughty, Steve, 'So Much For a New Lease of Life!' *Daily Mail*, 14 November 2013 (http://www.dailymail.co.uk/news/article-2507404/Joy-retirement-wears-just-TEN-MONTHS-bickering-daytime-TV-toll.html).

28. White, Steve, 'Great-grandmother Aged 76 Went On Four-Year Shoplifting Spree Because She Was "Bored" of Being Old', *Mirror*, 28 January 2014 (http://www.mirror.co.uk/news/weird-news/june-humphreys-crewe-went-four-year-3086703).

29. '100-Year-Old Man Continues to Work After "Boring" Retirement', BBC Essex, 29 January 2013 (http://www.bbc.co.uk/news/uk-england-essex-21246855).

Chapter Five: The Boredom-Prone Personality: Why Some People Get More Bored Than Others

1. Geen, Russell G., 'Preferred Stimulation Levels in Introverts and Extroverts: Effects on Arousal and Performance', *Journal of Personality and Social Psychology*, volume 46: 6 (June 1984), 1303–12.

2. Smith, Richard P., 'Boredom: A Review', *Human Factors: The Journal of the Human Factors and Ergonomics Society*, volume 23: 329 (1981).

3. Schubert, Daniel S., 'Creativity and Coping with Boredom, *Psychiatric Annals*, volume 8: 3 (March 1978), 46–54.

4. Drory, A., 'Individual Differences in Boredom Proneness and Task Effectiveness at Work', *Personnel Psychology*, 35 (1982), 141–151.

5. Crocker, T., 'Underachievement: Is Our Vision Too Narrowed and Blinkered? Fools Step In Where Angels Fear to Tread', *Gifted*, *131* (2004), 10–14.

6. Smith, P. C., 'The Prediction of Individual Differences in Susceptibility to Industrial Monotony', *Journal of Applied Psychology*, *39* (1955), 322–29.

7. Hill, A. B., 'Work Variety and Individual Differences in Occupational Boredom', *Journal of Applied Psychology*, *60* (1975), 129–31.

8. Zondag, H. J., 'Narcissism and Boredom Revisited: An Exploration of Correlates of Overt and Covert Narcissism Among Dutch University Students', *Psychol. Reports.*, volume 112: 2 (April 2013), 563–76.

9. Gana, Kamel, Trouillet, Raphael, Martin, Bettina and Toffart, Leatitia, 'The Relationship Between Boredom Proneness and Solitary Sexual Behaviors in Adults', *Social Behavior and Personality: An International Journal*, volume 29: 4 (2001).

10. Vodanovich, S. J. and Kass, S. J., 'A Factor Analytic Study of the Boredom Proneness Scale, *Journal of Personality Assessment*, *55* (1990), 115–23.

11. Watt, J. D. and Vodanovich, S. J., 'Boredom Proneness and Psychosocial Development', *Psychology*, volume 133: 3 (May 1999), 303–14.

12. Gosaline, Anna, 'Bored to Death: Chronically Bored People Exhibit Higher Risk-Taking Behavior', *Scientific American*, 26 February 2007 (http://www.scientificamerican.com/article/the-science-of-boredom).

13. LePera, Nicole, 'Relationships Between Boredom Proneness, Mindfulness, Anziety, Depression, and Substance Use', *Psychology Bulletin*, volume 8: 2 (2011).

14. Blaszcynski, A., McConaghy, N. and Frankova, A., 'Boredom Proneness in Pathological Gambling', *Psychol Reports*, volume 67:1 (August 1990), 35–42.

15. Mann, S. and Robinson, A., 'Boredom in the Lecture Theatre: An Investigation into the Contributors and Outcomes of Boredom Amongst University Students', *British Educational Research Journal*, volume 35: 2 (2009), 243–58.

16. Gana, Kamel, Deletang, Benedicte and Metais, Laurence, 'Is Boredom Proneness Associated with Introspectiveness?' *Social Behavior and Personality: An International Journal*, volume 28: 5 (1 January 2000).

17. Malkovsky, E., Merrifield, C., Goldberg, Y. and Danckert, J. A., 'Exploring the Relationship Between Boredom and Sustained Attention', *Journal of Experimental Brain Research*, volume 221: 1 (August 2012), 59–67.

18. Rupp, D. and Vodanovich, S. J., 'The Relationship Between Boredom Proneness and Self-reported Anger and Aggression', *Journal of Social Behavior and Personality*, 12 (1997), 925–36.

19. Sommers, J. and Vodanovich, S. J., 'Boredom Proneness: Its Relationship to Psychological and Physical Health Symptoms', *Journal of Clinical Psychology*, 56 (2000), 149–55.

20. Danckert, J.A. and Allman, A.A., 'Time Flies When You're Having Fun: Temporaral Estimation and the Experience of Boredom', *Brain and Cognition*, 59 (2005), 236–45.

21. Robinson, Joe, 'Don't Curb Your Enthusiasm: The Problem With Being Cool', *Huffington Post*, 13 October 2010 (http://www.huffingtonpost.com/joe-robinson/are-cool-people-more-in-se_b_757462.html).

22. von Hahn, Karen, 'Style With a Sneer: Models Stalk Down Runway Looking Surly', The Star.com, 16 April 2014 (http://www.thestar.com/life/2014/04/16/style_with_a_sneer_models_stalk_down_run_way_looking_surly.html).

23. Branch, Shelly, 'Forget Standing Tall, Female Models Make Slouching Look Good', *Wall Street Journal*, 30 September 2004 (http://online.wsj.com/articles/SB109648714805031561).

Chapter Six: 'Mum, I'm Bored': How We Are Growing a Nation of Bored Kids

1. Hobel, C. J., Goldstein, A. and Barrett, E. S., 'Psychosocial Stress and Pregnancy Outcome', *Clinical Obstetrics and Gynecology*, 51(2) (2008), 333–48.

2. Binoche, Jill, 'Make Baby Smarter in the Womb', *Smart Babies*, 1 February 2015 (http://www.smartbabynews.org/make-baby-smarter-in-the-womb).

3. Rauscher, Frances H., Shaw, Gordon L. and Ky, Catherine N., 'Music and Spatial Task Performance', *Nature 365, 6447* (1993), 611.

4. Hughes, Jane, 'World: Americas: The Mozart Effect Debunked', BBC News, 9 September 1999 (http://news.bbc.co.uk/1/hi/world/americas/442347.stm).

5. Crone, Jack, 'Will the Librarian PLEASE Keep the Noise Down! Anger Over Silence in Libraries Being Shattered By Creches, Concerts and Dance Classes Held to Attract More Visitors', *Daily Mail*, 8 November 2001.

6. Lang, Heide, 'The Trouble With Day Care', *Psychology Today*, 1 May 2005 (http://www.psychologytoday.com/articles/200505/the-trouble-day-care).

7. Macrae, Fiona, 'Putting Baby in Nursery "Could Raise Its Risk of Heart Disease" Because It Sends Stress Levels Soaring', *Mail Online*, 12 September 2011 (http://www.dailymail.co.uk/health/article-2036266/Putting-baby-nursery-raise-heart-disease-risk-sends-stress-levels-soaring.html).

8. McDonough, P., 'TV Viewing Among Kids at an Eight-year High', Nielsenwire, 26 October 2009 (available at: http://blog.nielsen.com/nielsenwire/media_entertainment/tv-viewing-among-kids-at-an-eight-year-high).

9. Rideout, V. J., Foehr, U. G. and Roberts, D. F., 'Generation M2: Media in the Lives of 8- to 18-year-olds', Kaiser Family Foundation, January 2010 (http://www.kff.org/entmedia/upload/8010.pdf).

10. Levy, Andrew, 'Parents' Anxieties Keep Children Playing Indoors: Fears About Traffic and Strangers Leading to "Creeping Disappearance" of Youngsters From Parks', *Daily Mail*, 7 August 2013 (http://www.dailymail.co.uk/news/article-2385722/Parents-anxieties-children-playing-indoors-Fears-traffic-strangers-leading-creeping-disappearance-youngsters-parks.html).

11. 'Parents Admit to "Using TV as Babysitter"', BBC News, 9 May 2011 (http://www.bbc.co.uk/news/education-13308737).

12. 'Children and Watching TV', Facts for Families, December 2011 (http://www.aacap.org/AACAP/Families_and_Youth/Facts_for_Families/Facts_for_Families_Pages/Children_And_Wat_54.aspx).

13. 'Entertainment Media Diets of Children and Adolescents May Impact Learning', Commonsense, 2012 (https://www.commonsensemedia.org/about-us/news/press-releases/entertainment-media-diets-of-children-and-adolescents-may-impact).

14. 'How Teens Do Research in the Digital World', Pew Research Center, 1 November 2012 (http://www.pewinternet.org/2012/11/01/how-teens-do-research-in-the-digital-world).

15. Christakis, Dimitri A., Zimmerman, Frederick J., DiGiuseppe, David L. and McCarty, Carolyn A., 'Early Television Exposure and Subsequent Attentional Problems in Children', *Pediatrics,* volume 113: 4 (1 April 2004), 708–13.

16. Swing, Edward L., Gentile, Douglas A., Anderson, Craig A. and Walsh, David A., 'Television and Video Game Exposure and the Development of Attention Problems', *Pediatrics, 126* (2010), 214.

17. Anderson, D. R., Levin, S. R. and Lorch, E. P., 'The Effects of TV Program Pacing on the Behavior of Preschool Children', *AV Commun Rev.*, volume 25: 2 (1977), 159–66.

18. Schumann, Rebecca, 'Fisher Price Baby Seat Recalled? "Electronic Babysitter" iPad Product Recall Requested By Parents, Petition Issued By CCFC', *International*, 11 December 2013 (http://www.

ibtimes.com/fisher-price-baby-seat-recalled-electronic-baby
sitter-ipad-product-recall-requested-parents-petition).

19. Schurgin O'Keeffe, Gwenn, Clarke-Pearson, Kathleen and
    Council on Communications and Media, 'Clinical Report: The
    Impact of Social Media on Children, Adolescents, and Families,'
    Pediatrics, published online, 28 March 2011 (http://www.
    longislandweb.com/peachykeen/pdf/PediatricsClinicalRpt..
    ImpactOfSocialMedia.pdf).

20. Williams, Rhiannon 'Children Using Social Networks Underage
    "Exposes Them to Danger"', *Daily Telegraph*, 6 February 2014
    (http://www.telegraph.co.uk/technology/news/10619007/
    Children-using-social-networks-underage-exposes-them-to-
    danger.html).

21. 'Study: Tablets, Smartphones are the New Electronic Baby-
    sitters', CBS New York, 29 October 2013 (http://newyork.
    cbslocal.com/2013/10/29/study-tablets-smartphones-are-the-
    new-electronic-babysitters).

22. Goldberg, Stephanie, 'Parents Using Smartphones to Entertain
    Bored Kids', Special to CNN, 27 April 2010 (http://edition.cnn.
    com/2010/TECH/04/26/smartphones.kids).

23. 'Tablets: The Electronic Babysitter', *Computer Business Review*,
    9 August 2013 (http://www.cbronline.com/news/mobile-and-
    tablets/tablets-the-electronic-babysitter).

24. 'After-School Activities: Dubai Kids Discover Antidote to
    After-School Boredom', *Mathnasium*, 18 February 2014 (http://
    mathnasium.ae/school-activities-dubai-kids-discover-antidote-
    school-boredom).

25. 'The Cost of After-School Activities in the UK: How Much Do
    Parents Spend?' *Maths Doctor*, September 2014 (http://www.
    mathsdoctor.co.uk/after-school/report).

26. Odone, Cristina, 'Children Need Warmth, Not the Cruelty of
    "Hothousing"', *Daily Telegraph*, 3 March 2013 (http://www.

telegraph.co.uk/education/9906487/Children-need-warmth-not-the-cruelty-of-hothousing.html).

27. Edgar, James, 'Give Your Child Time to Be Bored, Pushy Parents are Urged', *Telegraph*, 7 January 2014 (http://www.telegraph.co.uk/education/educationnews/10556523/Give-your-child-time-to-be-bored-pushy-parents-are-urged.html).

28. 'Overscheduled Child May Lead to a Bored Teen', WebMDArchive (http://www.webmd.com/parenting/features/overscheduled-child-may-lead-to-bored-teen?page=3).

29. Richardson, Hannah, 'Children Should Be Allowed to Get Bored, Expert Says', BBC News, 23 March 2013 (http://www.bbc.co.uk/news/education-21895704).

30. Davies, Emily, 'Why Boredom is Good for Children: Quiet Time Can Prepare Youngsters for Dull Moments in Adulthood', *Daily Mail*, 8 January 2014 (http://www.dailymail.co.uk/news/article-2535675/Why-boredom-good-children-Quiet-time-prepare-youngsters-dull-moments-adulthood.html).

31. Collier, Edward, 'The Importance of Being Bored', *Guardian*, 30 July 2010 (http://www.theguardian.com/commentisfree/2010/jul/30/bored-children-boredom-parents).

Chapter Seven: Boredom and the Rise of ADHD and Autistic Spectrum Disorder

1. Lilienfeld, Scott O. and Arkowitz, Hal, 'Are Doctors Diagnosing Too Many Kids with ADHD? *Scientific American*, 11 April 2013 (http://www.scientificamerican.com/article/are-doctors-diagnosing-too-many-kids-adhd).

2. Berger, Sarah, 'A Look into the Rise of ADD and ADHD', Harbinger Online, 5 March 2012 (http://smeharbinger.net/features/a-look-into-the-rise-of-add-and-adhd).

3. Schwarz, Alan, 'The Selling of Attention Deficit Disorder', *New*

York Times, 14 December 2013 (http://www.nytimes.com/2013/ 12/15/health/the-selling-of-attention-deficit-disorder.html? pagewanted=all&_r=0).

4. -- and Cohen, Sarah, 'A.D.H.D. Seen in 11% of U.S. Children as Diagnoses Rise', *New York Times*, 31 March 2013 (http://www. nytimes.com/2013/04/01/health/more-diagnoses-of-hyper activity-causing-concern.html?pagewanted=all&_r=0).

5. Dimitri, A., Christakis, Frederick J., Zimmerman, David L. and DiGiuseppe, Carolyn A. McCarty 'Early Television Exposure and Subsequent Attentional Problems in Children', *Pediatrics,* volume 113: 4 (1 April 2004), 708–13.

6. Robinson, Belinda, 'Doctors Say Parents and Schools are Pushing Them to Label Children Who are Just Shy or Bookish as Mentally Ill', *Daily Mail*, 21 June 2014 (http://www.dailymail.co.uk/news/ article-2664374/Doctors-say-parents-schools-pushing-label-children-just-shy-bookish-mentally-ill.html#ixzz3MuYzPV4M).

7. McKinstry, Leo, 'Why a Diagnosis of ADHD is Welcomed By Some Parents', *Daily Express*, 15 August 2013 (http://www. express.co.uk/comment/columnists/leo-mckinstry/422158/ Why-a-diagnosis-of-ADHD-is-welcomed-by-some-parents).

8. Friedman, Richard A., 'A Natural Fix for ADHD', *New York Times*, 31 October 2014 (http://www.nytimes.com/2014/11/02/opinion/ sunday/a-natural-fix-for-adhd-html).

9. Wedge, Marilyn, 'Why French Kids Don't Have ADHD' *Psychology Today*, 8 March 2012 (https://www.psychologytoday.com/blog/ suffer-the-children/201203/why-french-kids-dont-have-adhd).

10. Eisenberg, Kenya D., Campbell, B., Gray, P. and Sorenson, M., 'BMC Dopamine Receptor Genetic Polymorphisms and Body Composition in Undernourished Pastoralists: An Exploration of Nutrition Indices Among Nomadic and Recently Settled Ariaal Men of Northern Kenya', *Evolutionary Biology*, volume 8: 1 (2008), 173.

11. Poppy, L.A., Schoenberga, C., Sevket Hepark, B., Cornelis, C., Kanb, Henk P., Barendregta, Jan K., Buitelaarb, C., Anne, E.M. and Speckens, B., 'Effects of Mindfulness-based Cognitive Therapy on Neurophysiological Correlates of Performance Monitoring in Adult Attention-Deficit/Hyperactivity Disorder)', *Clinical Neurophysiology*, volume 125: 7 (July 2014), 1407–16.

12. Bögels, Susan M., Peijnenburg, Dorreke and van der Oord, Saskia, 'The Effectiveness of Mindfulness Training for Children with ADHD and Mindful Parenting for Their Parents', *Journal of Child and Family Studies*, volume 21: 1 (February 2012), 139–47.

13. Zylowska, Lidia, Ackerman, Deborah L., Yang, May H., Futrell, Julie L., Horton, Nancy L., Hale, T., Sigi Pataki, Caroly and Smalley, Susan L., 'Mindfulness Meditation Training in Adults and Adolescents With ADHD: A Feasibility Study', *Journal of Attention Disorders*, volume 11: 6 (2008), 737–46.

14. Travis, Frederick, Grosswald, Sarina and Stixrud, William, 'ADHD, Brain Functioning, and Transcendental Meditation Practice', *Mind & Brain, The Journal of Psychiatry*, volume 2: 1 (2011), 73–81.

15. 'New Study Shows Transcendental Meditation Improves Brain Functioning in ADHD Students', EurekAlert! Maharishi University of Management, 26 July 2011 (http://www.eurekalert.org/pub_releases/2011-07/muom-nss072611.php).

16. Golden, G. K. and Hill, M. A., 'Only Sane: Autistic Barriers in "Boring" Patients', *Clinical Social Work Journal*, volume 22: 1 (1994), 9–26.

17. Biever, Celeste, 'Device Warns You If You're Boring or Irritating', *New Scientist*, 29 March 2006 (http://www.newscientist.com/article/mg19025456.500-device-warns-you-if-youre-boring-or-irritating.html).

18. Roth, Mark, 'TSA May Have the Perfect Job for Autistic Workers', *Pittsburgh Post-Gazette*, 9 October 2013 (http://www.post-gazette.com/news/health/2013/10/09/TSA-may-have-the-perfect-job-for-autistic-workers/stories/201310090039).

19. Szalavitz, Maia, '"Resting" Autism Brains Still Hum With Activity', Simons Foundation Autism Research Initiative, 21 February 2014 (http://sfari.org/news-and-opinion/blog/2014/resting-autism-brains-still-hum-with-activity).

20. 'Autism Cases on the Rise; Reason for Increase a Mystery', WebMD Archive (http://www.webmd.com/brain/autism/searching-for-answers/autism-rise?page=2).

21. Magee, Anna, 'Husband a Right Old Grump? He Could Be One of Thousands Who Have Asperger's Without Realising', *Daily Mail*, 5 June 2012 (http://www.dailymail.co.uk/health/article-2154689/Husband-right-old-grump-Aspergers-Thousands-realising.html).

Chapter Eight: The Plague of Interactive Whiteboards: Why Boredom in Schools and Further Education is Booming

1. High School Survey of Student Engagement, 2009 (http://ceep.indiana.edu/hssse/images/HSSSE_2010_Report.pdf).

2. 'Most Teens Associate School With Boredom, Fatigue', Gallup, 8 June 2004 (http://www.gallup.com/poll/11893/most-teens-associate-school-boredom-fatigue.aspx).

3. 'The Silent Epidemic', Bill & Melinda Gates Foundation (https://docs.gatesfoundation.org/Documents/TheSilentEpidemic3-06FINAL.pdf).

4. Bryner, Jeanna, 'Most Students Bored at School', Livescience, 28 February 2007 (http://www.livescience.com/1308-students-bored-school.html).

5. OECD Indicators, 2002 (http://www.keepeek.com/Digital-Asset-Management/oecd/education/education-at-a-glance-2002/the-learning-environment-and-organisation-of-schools_eag-2002-6-en#page1).

6. Education in Japan Community Blog (https://educationin japan.wordpress.com/edu-news/boredom-main-reason-for-pte-school-exodus).

7. Daschmann, E.C., Goetz, T. and Stupnisky, R. H., 'Testing the Predictors of Boredom at School: Development and Validation of the Precursors to Boredom Scales', *British Journal of Educational Psychology*, volume 81, part 3 (September 2011) 421–40.

8. 'School: It's Way More Boring Than When You Were There', Salon. com, 2011 (http://www.salon.com/2011/09/14/denvir_school).

9. Paton, Graeme, 'Schools Using Dance and Fashion to Get Bored Pupils Interested in Maths', *Daily Telegraph*, 15 January 2010 (http://www.telegraph.co.uk/education/educationnews/6990115/Schools-using-dance-and-fashion-to-get-bored-pupils-interested-in-maths.html).

10. Preckel, F., Götz, T. and Frenzel, A., 'Ability Grouping of Gifted Students: Effects on Academic Self-concept and Boredom', *British Journal of Educational Psychology*, volume 80, part 3 (September 2010), 451–72.

11. Vogel-Walcutt, Jennifer J., Fiorella, Logan, Carper, Teresa and Schatz, Sae, 'The Definition, Assessment, and Mitigation of State Boredom Within Educational Settings: A Comprehensive Review', *Educational Psychology Review*, volume 24: 1 (March 2012), 89–111.

12. Fisher, Anna V., Godwin, Karrie E. and Seltma, Howard, 'Visual Environment, Attention Allocation, and Learning in Young Children When Too Much of a Good Thing May Be Bad', *Psychological Science*, volume 25: 7 (July 2014), 1362–70.

13. Sparks, Sarah D., 'Researchers Argue Boredom May Be a "Flavor of Stress"', *Education Week*, volume 32: 7 (10 October2012).

14. EuropArchive.org (http://collection.europarchive.org/tna/20040722012352/http://partners.becta.org.uk/upload-dir/downloads/page_documents/research/harnessing_technology_schools_survey07.pdf).

15. 'Leveraging Interactive Whiteboards as a Core Classroom Technology' (http://downloads01.smarttech.com/media/site-core/en/pdf/research_library/k-12/leveraging_ibws.pdf).

16. Stewart, William, 'Pedagogy – "Disillusioned" Teachers Bored by Chalk and Talk', *TES* magazine, 24 January 2014 (https://www.tes.co.uk/article.aspx?storycode=6395637).

17. Goff, Hannah, 'Too Much Technology in the Classroom?' *BBC News Education*, 15 January 2007 (http://news.bbc.co.uk/1/hi/education/6241517.stm).

18. Paton, Graeme, 'Ofsted: Mixed-ability Classes "A Curse" on Bright Pupils', *Daily Telegraph*, 20 September 2012 (http://www.telegraph.co.uk/education/educationnews/9553764/Ofsted-mixed-ability-classes-a-curse-on-bright-pupils.html).

19. Boaler, Jo (Stanford University, California); Wiliam, Dylan (King's College London) and Brown, Margaret (King's College London), '40 Students' Experiences of Ability Grouping – Disaffection, Polarisation and the Construction of Failure (http://www.nottingham.ac.uk/csme/meas/papers/boaler.html).

20. Shepherd, Jessica, 'Dividing Younger Pupils By Ability Can Entrench Disadvantage, Study Finds', *Guardian*, 9 February 2012 (http://www.theguardian.com/education/2012/feb/09/dividing-pupils-ability-entrench-disadvantage).

21. Kanevsky, L. and Keighley, T., 'To Produce Or Not to Produce? Understanding Boredom and the Honor in Underachievement', *Roper Review*, 2003, 0278-3193 26 (1).

22. Fallis, R. K. and Optotow, S., 'Are Students Failing Schools Or Are Schools Failing Students? Class Cutting in High School', *Journal of Social Issues*, volume 59: 1 (2003), 103–19.

23. Curtis, Polly, 'Ofsted's New Mission – To Get Rid of Boring Teachers', *Guardian*, 5 January 2009 (http://www.theguardian.com/education/2009/jan/05/ofsted-boring-teachers).

24. Marshall, Konrad, 'Burnout Hits One in Four Teachers', *The Age*,

6 October 2013 (http://www.theage.com.au/victoria/burnout-hits-one-in-four-teachers-20131005-2v13y.html).

25. 'Obama Says Too Much Testing Makes Education Boring; Sees Tests As Punishment', *CNS News*, 29 March 2011 (http://cns news.com/news/article/obama-says-too-much-testing-makes-education-boring-sees-tests-punishment).

26. 'Finland: Typing Takes Over as Handwriting Lessons End', *BBC News*, 21 November 2014 (http://www.bbc.co.uk/news/blogs-news-from-elsewhere-30146160).

27. Schank, Roger C., 'Why Kids Hate School — Subject By Subject' *Washington Post*, 7 September 2012 (http://www.washingtonpost.com/blogs/answer-sheet/post/why-kids-hate-school--subject-by-subject/2012/09/06/0bflacc4-f5d6-11e1-8398-0327ab83ab91_blog.html).

28. 'Classroom Maths Irrelevant to Workplace' (http://www.news.com.au/national/queensland/classroom-maths-irrelevant-to-workplace-says-professor-ian-chubb/story-fnii5v6w-1227164607227).

29. Paton, Graeme, 'Teachers Should "Ignore Shakespeare's Boring Scenes"', *Daily Telegraph*, 3 May 2013 (http://www.telegraph.co.uk/education/educationnews/10035821/Teachers-should-ignore-Shakespeares-boring-scenes.html).

30. Hodges, Lucy 'Another Boring Lecture...' *Independent*, 9 September 2004.

31. Mann, S. and Robinson, A., 'Boredom in the Lecture Theatre: An Investigation into the Contributors and Outcomes of Boredom Amongst University Students', *British Educational Research Journal*, volume 35: 2 (2009), 243–58.

32. Van der Velde, E. G., Feij, J. A. and Toon, W., 'Stability and Change of Person Characteristics Among Young Adults: The Effect of the Transition From School to Work', *Personality and Individual Differences*, volume 18: 1 (1995), 89–99.

33. Vygotsky, L. S., *Mind in Society: The Development of Higher Psychological Processes* (Cambridge, MA: Harvard University Press, 1978).

34. Baillie, C. and Hazel, E., 'Teaching Materials Laboratory Classes', Higher Education Academy UK Centre for Materials Education Website, 2006 (http://www.materials.ac.uk/guides/labclasses.asp).

35. Susskind, J. E. and Gurien, R. A., 'Do Computer-generated Presentations Influence Psychology Students' Learning and Motivation to Succeed?': poster presentation at the Annual Convention of the American Psychological Society, Denver, CO, 1999.

36. Bartlett, R. M., Cheng, S. and Strough, J., 'Multimedia Versus Traditional Course Instruction in Introductory Psychology', poster presented at Annual American Psychological Association, Washington, DC, 2000.

37. Kanevsky, L. and Keighley, T., 'To Produce Or Not to Produce? Understanding Boredom and the Honor in Underachievement', *Roeper Review*, volume 26: 1 (Fall 2003).

38. Ward, T., 'I Watched in Dumb Horror', *Guardian*, 20 May 2003.

39. Wolff, J., 'Room for Improvement Among Lecturers', *Guardian Education Supplement*, 4 July 2006.

40. Ramsden, P. *Learning to Teach in Higher Education* (London: Routledge, 2003).

41. Gjesne, T., 'General Satisfaction and Boredom at School as a Function of the Pupil's Personality Characteristics', *Scandinavian Journal of Educational Research*, 21, 113–146.

42. Mikulas, W. L. and Vodanovich, S. J. (1993) 'The Essence of Boredom', *Psychological Record*, volume 43: 1 (1977), 3–13.

43. Watt, J. D. and Vodanovich, S. J., 'Boredom Proneness and Psychosocial Development', *Journal of Psychology*, 133 (1999), 303–14.

44. Larson, R. W. and Richards, M. H., 'Boredom in the Middle School Years: Blaming Schools Versus Blaming Students', *American Journal of Education*, 99 (1991), 418–43.

45. Handelsman, M. M., Briggs, W. L., Sullivan, N. and Towler, A., 'A Measure of College Student Course Engagement', *The Journal of Educational Research*, volume 98: 3 (2005), 184–191.

46. Pekrun, Reinhard, Goetz, Thomas, Daniels, Lia M., Stupnisky, Robert H. and Perry, Raymond P., 'Boredom in Achievement Settings: Exploring Control–Value Antecedents and Performance Outcomes of a Neglected Emotion', *Journal of Educational Psychology*, volume 102: 3 (August 2010), 531–49.

47. Bajak, Aleszu, 'Lectures Aren't Just Boring, They're Ineffective Too, Study Finds', *Science Insider*, 12 May 2014 (http://news.sciencemag.org/education/2014/05/lectures-arent-just-boring-theyre-ineffective-too-study-finds).

48. Marquis, Justin, 'Is the College Lecture Dead, Dying, or Just Lying Low?' Ph.D. thesis, 20 March 2012 (http://www.online universities.com/blog/2012/03/is-the-college-lecture-dead-dying-or-just-lying-low).

Chapter Nine: Boredom in the Boardroom: Why Boredom in the Workplace is Rising

1. Blacksmith, Nikki and Harter, Jim, 'Majority of American Workers Not Engaged in Their Jobs', Gallup, 28 October 2011 (http://www.gallup.com/poll/150383/majority-american-workers-not-engaged-jobs.aspx).

2. O'Hanlon, J. F., 'Boredom: Practical Consequences and a Theory', *Acta Psychologica*, 49 (1981), 53–82.

3. Drory, A., 'Individual Differences in Boredom Proneness and Task Effectiveness at Work', *Personnel Psychology*, 35 (1982), 141–51.

4. Branton, P., 'A Field Study of Receptive Manual Work in Relation to Accidents at the Work Place', *International Journal of Production Research*, *8* (1970), 93–107.

5. Dyer-Smith, M. and Wesson, D., 'Resource Allocation Efficiency as an Indicator of Boredom, Work Performance and Absence', *Ergonomics*, *40* (1997), 515–21.

6. Grubb, E. A., 'Assembly Line Boredom and Individual Differences in Recreation Participation', *Journal of Leisure Research*, *7* (1975), 256–69.

7. Lee, T. W., 'Toward the Development and Validation of a Measure of Job Boredom', *Manhattan College Journal of Business*, *15* (1986), 22–8.

8. McBain, W. N., 'Arousal, Monotony, and Accidents in Line Driving', *Journal of Applied Psychology*, *54* (1970), 509–19.

9. Hill, A. B., 'Work Variety and Individual Differences in Occupational Boredom', *Journal of Applied Psychology*, *60* (1975), 129–31.

10. Steinauer, J. M., 'Bored Stiff', *Incentive*, volume 173: 11 (November 1999), 7

11. *Faking It*, Development Dimensions International, Research Report, Autumn 2004.

12. Joyce, A., 'Boredom Numbs the Work World', *Washington Post*, 10 August 2005 (http://www.washingtonpost.com/wp-dyn/con tent/article/2005/08/09/AR2005080901395.html).

13. Teacher Training Agency, 2004 (http://www.tda.gov.uk/about/ mediarelations/2004/20040713.aspx).

14. Joyce, A., 'Boredom Numbs the World of Work', *Washington Post*, 10 August 2005.

15. Vodanovich, S. J., 'Psychometric Measures of Boredom: A Review of the Literature', *Journal of Psychology*, *137* (2003), 569–95.

16. Brisset, D. and Snow, R. P., 'Boredom: Where the Future Isn't', *Symbolic Interaction*, 16 (1993), 237–56.

17. Saito, H., Kashida, K., Endo, Y. and Saito, M., 'Studies on a Bottle Inspection Task', *Journal of Science of Labor*, 48 (1972), 475–532.

18. Cox & 'Repetitive Work', in Cooper, C. L. and Payne, R. (eds.), *Current Concerns in Occupational Stress* (Chichester: Wiley, 1980).

19. Hamilton, J., 'Development of Interest and Enjoyment in Adolescence. Part 11. Boredom and Psychopathology', *Journal of Youth and Adolescence*, 12 (1983), 363–72.

20. Orcutt, J. D., 'Contrasting Effects of 2 Kinds of Boredom on Alcohol Use', *Journal of Drug Issues*, 14 (1984), 161–73.

21. Wasson, A. S., 'Susceptibility to Boredom and Deviant Behaviour at School', *Psychological Reports*, 48 (1981), 901–02.

22. Grose, V. L., 'Coping with Boredom in the Cockpit Before It's Too Late', *Professional Safety*, volume 34: 7 (1989), 24–6.

23. Alfredsson, L., Karasek, R. A. and Theorell, T., 'Myocardial Infarction Risk and Psychosocial Work Environment: An Analysis of the Male Swedish Working Force', *Social Science & Medicine*, 16 (1982), 463–7.

24. Caplan, R. D., Cobb, S., French, J. R. P., van Harrison, R. and Pinneau, S. R., *Job Demands and Worker Health*, Washington DC: US Department of Health, Education and Welfare, 1975.

25. 'Feeling Bored at Work? Three Reasons Why and What Can Free You', *Psychology Today*, 3 May 2010 (http://www.psychologytoday.com/blog/the-new-resilience/201005/feeling-bored-work-three-reasons-why-and-what-can-free-you).

26. Bruursemaa, Kari, Kesslerb, Stacey R. and Spector, Paul E., 'Bored Employees Misbehaving: The Relationship Between Boredom and Counterproductive Work Behaviour', *Work & Stress: An International Journal of Work, Health & Organisations*, volume 25: 2 (2011), 93–107.

27. Mann, S., 'Counting Window Panes: An Investigation into Boredom-reducing Strategies Used by Teachers and the Causes and Consequences of Their Workplace Boredom', presentation at the Annual Conference of the Division of Occupational Psychology of the British Psychological Society, Glasgow, January 2006.

28. Elsbach, Kimberly D. and Hargadon, Andrew B., 'Enhancing Creativity Through "Mindless" Work: A Framework of Workday Design', *Organization Science* (2006), 470–83.

29. 'Cockpit Boredom: A Risk *All* Managers Face', *Irmi*, February 2014 (http://www.irmi.com/expert/articles/2014/grose02-risk-management-systemic-approach.aspx).

30. Kass, Steven J., Vodanovich, Stephen J. and Callender, Anne, 'State-Trait Boredom: Relationship to Absenteeism, Tenure, and Job Satisfaction', *Journal of Business and Psychology*, volume 16: 2 (December 2001), 317–27.

31. Hackman, J. R. and Oldham, G. R., *Work Re-design* (Reading, MA: Addison-Wesley, 1980).

32. Fisher, C., *Boredom: Construct, Causes and Consequences*, Technical report ONR-9, Texas A&M University, 1987.

33. Loukidou, Lia, Loan-Clarke, John and Daniels, Kevin, 'Boredom in the Workplace: More Than Monotonous Tasks', *International Journal of Management Reviews*, volume 11: 4 (December 2009), 381–405.

34. Gould, C. and Seib, H. M., 'Job Satisfaction as a Function of Boredom Proneness and Central Life Interests', paper presented at the 43rd Annual Southeastern Psychological Association meeting, Atlanta, 1997.

35. Fisher, Cynthia D. and Klinger, Eric, 'Effects of External and Internal Interruptions on Boredom at Work: Two Studies', *Journal of Organizational Behavior*, volume 19: 5 (September 1998) 503–22.

36. 'The Stream of Consciousness Emotions, Personality, and Psychotherapy 1978', *Modes of Normal Conscious Flow*, 225–58.

37. 'Drone Pilots May Need Distractions' *Robotics*, 13 December 2012 (http://news.discovery.com/tech/robotics/drone-pilots-distraction-121127.htm).

38. Robinson, Will, 'Is This the World's Most Boring Job? Meet the Woman Who is Actually Paid to Watch Grass Grow', *Daily Mail*, 21 October 2013) (http://www.dailymail.co.uk/news/article-2470107/Is-worlds-boring-job-Grass-seed-analyst-paid-watch-grow.html).

39. 'The Most Boring Job in the World? Scientist Finds Wonder in Watching Paint Dry', *Daily Star*, 7 July 2014 (http://www.dailystar.co.uk/news/latest-news/387727/Dulux-research-scientist-paid-to-watch-paint-dry).

40. Salary Explorer (http://www.salaryexplorer.com/most-boring-jobs.php).

41. Mann, S., 'The Boredom Boom', *The Psychologist*, volume 20: 2 (February 2007), 90–3 (http://www.thepsychologist.org.uk/archive/archive_home.cfm/volumeID_20-editionID_144-ArticleID_1144-getfile_getPDF/thepsychologist/0207mann.pdf).

42. Chadwick Jones, J. K., *Automation and Behaviour: A Social Psychological Study* (London: Wiley-Interscience, 1969).

43. 'Automated Cockpits May Drive "Bored" Pilots Crazy', Indo-Asian News Service, 8 May 2014 (http://gadgets.ndtv.com/science/news/automated-cockpits-may-drive-bored-pilots-crazy-520570).

44. Kavanagh, Jim, 'Airline Pilots Struggle to Stay Focused', CNN, 30 October 2009 (http://edition.cnn.com/2009/TRAVEL/10/28/pilots.cockpit/index.html?eref=rss_us).

45. British Chamber of Commerce, 2004.

46. 'UFU Fears Mounting Paperwork', *Farmers Weekly*, 29 March 2005 (http://www.fwi.co.uk/news/ufu-fears-mounting-paperwork.htm).

47. Martin, Nicole, 'Paperwork "Costs Time That Should be Spent With Patients"', *Telegraph*, 21 April 2001 (http://www.telegraph.co.uk/news/uknews/1316809/Paperwork-costs-time-that-should-be-spent-with-patients.html).

48. 'Cost of Paperwork Hits Housing Groups', Community Care, 9 March 2005 (http://www.communitycare.co.uk/2005/03/09/cost-of-paperwork-hits-housing-groups).

49. 'Nurses "Drowning in Sea of Paperwork"', BBC News, 21 April 2013 (http://www.bbc.co.uk/news/heath-22206882).

50. Rouse, Lucy, 'How Many Would-be Teachers Are Put Off Before They Even Start?' theguardian.com, 29 January 2011 (http://www.theguardian.com/commentisfree/2011/jan/29/teachers-paperwork).

51. 'Why Don't People Want to Be Teachers?' BBC News, 4 September 2001 (http://news.bbc.co.uk/1/hi/talking_point/1513140.stm).

52. McCartney, Robert, 'Paperwork Burden Plagues Teachers', *Washington Post*, 12 November 2011 (http://www.washingtonpost.com/local/paperwork-burden-plagues-teachers/2011/11/11/gIQALB3aFN_story.html).

53. 'Teachers Are Getting Buried Under Mountain of Paperwork', *News Herald*, 8 December 2012 (http://www.newsherald.com/opinions/letters-to-the-editor/teachers-are-getting-buried-under-mountain-of-paperwork-1.61650?page=1).

54. Lencioni, Patrick, *Death by Meeting: A Leadership Fable About Solving the Most Painful Problem in Business* (San Francisco: Jossey-Bass, 2004).

55. Steelcase Workplace Index Survey, December 2000.

56. Walker, Duncan, 'Why Are Meetings So Boring?' *BBC News Magazine*, 9 November 2004 (http://news.bbc.co.uk/1/hi/magazine/3993483.stm).

57. 'Tory MP Apologises for Playing Candy Crush During Committee',

BBC News, 8 December 2014 (http://www.bbc.co.uk/news/uk-politics-30375609).

58. Read, Simon, 'Time for the Government to Step In? The Dark Side of The Call Centre', *Independent*, 11 June 2013 (http://www.independent.co.uk/news/uk/politics/time-for-the-government-to-step-in-the-dark-side-of-the-call-centre-8654571.html).

59. 'Business: The Economy Boom-time for Call Centres', BBC News, 18 August 1999 (http://news.bbc.co.uk/1/hi/business/423930.stm).

60. CallCenterOps (http://www.callcenterops.com/obs-boredom.htm).

61. Call Center College (http://www.ecustomerserviceworld.com/earticlesstore_articles.asp?type=article&id=443).

62. Carvel, John, 'Graduates Find Prized Jobs Are Rather Boring, Says Survey', *Guardian*, 27 July 2006 (http://www.theguardian.com/money/2006/jul/27/workandcareers.graduation).

63. 'Paperwork "Slowing Crime Fight"', BBC News, 20 March 2005 (http://news.bbc.co.uk/1/hi/england/southern_counties/4366287.stm).

64. 'Bid to Cut GP Paperwork Launched', BBC News, 29 December 2004 (http://newsbbc.co.uk/1/hi/health/4121751.stm).

65. 'Teachers Face Handheld Revolution', BBC News, 10 September 2005 (http://newsbbc.co.uk/1/hi/uk_politics/4230832.stm).

66. Fisher, Cynthia D., 'Boredom at Work: A Neglected Concept', *Human Relations*, 46 (March 1993), 395–417.

67. Collinson, D., 'Managing Humour', *Journal of Management Studies*, volume 39: 3 (May 2002), 269–88.

68. Butler, Nick, Olaison, Lena, Śliwa, Martyna, Meier, Bent and Sverre, Spoelstra Sørensen, 'Work, Play and Boredom', *Ephemera Theory and Politics in Organization*, volume 11: 4 (November 2011).

69. McGhee, P. 'The Key to Stress Management, Retention and

Profitability? More Workplace Fun', *HR Focus*, volume 77: 9 (2000), 5–6.

70. Deal, T. and Key, M. K., 'Corporate Celebration: Play, Purpose and Profit at Work' (San Francisco, CA: Berrett-Koehler, 1998).

71. Burkeman, Oliver, 'Who Goes to Work to Have Fun?' *New York Times*, 11 December 2013 (http://www.nytimes.com/2013/12/12/opinion/burkeman-are-we-having-fun-yet/html?_r=0).

72. 'The 25 Best Companies to Work for in America' (http://www.businessinsider.com/best-companies-to-work-for-2011-2?op=1#ixzz3LcgFUrjx).

73. 'Quad/Graphics Featured in Book That Highlights Fearless Companies' (http://whattheythink.com/news/5003-quadgraphics-featured-book-highlights-fearless).

74. Santovec, M. L., 'Yeeaa-Haw!' *Credit Union Management*, volume 24: 3 (March 2001).

75. Miller, J., 'Humour: An Empowerment Tool for the 1990s', *Management Development Review*, volume 9: 6 (1996), 36–40.

76. Caudron, S., 'Humour is Healthy in the Workplace', *Personnel Journal*, June 1992, 63–8.

77. 'When Sun Microsystems Has Fun' (http://www.nytimes.com/2008/04/01/business/worldbusiness/01iht-techfools.4.11593549.html).

78. 'He's No Fool (But He Plays One Inside Companies)' (http://www.fastcompany.com/35777/hes-no-fool-he-plays-one-inside-companies).

79. Rushe, D., 'Forget Work, Just Have Some Fun', *Sunday Times*, 16 September 2007 (http://www.thesundaytimes.co.uk/sto/business/article71497.ece).

80. 'Six Cool Companies to Work For' (http:www.cnbc.com/id/39573304/Six_Cool_Companies_to_Work_For?slide=3).

81. NMPLive (http://www.nmplive.co.uk/john-cleese).

Chapter Ten: I'm Not Boring You, Am I?

1. '9 Ways to Tell If You Are Boring', *Weekly World News*, 8 December 2009 (http://weeklyworldnews.com/headlines/14251/9-ways-to-tell-if-youre-boring).

2. Leary, M. R., Rogers, P. A., Canfield, R. W. and Coe, C., 'Boredom in Interpersonal Encounters: Antecedents and Social Implications', *Journal of Personality and Social Psychology*, volume 51: 5 (1986), 968–75.

3. Kwan-Liu Ma et al. 'Scientific Storytelling Using Visualization' (http://vis.cs.ucdavis.edu/papers/Scientific_Storytelling_CGA.pdf).

4. Melnick, M., 'Want to Be Heard? Try Changing the Way You Talk', *Time*, 20 May 2011 (http://healthland.time.com/author/meredithmelnick and http://healthland.time.com/2011/05/20/want-to-be-heard-try-changing-the-way-you-talk/#ixzz2Qhkmn141).

5. Gladwell, Malcolm, *Blink* (New York: Back Bay Books, 2005).

6. Llewellyn Smith, J., 'Women and Divorce: Goodbye Darling, You're Just Too Dull', *Daily Telegraph*, 4 September 2011.

7. Tamir, D. I. and Mitchell, J. P., 'Disclosing Information About the Self is Intrinsically Rewarding', *Proceedings of the National Academy of Sciences*, volume 109: 21 (2012), 8038–43.

8. Epstein, Mike, 'Listening to People Complain Drains Intelligence, Researchers Complain', *The Mary Sue*, 14 October 2012 (http://www.geekosystem.com/complaining-makes-you-dumb).

9. Child, Ben, 'Bruce Willis Says Sorry For "Boring" Interview On BBC's *The One Show*', *Guardian*, 14 February 2013.

10. Kroes, S., 'Detecting Boredom in Meetings', University of Twente, Enschede, Netherlands, 2005, 1–5.

11. Murphy Paul, Annie, 'Your Brain on Fiction', *New York Times Sunday Review*, 17 March 2012.

12. de Bono, Edward, *The Mechanism of the Mind* (London: Penguin, 1971) and *I Am Right, You Are Wrong* (London: Viking, 1990).

13. Asimov, Isaac, *Treasury of Humor: A Lifetime Collection of Favorite Jokes* (New York: Houghton Mifflin, 1971).

14. Vertegaal, Roel et al., 'Eye Gaze Patterns in Conversations: There is More to Conversational Agents Than Meets the Eyes', Proceedings of the SIGCHI Conference on Human Factors in Computing Systems, 2001, 301–8.

15. Fullwood and Doherty-Sneddon, 'Effect of Gazing at the Camera During a Video Link on Recall', *Applied Ergonomics*, volume 37: 2 (March 2006), 167–75.

16. *US Weekly*, 12 December 2012.

17. Obama, Barack, *Dreams from My Father: A Story of Race and Inheritance* (New York: Broadway Books, 2004).

18. 'What Makes President Barack Obama Successful', Oprah. com (http://www.oprah.com/money/What-Makes-President-Barack-Obama-Successful).

19. 'Semantic Enigmas', guardian.co.uk (http://www.theguardian. com/notesandqueries/query/0,5753,-19185,00.html).

20. 'Is This the Most Boring Man in Britain?' *Daily Mirror*, 11 May 2012 (http://www.mirror.co.uk/news/uk-news/retired-postman-to-photograph-every-postbox-827564).

21. Coughlan, Sean, 'Boring Conference "Too Interesting" Fear', BBC News, 15 November 2011 (http://www.bbc.co.uk/news/education-15722197).

Chapter Eleven: The Benefits of Boredom

1. Hoover, M. (1986) 'Extreme Individualisation, False Subjectivity and Boredom', *Virginia Journal of Sociology*, 2, pp. 35–51.

2. 'Do Bored Teenage Daughters Get a Pardon Too? Sasha and Malia Can't Hide Their Disdain as Obama Saves Turkeys From the Slaughterhouse', *Daily Mail*, 26 November 2014 (http://www. dailymail.co.uk/news/article-2850776/Cheese-turkey-rests-crowned-National-Thanksgiving-Turkey.html).

3. Bornstein, R. F., 'Exposure and Affect: Overview and Meta-analysis of Research 1968–1987', *Psychological Bulletin*, 106 (1989), 265–89.

4. Brisset, D. and Snow, R. P., 'Boredom: Where the Future Isn't', *Symbolic Interaction*, 16 (1993), 237–56.

5. Bell, G., 'The Value of Boredom', *TED x Sydney Conference*, 2011. Available at: http://www.youtube.com/watch?v=Ps_YUElM2EQ.

6. Toohey, P., *Boredom: A Lively History* (New Haven & London: Yale University Press, 2011).

7. Smallwood, J. S. and Schooler, J. W., 'The Restless Mind', *Psychological Bulletin*, 132 (2006) 946–58.

8. Tushup, Richard J. and Zuckerman, Marvin, 'The Effects of Stimulus Invariance on Daydreaming and Divergent Thinking', *Journal of Mental Imagery*, volume 1: 2 (1977), 291–301.

9. Smith, R. P., 'Boredom: A Review', *Human Factors*, volume 23: 3 (June 1981), 329–40.

10. Singer, J. L., *The Inner World of Daydreaming* (New York: Harper & Row, 1975).

11. Schank, R.C., *Dynamic Memory* (Cambridge: Cambridge University Press, 1982).

12. Begley, S., Bailey, H., Sone, D. and Interlandi, J., 'Will the BlackBerry Sink the Presidency?' *Newsweek*, volume 153: 7 (16 February 2009), 36–9.

13. Mann, S. and Cadman, R., 'Does Being Bored Make Us More Creative?' *Creativity Research Journal*, volume 26: 2 (2014), 165–73.

14. Andrade, J., 'What Does Doodling Do?' *Applied Cognitive Psychology*, volume 24: 1 (January 2010), 100–6.

15. Nietzsche, F., *The Gay Science* (New York: Vintage, 1974).

16. Gaylin, W. (ed.), 'Feeling Bored', in *Feelings: Our Vital Signs* (New York: Harper & Row, 1979), 113–129.

17. Vodanovich, S. J., 'On the Possible Benefits of Boredom: A Neglected Area of Personality Research', *Psychology and Education – An Interdisciplinary Journal*, volume 40, parts 3–4 (2003), 28–33.

18. Harris, M. B., 'Correlates and Characteristics of Boredom Proneness and Boredom', *Journal of Applied Social Psychology 30* (2000), 576–98.

19. Hill, Amelia, 'Boredom Is Good For You, Study Claims', *Guardian*, 6 May 2011 (http://www.theguardian.com/science/2011/may/06/boredom-good-for-you-claims-study).

20. 'The Secret Benefits of a Curious Mind', *Psychology Today*, 8 October 2014 (https://www.psychologytoday.com/blog/thriving 101/201410/the-secret-benefits-curious-mind).

21. 'Why I Want a Digital-free Sunday... by Sister of Facebook Founder Mark Zuckerberg', *Daily Mail*, 10 November 2013 (http://www.dailymail.co.uk/debate/article-2496091/Why-I-want-digital-free-Sunday--sister-Facebook-founder-Mark-Zuckerberg.html).

22. 'Taking Time Out With a Digital Detox', *Daily Telegraph*, 28 December 2014 (http://www.telegraph.co.uk/news/predictions/technology/11306785/digital-detox.html).

23. 'Best Unplugged Vacations', Travel Channel (http://www.travelchannel.com/interests/wellness-and-renewal/articles/best-unplugged-vacations).

24. Wakefield, Jane, 'Turn Off E-mail and Do Some Work', *BBC News*, 19

October 2007 (http://news.bbc.co.uk/1/hi/technology/7049275. stm).

25. Mcmahan, Dana, 'Connected Travelers Seek Out Digital Detox on Vacation', NBC News, 29 May 2014 (http://www. nbcnews.com/feature/carry-on/connected-travelers-seek-out-digital-detox-vacation-n117771).

26. 'Digital Detox Retreats: Unplug & Recharge at 8 Tech-Free Getaways', *Huffington Post*, 24 April 2013 (http://www.huffington post.com/2013/04/24/digital-detox-retreats-un_n_3147448. html).

27. 'Digital Detox Retreats Let Stressed Japanese Log Out', *Japan Times*, 26 December 2014 (http://www.japantimes.co.jp/news/ 2014/12/26/national/social-issues/digital-detox-retreats-let-stressed-out-japanese-log-out/#.VKBsJ2AgCk).

28. 'Nature is the Antidote to Boredom', *Outdoor Nation*, 5 April 2013 (http://outdoornation.org.uk/2013/04/05/nature-is-the-anti dote-to-boredom).

29. Csikszentmihalyi, Mihaly, *Beyond Boredom and Anxiety: Experiencing Flow in Work and Play* (San Francisco, Jossey-Bass, 2000).

30. 'You Never Graduate From the School of Christ', One Story Ministries, 11 May 2015 (http://onestoryministries.wordpress. com).

31. Premack, D., 'Toward Empirical Behavior Laws: I. Positive Reinforcement', *Psychology Review, 66* (1959), 219–33.

INDEX